EGYPT
1801

EGYPT
1801

THE END OF NAPOLEON'S EASTERN EMPIRE

STUART REID

FRONTLINE
BOOKS

EGYPT 1801
The End of Napoleon's Eastern Empire

This edition published in 2021 by

Frontline Books,
An imprint of
Pen & Sword Books Ltd,
47 Church Street, Barnsley, S. Yorkshire, S70 2AS,

This book is based on file reference CAB 44/324 , which is held at The National Archives, Kew, and is licensed under the Open Government Licence v3.0.

ISBN: 978 1 52675 846 0

Typeset in 10.5/13 pt Palatino
by SJmagic DESIGN SERVICES, India.

Printed and bound in Great Britain by CPI Group (UK) Ltd, Croydon, CR0 4YY

Pen & Sword Books Ltd incorporates the imprints of Air World Books, Pen & Sword Archaeology, Atlas, Aviation, Battleground, Discovery, Family History, History, Maritime, Military, Naval, Politics, Social History, Transport, True Crime, Claymore Press, Frontline Books, Praetorian Press, Seaforth Publishing and White Owl

For a complete list of Pen & Sword titles please contact:

PEN & SWORD BOOKS LTD
47 Church Street, Barnsley, South Yorkshire, S70 2AS, UK.
E-mail: enquiries@pen-and-sword.co.uk
Website: www.pen-and-sword.co.uk

Or

PEN AND SWORD BOOKS,
1950 Lawrence Road, Havertown, PA 19083, USA
E-mail: Uspen-and-sword@casematepublishers.com
Website: www.penandswordbooks.com

Contents

Introduction

On 8 March 1801, just a bare matter of weeks into the new century, the British Army won an unlikely victory over what until then was regarded as the foremost army in Europe; through an opposed beach landing in far off Egypt no less.

Within days it then proceeded to demonstrate that this first triumph had been no fluke by winning two more major battles in the open field, each just a week apart. Then, in a strange campaign waged over the space of the next seven months, it surmounted all difficulties to march up the Nile, capture the fabled city of Cairo and then, amidst the ruins of antiquity, compel a French army, superior to it in numbers, to capitulate and evacuate Napoleon Bonaparte's eastern empire. This sustained series of victories in such bizarre circumstances – which at one point included the desperate defence of a two-millennia-old Roman fortress – was all the more dramatic because except in far-off India, the preceding decade had seen Britain and its armies reach the nadir of its fortunes as a military power. It had been defeated in Europe and unsuccessful in the Caribbean – at an awful cost – and yet now not only came a stunning series of battles in Egypt but the confidence and expertise that it gained there then in turn ushered in the yet more famous campaigns in the Spanish Peninsula and the crowning glory of Waterloo.

And yet this transformative experience was supposedly the work of just two men, one old and effectively blind, and the other a painfully inexperienced nonentity. Neither of them, if judged dispassionately, should have been allowed anywhere near the command of an army.

Explaining how this remarkable victory came about therefore goes far beyond the chessboard moves on the battlefield, for in truth, although the French made a succession of bad decisions, there was precious little in the way of fertile genius displayed by the British high command either. Instead, the victory – and it was a very real one – was brought about, just as it would be at Inkerman fifty years later, by the brigadiers, such as John Moore and John Stuart, by the colonels and the captains and above all by the sheer hard fighting and determination of the ordinary British soldiers amidst the most arduous conditions.

Napoleonic-era campaigns are often seen in terms of the sweeping but disciplined manoeuvres laid down in the drill books of the day, resulting in dramatic charges or dogged retreats, and above all, movement. Yet the Egypt business was different, and not just due to its exotic setting. The operations against the French-held city of Alexandria time and again seem to provide a foretaste of the First World War, with heavy casualties expended to achieve advances measured in just yards before victory suddenly came, just as it would do in 1918 with a catastrophic failure in enemy morale. The parallels are fascinating and so too is the desert war, where a ramshackle Turkish army was led to a wholly unexpected victory by a handful of British officers and gunners; adventurers far from home who, like later empire-builders, exchanged their glittering regimentals for Tatar dress and managed local forces way above their pay scale.

As always, a great many people contributed to the making of this study; some through direct contributions and suggestions, others less directly but no less importantly, including Sir Tim Berners Lee, whose internet allowed me to continue to access some very important texts despite the massive lockdown imposed by a malignant epidemic.

Stuart Reid
Monkseaton 2020

Chapter 1

The Mediterranean War

No one would ever accuse Napoleon Bonaparte of a lack of imagination. In 1796, at the age of 26, he was given command of the French army's ramshackle *Armee d'Italie* and, much to everyone's surprise, promptly inspired it to win a dazzling series of victories over the Austrians at Lodi, Castiglione, Arcola and Rivoli. By January 1797 he was just 95 miles from Vienna, and Austria was suing for peace. The Treaty of Campo Formio, which he imposed (largely without any meaningful reference to his government) was not to be signed until 17 October 1797, but in the meantime General Bonaparte's thoughts were ranging ever further afield and in August he enthusiastically wrote that, 'The time is not far distant when we shall find that the only way to destroy England is by occupying Egypt.'[1]

At first sight that might appear an extraordinary statement. However, the great war in Europe was now all but over and he argued that once in French hands, Egypt potentially offered a short route from the Mediterranean to the Indian subcontinent. And that in turn offered the enticing prospect of an alliance there with Tippoo Sahib, the Tiger Sultan of Mysore. Tippoo already represented a very substantial threat to Britain's mighty East India Company and with French assistance the Sultan might very well destroy it, thereby cutting off a major source of the wealth that underpinned all the alliances and combinations raised by Perfidious Albion against France.

That bold and even fantastical suggestion was then followed up on 13 September with a more substantial memorandum addressed to the French Foreign Minister, Charles-Maurice de Talleyrand-Périgord. 'If when a treaty of peace is concluded with England we have to surrender the Cape of Good Hope (seized by Britain from the Dutch in 1795), we ought to take Egypt,' Bonaparte declared in his usual style. 'That country

1

has never belonged to a European nation. The Venetians have had a certain preponderance there for many centuries, but such has only been precarious. We might have this with 25,000 men, taken from Northern Italy, escorted by eight or ten Venetian ships of the line, or frigates, and possess ourselves of it. Egypt no longer belongs to the Grand Signor [the Sultan]; I desire, Citizen Minister, that you will make inquiries and inform me what effect an expedition to Egypt might have at the Porte.'[2]

The Sublime Porte, or Turkish government's, views on the proposal were important, for although Egypt remained a somewhat tenuous possession of the Ottoman Empire, and there was still a Turkish pasha resident in Cairo, for centuries the real rulers of the country had been the *Mamlūks*. Ironically, the term identifies them as slave soldiers, traditionally imported from the North Caucasus, and now forming a closed military caste, loyal now only to their own beys or chieftains. 'To be a Mamaluke,' wrote Captain Thomas Walsh, 'it was indispensably necessary to have been a slave: and even the child of a Mamaluke could not hold any employment among them. The beys, kiachefs, and other officers among the Mamalukes, purchased these slaves from merchants, who brought them to Egypt. They were of all nations and countries, some Germans and Russians, but chiefly Georgians, Circassians, and from other parts of Mount Caucasus. After serving their masters with fidelity, they were made free, and then had the right of buying slaves. The power and influence of the beys were proportionate to the number of Mamelukes that composed their household.'

Their governance of Egypt was both despotic and chaotic as the various beys vied among themselves for power at the expense of the mercantile communities and the wretched native *fellahin*. Consequently, as the servant of a republic publicly committed to spreading the virtues of *liberté, egalitié et fraternitié*, the General had no difficulty in justifying his proposed expedition to Egypt not only as a matter of national policy, but as a *mission civilisatrice*.

Not surprisingly, at first the French government was unimpressed by this rhodomontade, and when Bonaparte returned to Paris on 5 December 1797, he instead found himself assigned to take the command of a proposed seaborne expedition to be mounted against Great Britain. Dutifully, he proceeded to Dunkirk and commenced preparations, with a great show of activity, before unequivocally announcing at the end of February that the expedition could not possibly take place until the following year at the earliest. 'Make what efforts we will,' were the opening words of his report, 'we shall not for many years gain control of the sea. To make a descent upon England without mastery of the

2

sea is the boldest and most difficult operation ever attempted.' Having thus peremptorily dismissed the expedition to England as totally impractical, he instead advocated his own pet scheme to invade Egypt.

After two days of discussion the Directory, perhaps a little wearily, eventually agreed. On 2 March 1798, the expedition to England was formally abandoned, and General Bonaparte was given the go-ahead to conquer Egypt instead.

It still took some time to prepare such an ambitious expedition, but now a supposed Irish expedition served in the meantime as a convenient cover story, and on 19 May 1798, the great adventure began. The invasion fleet sailed from Toulon, and headed south-east into the Mediterranean, picking reinforcements en route. The main body of the army that had embarked at Toulon numbered 10,473 infantry, 880 cavalry, and 1,365 artillerymen, while from Marseilles came another 3,900 infantry and 680 cavalry; at Genoa 5,419 more infantry, 683 cavalry, and 150 artillery were embarked; and at Civita Vecchia [the port of Rome], another 5,053 infantry and 799 cavalry joined; making an initial grand total of 29,402 men. However, even this number was eventually increased to 36,826 soldiers, and a further 12,782 men formed the crews of the fleet, making a grand total for the expedition of 49,608 men together with an unknown number of women and children. There were also 171 guns, at least one balloon and a coterie of *savants* all eager to explore the fabled land of the Pharaohs.

En route to Egypt, however, General Bonaparte paused to seize the strategically important island of Malta. This was not an opportunistic afterthought, but a carefully considered part of his plan. Situated midway between Sicily and Tunisia, and held by the Order of the Knights Hospitaller of St John of Jerusalem since 1530, it was once a vital bastion against the Ottoman Turks, but those days were long gone now and the island's real significance forgotten.

The Grand Master of the Knights in 1798 was Ferdinand Joseph Antoine Herman Louis von Hompesch zu Bolheim,[3] a German princeling from the Eifel. He had been aware for some time of the increased French activity in the Mediterranean ports, but he also believed or was encouraged to believe the cover story that the objective of the expedition was Ireland. As a result, it was not until the French fleet was actually sighted off the Island on 6 June that Hompesch finally recognised the danger and called out the militia. His resources, however, were meagre:

All men in the four cities and Floriana should be divided into 24 companies of 150 men each, to be commanded by a captain, lieutenant, and sub-lieutenant, all Knights of the Order; 150 of the Grand Master's guard should defend the palace with a company of the Regiment of the Bolla [coastguard]: the remainder of the guard to be located in St Elmo; 700 men of the chasseurs, of which the colonel and majors were Maltese, should be divided between Manoel, Tigne, and Ricasoli; 250 marines from the galleys, together with such men as might be obtained from the warships, should defend San Angelo and Cottonera; 1,000 men of the Malta Regiment, and two companies of that of the Bolla, should be distributed on the ramparts of Valletta and Floriana; 250 gunners should occupy the forts, whilst the towns on the coast-line should be defended by the country militia, commanded by Knights belonging to the sea forces of the Order.[4]

Much good they did him. Bonaparte's agents had been active for some time at the very highest levels of the Maltese government and when the French landed four days later, resistance was nominal at best. There was just enough fighting to make the conquest respectable but, as Bonaparte expected, the emergent Maltese bourgeoisie at first saw the French as liberators, who would deliver them from the despotic rule of the Knights. Moreover, a surprising number of the Knights themselves had already been bought and were keen to reach a speedy accommodation with the invaders and so, for a variety of motives, they all conspired to bring about a capitulation of the island on 10 June 1798.

The remaining Maltese regular troops were swept into a new *Legion Maltaise*, partly officered by some of the French-born Knights, and absorbed into the *Armée d'Orient*.[5] In their place Bonaparte left a substantial garrison of his own commanded by General Claude-Henri Belgrand de Vaubois, comprising five regiments of infantry, totalling 3,053 men, supported by five companies of artillery and a locally raised National Guard.[6]

Blessed by his usual good luck, after leaving Malta, Bonaparte and his huge expeditionary force narrowly avoided being intercepted at sea by the British Navy. By the Treaty of San Ildefonso in August 1796, Revolutionary France and Bourbon Spain had become unlikely allies and Britain's fleets and garrisons beyond Gibraltar were rendered untenable and forced to withdraw. However, word of General Bonaparte's preparations at Toulon and his probable destination of Ireland saw a reversal of this policy. On 24 May, Admiral Lord St Vincent, who was blockading the Spanish port of Cadiz, received sufficient reinforcements to detach a squadron of twelve warships under Rear Admiral Nelson

4

to go first to Toulon, and then, finding the French gone from there, to afterwards pursue them. In the event, the two fleets literally passed in the night and Bonaparte arrived safely off the ancient port of Alexandria on 30 June 1798. The word from the French consul there was that the British too had also touched at the port and left just twenty-four hours before, but no doubt they would be back, so ignoring the advice of his own naval officers and the rough seas, Bonaparte insisted on landing his advance guard immediately. By midnight some 5,000 men were ashore at the western end of the Old Harbour, sometimes known as Marabout Bay, some 7 miles west of Alexandria. The local *Bedouin* harassed them on their march but otherwise opposition was non-existent and next day he briskly fought his way into the town with the loss of just 60 men.

Within two more days the rest of the army was safely landed and the French had begun moving inland with the ultimate goal of seizing Cairo. General Desaix marched across the desert with his division and two pieces of artillery, arriving at Damanhūr, some 15 miles from Alexandria, on 6 July. Bonaparte soon followed, leaving Alexandria under General Kléber's command, while General Dugua marched on Rosetta at the mouth of the western channel of the Nile. Its bloodless capture then allowed a flotilla of supply boats to pass into the river and rejoin the army at Ramanieh by 12 July. The French army then resumed its advance up the Nile, travelling by night to avoid the worst of the blistering summer heat. In the meantime, contact with the Turks was sporadic, with the most substantial skirmish taking place on the Nile north of Cairo at Shubra Khit on 15 July. The Turks were brushed aside there and by 21 July 1798 the French were approaching the village of Imbāba, where a *Mamlūk* army was waiting.

The most senior of the *Mamlūk* leaders, Ibrāhīm-Bey was still encamped on the right bank of the Nile, where he was reputed to have an improbable 100,000 men; *Mamlūks*, Turks and Egyptians gathered in and around Cairo itself. On the left bank, his long-time rival, Murād Bey, was left to oppose the French with only some 6,000 *Mamlūk* and *Bedouin* cavalry, supported by several thousand more or less useless Egyptian infantry and somewhat tougher Greek and Albanian infantry that landed from the Nile flotilla.

What was afterwards to be rather grandiloquently styled, the battle of the Pyramids was a one-sided massacre. The *Mamlūks* were an undisciplined mediaeval host. The best of their cavalry were individually brave and skilful warriors, well-mounted and heavily armed, not only with remarkably sharp scimitars (which would soon become must-have accessories for French and British veterans alike) but also with pistols, carbines, light lances, axes and even javelins. However, their sole notion of fighting battles was to charge furiously in a loose swarm straight at the enemy, while their infantry cheered them on as interested spectators before coming forward to finish off the wounded and scavenge the dead. Against a well-armed and well-disciplined modern European army they were hopelessly outclassed. This was not an unusual experience in colonial warfare, but on this occasion the French also managed to outnumber their 'savage' foes by a very considerable margin.

Even allowing for the infantry division left behind at Malta, and the very necessary garrisons planted in Alexandria and Rosetta, Bonaparte still had something like 25,000 fighting men with him that day. They were formed in five infantry divisions, each comprising three demi-brigades or regiments, mustering three battalions apiece. In addition, of course, he had his well-served cannon together with two regiments of light cavalry and five regiments of dragoons, totalling some 2,700 horsemen, albeit most had still to actually find mounts and were trudging unhappily on foot.

Conscious that they were going to be assailed by a great host of mounted cavalry, the French sensibly drew upon Austrian and Russian experience of fighting the Turks, and each infantry division was formed into a large square, with a complete demi-brigade drawn up in six ranks forming the front face, a second one forming the rear and the third demi-brigade split between the two flanks, with all the cavalry and the baggage crammed inside the squares and safely out of harm's way. Only the light field artillery was posted immediately outside the squares, protected by companies of grenadiers detached from their parent battalions.[7]

When all was ready, the French then advanced southwards in echelon, with their right flank leading and the left flank guiding itself off the Nile. From right to left, Napoleon posted the divisions of Generals Desaix, Reynier, Dugua, Vial and Bon. And then, for added security Desaix also sent a small detachment to occupy the village of Biktil, a little to the west of his right flank.

For his part, Murād Bey anchored his right flank on the Nile at the village of Imbāba, which was substantially fortified in traditional Ottoman style with ditches and palisades and was held by infantry and some cannon landed from the Nile flotilla. At about halfway through the afternoon his *Mamlūks* suddenly launched a characteristically violent attack without warning. It was a colourful and impressive sight, but it was also an exercise in bloody futility. The divisional squares of

6

Desaix, Reynier and Dugua held firm and mowed down the horsemen with volleys of musketry and artillery fire delivered at point-blank range. 'The earth was covered with the bodies of men and horses,' wrote Captain Doguereau, of the Artillery afterwards; 'those who had not been hit passed between the divisions ... and again came under fire.'[8] The *Mamlūks* quickly realised they were overmatched and if their vainglorious tactics had a redeeming feature, it was that they knew when to break off, and so their furious attacks soon receded. Bon's division then deployed into battalion columns and assaulted Imbāba. Breaking into the fortified village at the first rush, the French routed the infantry without difficulty and soon the battle was all over.

Against a reported a loss of just twenty-nine Frenchmen killed and 260 wounded, a reputed 700 to 800 of Murad Bey's shambolic host were said to have fallen in the battle or were drowned in the Nile. Warily acknowledging his own cavalry's inferiority, Bonaparte refrained from an immediate pursuit, but once he had established that the other *Mamlūk* leader, Ibrāhīm-Bey, would not stand and face him, he set about passing his army over on to the right bank of the Nile. Three days later, and without any opposition, the General entered Cairo, while Ibrāhīm-Bey fled into the wastes of Sinai and Murād Bey retired into Upper Egypt, where he maintained a spirited but ultimately doomed resistance, before making his peace with General Kleber in May 1800.

The French triumph, alas, was marred just over a week later on the night of 1 August, when the battle of the Pyramids found its counterpoint in the battle of the Nile and Admiral de Brueys' fleet was literally annihilated by the Royal Navy as it lay at anchor in Aboukir Bay. Astonishingly, only three ships escaped. The rest were all sunk or captured, including Brueys' flagship *l'Orient*, which famously blew up. Yet the fleet had served its purpose. The French army was now successfully established in Egypt and while there is no doubting the scale of Nelson's victory and the fact that the Royal Navy was now in undisputed control of the Mediterranean, the loss of the battle at first had surprisingly little practical effect ashore.

Thus, when the Porte's belated declaration of war on France led to a dutiful uprising in Cairo in October, the insurrection was ruthlessly crushed and afterwards a far from beleaguered Bonaparte led an expedition into the Levant in a spoiling attack against the assembling Turkish forces. The towns of Jaffa and Haifa were taken in quick succession and their garrisons brutally massacred in cold blood, but at Acre he was frustrated by its septuagenarian governor, Ahmad Pasha al-Jazzar, assisted by an English naval officer, Captain Sidney

Smith. In his own estimation at least, Smith was the dashing hero who stopped Napoleon's career in its tracks, but although 'The Swedish Knight'[9] (as he was mercilessly lampooned by some of his colleagues) certainly played his part in the defeat, it is difficult to avoid the feeling that al-Jazzar (the Butcher), the tough old Bosnian soldier of fortune, probably had a rather better claim to be the real hero as he and his men withstood the worst that Bonaparte could throw against them. At any rate, afterwards General Bonaparte took a more sanguine view of the setback. Notwithstanding his own later boasts, he was never going to overthrow the vast Ottoman Empire all by himself, but he had successfully accomplished his immediate aim of firmly discouraging any immediate counterattack by land. Returning to Egypt, he also decisively defeated a landing by the Turks in Aboukir Bay; in 14 July 1799 an estimated 16,000 Turkish troops came ashore there, seized the castle and then dug in, only for Bonaparte to counterattack and destroy them in their fortified beachhead a little over a week afterwards.

Having thus secured his Oriental empire for the moment and proclaimed his latest triumph to the world, it was only a month later when the General left a reluctant Kleber in full charge, and boarded a frigate to run the British blockade and return to France! Unsurprisingly, many characterised Napoleon Bonaparte's sudden exit from Egypt in an ugly light; not least his successor, General Kleber, who only learned of his chief's departure by letter! For Napoleon, however, it was a matter of pragmatism. He came, he saw and he conquered Egypt, exactly as he had said he would. It is true that his fleet had been destroyed by the Royal Navy, but he was leaving Egypt firmly under French control and he could now best support his Egyptian army first by employing his formidable talents in securing reinforcements and supplies for it, and more importantly by bringing about a universal peace in Europe that would formally acknowledge France's possession of his conquests. And he could best achieve both those objectives by returning home and becoming ruler of France.

In the meantime, having returned to the Mediterranean, Britain was determined to stay. For a great many years she had maintained a forward naval base on the island of Minorca, but then lost it temporarily in 1756 and again, apparently for good in 1783. Now the present war offered an opportunity to recover it again.

Sir Charles Stuart was accordingly appointed commander-in-chief Mediterranean and sent to Lisbon, where he made his preparations for the attack on Minorca. Incredibly enough, he was initially accompanied only by the 51st Regiment. However, once arrived he was able to exercise his authority as commander-in-chief by taking the 28th, 42nd, 58th and 90th Regiments from Gibraltar and sailing eastwards at the end of October 1798. By 7 November he was off the north coast of the island and, notwithstanding all too evident signs that the Spaniards had been forewarned and were waiting for him, he had the ships' boats hoisted out to land his men in Adaya Bay.

Some 800 men went ashore in the first wave and although a force estimated at 2,000 strong gathered against, them no real attempt was made to oppose the landing. On the contrary, even on that first day 100 deserters came in from one of the Swiss regiments on the Spanish side. Beyond confirming that the garrison comprised six battalions in all,[10] these deserters were unable to provide much useful information, but it was evident that neither the governor nor the garrison were inclined to a resolute defence. Some manoeuvring followed and a fair bit of bluff on Stuart's part (including the mounting of light battalion guns in his 'siege batteries') resulted in the surrender of the island on 15 November, on condition that the garrison should be shipped to the nearest Spanish port. About 3,600 were duly embarked, but another 1,000 'Swiss' remained behind. They were in fact German prisoners of war from the Austrian service who had been trafficked by the French at two dollars a head, and were now readily enlisted into a new regiment formed by Stuart for the British Army, which would later serve with some distinction in Egypt.

With Minorca once more in British hands, the government was able to contemplate a more aggressive forward policy in the Mediterranean. On 22 January 1799, the French occupied Naples and established the short-lived Parthenopean Republic, and so the 30th and the 89th Regiments were ordered from Minorca to Sicily there to prop up King Ferdinand's tottering regime. As it happens, no sooner did they arrive there than an uprising on the mainland temporarily returned Ferdinand to Naples and this meant that the two battalions, under Brigadier General Thomas Graham, were very conveniently at hand for a redeployment to Malta.

In retrospect it was perhaps not surprising that it took just eighty-two days for the Maltese people to rise up in revolt against their liberators. Having seized the island en route to Egypt, Bonaparte had established a new government for it in the approved republican style, but there was no doubting that the French, not the native Maltese, were firmly in charge and they not only took over all the reins of government but set about plundering the island's moveable assets with a rapacity honed by long and happy experience in Italy. The trouble really began on 28 August when three French warships commanded by Admiral Villeneuve, crept into the Grand Harbour of Valletta and announced themselves the only survivors of the disaster in Aboukir Bay. Five days later the revolt began, the garrison of Mdina was massacred, an intended relief force ambushed and the French were thereafter confined to the formidable Valletta defences.

It was a good start but at first the Maltese were on their own. The nearest and most obvious source of assistance was the adjacent Kingdom of the Two Sicilies, whose ruler was still the island's notional suzerain – the Knights having held Malta in return for an annual fee of one falcon. However, obtaining that help proved surprisingly problematic. All of Italy was then in the grip of military and social upheaval as the old kingdoms, duchies and republics were conquered and remade in the revolutionary model and at this point in time Ferdinand lacked both the resources and the willingness to assist the Maltese. On the contrary, viewing the insurgents as a species of Jacobin mob who had at the very least acquiesced in the expulsion of the Knights, the immediate reaction in Naples was to place an embargo on Maltese shipping!

Fortunately, a small Portuguese squadron intended as a reinforcement for Admiral Nelson's fleet was diverted to Malta and on 18 September 1798, Admiral the Marquis de Niza commenced a blockade of the Grand Harbour and would remain off Malta until 18 December 1799. In the interim he disembarked his marines, twenty artillerymen and two officers, and gave the Maltese a quantity of firelocks and gunpowder. Then, at the end of the month, Captain Sir James Samaurez, en route to Gibraltar, convoying the French ships captured at the Nile, also turned over 1,062 firelocks to the insurgents.[11] This was the first real assistance they received, but it was only the start. On 12 October came the arrival of another Royal Navy officer, Captain Alexander John Ball, a favourite of Nelson, with four more ships and orders to join de Niza's blockading force.

Soon afterwards even Nelson himself turned up for a look and 'learned with astonishment that not the smallest supply of arms or ammunition had been sent from Sicily by the King of Naples'. In response, he too landed a quantity of ammunition, and irked by the sight of a large French tricolour flying over the citadel on the adjacent island of Gozo, he instructed Captain Ball to capture the island at once. After the massacre of the Mdina garrison at the outset of the uprising, *Chef de Bataillon* (Major) Lochey and his 217 men were understandably wary of submitting to the Maltese, but surrendering to the Royal Navy was a different matter entirely and on 28 October 1798 Captain John Cresswell of the marines[12] raised the British flag over the fortress.

Valletta, however, still remained in French hands, but on 20 December 1798, the bomb vessels *Strombolo*, *Perseus* and *Bulldog* arrived. These were ketch-rigged, with what would have been the foremast replaced by a specially strengthened hold mounting a couple of heavy mortars, intended for bombarding enemy harbours. Each vessel had also embarked a subaltern, an NCO, and nine or ten specialist gunners, belonging not to the Navy but to the Royal Artillery, for the purpose of working the mortars.

After some discussion, on 29 December, the *Strombolo* landed both her 13in and 10in mortars and all three vessels between them contributed Lieutenant John Vivion and eleven men of the Royal Artillery.[13] Despite his junior rank, Vivion soon made himself indispensable. While Ball attended to civil and diplomatic matters, henceforth it was Vivion who took charge of the land-based military operations.

Unfortunately, on 11 January 1799, a plot to take Valletta from within failed. The gates of Marsamxett Harbour and Porta Reale were to be opened, but the conspirators were discovered and afterwards as many as forty-five of the would-be insurgents were rounded up and shot. Afterwards, the Maltese outside the city seemed more exercised by the fact that if successful, the conspirators had intended to raise the Russian flag, signifying their adherence to the Order, which elected the Tsar to be their Grand Master in succession to Hompesch,[14] and Nelson, never far from the Neapolitan Court (and the British ambassador's wayward wife), was quick write to Ball reminding him that:

Respecting the situation of Malta with the King of Naples it is this – he is the legitimate Sovereign of the Island: therefore, I am of opinion his Flag should fly. At the same time, a Neapolitan garrison would betray it to the first man who would bribe him. I am sure the King would have no difficulty in giving his Sovereignty to England; and I have lately with Sir William Hamilton got a Note that Malta should never be given to any Power without the consent of England … P.S. – In case of the Surrender of Malta, I beg you will not do anything which can hurt the feelings of their Majesties. Unite their Flag with England's, if it cannot, from the disposition of the Islanders, fly alone.

The insurgents responded in their own fashion, on the night of 15 February 1799, with an attempted escalade of the Cottonera Lines, forming the outer defences of the Three Cities of Birgu, Senglea and Cospicua, along the eastern shore of the Grand Harbour. These lines had never been completed and comprised no more than a bastioned wall without outworks. At first it seemed a straightforward operation, if a touch uncertain, but unfortunately, the French, observing that most of the Maltese soldiery were barefoot, had very sensibly strewn the ditches with broken glass, and it appears that although some of the assaulting force got over the first ditch, they failed to seize and open the gates. Panic followed and the whole operation collapsed ignominiously and although the Maltese were afterwards still reported to be 'practising the charge of the bayonet', there was no taste for another attempt.

Instead, Ball persuaded the Deputies meeting in Mdina to restyle themselves a National Congress and so on 28 February 1799 Captain Alexander John Ball RN was elected its President. King Ferdinand, for his part, also appointed him to be his Governor of the Island, while on the British side he was rather more modestly styled the Civil Commissioner and temporarily relieved of his immediate Naval duties in order to concentrate on these dual roles. Malta was thus to become Captain Ball's island.

Afterwards there was constant but desultory skirmishing. Left in complete charge for a six-week period during the summer when Ball was called away, Captain Vivion ensconced himself (with the entire powder supply) in the San Antonio Palace, midway between Valletta and the old capital of Mdina, and did his best to keep things moving. At the beginning of July, he cheerfully recounted to Ball how on two successive nights he launched false attacks on the outworks of Fort Manoel, a large but isolated island position within the Marsamxett Harbour on the western side of Valletta. On the third night he attempted a real attack against the bridge linking it with the mainland. Once again, iron caltrops scuppered the barefoot Maltese, but at least he had the satisfaction of chasing the French inside the fort itself and carrying off the sentries' watch cloaks and lanterns as prizes. That particular exploit earned him a summons to Mdina on the Saturday following, being St Paul's Day (29 June) where to his amusement he received 'all the honours in the church, procession &c. of commandant'.[15]

Otherwise it was minor stuff and tedious work. After the first few days of the revolt the French defence was passive in the extreme and there was a marked disinclination to set foot outside the walls. On both sides the real struggle was all about supplies. The French lived off their dwindling stockpiles but the diet was monotonous and deficient in vitamins, leading to scurvy, skin diseases and other ailments. On 31 December 1799, a multi-talented professional soldier, Lieutenant Colonel Lewis Lindenthal[16] reported the strength of the French garrison to be some

2,500 soldiers, 1,500 sailors, 130 *Garde Nationale* and 70 Maltese; for a total of 4,280 men, albeit at least 200 were said to be in hospital.

In the meantime, those two battalions under Brigadier Graham were landed on the Island by 10 December 1799[17] and by 19 May 1800, Graham was able to report he had under his command:

> 2,092 rank and file fit for duty, of whom 400 are new raised Maltese, and above 700 are Neapolitans, on whom I cannot place much dependence. There are, besides, about 2,000 armed peasants under the Governor's [Captain Ball's] command; half of them at least are allowed to go to work during the day, so that they are dispersed, and of course useless on a sudden emergency, and are tired and sleepy at night. They have no other officers but sergeants, and, though active, brave, hardy fellows, under no discipline nor restraint. It is a matter of doubt and accident whether they would act in case of a sortie so as to be of use even in the daytime; during the night I am sure they would only create confusion ... you will not wonder at my anxiety. I have every reason to hope for a reinforcement of one regiment at least from Minorca, besides the expectation of positive security from the arrival of the Russians. Disappointed of these, the urgency of the case made me undertake a levy of Maltese independent companies entirely at my own risk for the expense of raising, clothing, and arming them; four are completed, and four more are going on.[18]

Meanwhile, in the outside world matters were proceeding apace. Napoleon Bonaparte, having safely returned to France, engineered a coup in November of 1799, which saw him appointed First Consul and *de facto* ruler of France, and now he was once again fighting the Austrians in northern Italy. On 5 May 1800 Lieutenant General Sir Ralph Abercromby succeeded Sir Charles Stuart as commander in chief in the Mediterranean, and his initial instructions laid down four objectives. The first was to strengthen the British troops at Malta by two or three battalions, in order to bring about its surrender, primarily at this stage in order to release the blockading squadron for operations elsewhere. Secondly, after allowing 3,000 to 4,000 men as an adequate garrison for Minorca, he and the Royal Navy were to give every assistance to General Melas and the Austrian army in Italy. Thirdly (and seemingly at one and the same time), he was to co-operate with any pro-Royalist uprising in the southern provinces of France, while avoiding any future commitment by the British government; and then fourthly, in the event of the Austrians being reduced to the defensive in northern Italy, he was to instead employ his forces in rendering assistance to both Naples and Portugal, should either of their territories be threatened or invaded by the enemy! He was also encouraged to contemplate the seizure of Tenerife, but wisely ignore that suggestion entirely.

In any case the necessary preparations for the Malta reinforcement had already been made and within twenty-four hours of the general's arrival on Minorca on 22 May, both battalions of the 35th Regiment, under Major General Henry Pigot and Lieutenant Colonel John Oswald, were duly despatched to Malta.[19] The rest of Abercromby's force then sailed for Genoa, only to learn a couple of days into the voyage that it was already too late. In a hard-fought battle at Marengo, near Alessandria, on 14 June, General Bonaparte had been badly beaten and sent tumbling back in retreat, before the arrival of reinforcements under General Desaix a few hours later dramatically reversed the result and turned defeat into a decisive French victory. Genoa was immediately evacuated by the Allies and Admiral Lord Keith, with the Mediterranean Fleet, withdrew further down the coast to Livorno. Pursuing him there, Abercromby discovered that hostilities between the French and Austrians in Italy were already suspended by the convention of Alessandria, which had been signed only the day after the battle! The Italian war was clearly lost and despite the impassioned pleading of King Ferdinand, his Queen and a deeply compromised Horatio Nelson, Abercromby firmly declined to become involved in a doomed defence of Naples. Instead, sending most of his men straight back to Minorca, he despatched the 48th Regiment to Malta[20] and then followed them there to have a look at the situation for himself.

On viewing the massive fortifications surrounding Valletta, he ruled out landing troops in the vicinity of the Forts St Elmo or Ricasoli to take either of them by storm or to attack the Cottonera lines on its land front. In fact, he gloomily concluded that Valletta was all but impregnable and decided that if the French had not surrendered by October, he would withdraw all five British battalions and abandon the blockade. Fortunately, in the event, having finally run out of food, General Vaubois did in fact capitulate on 5 September 1800.[21]

By then it had dawned upon the British government that the island of Malta might actually represent an incomparable strategic asset, of far greater value than Minorca. And so, in a fresh set of instructions signed on 1 August, Henry Dundas made it clear to Abercromby that the blockade of Malta was not to be given up in October and that when it did fall it was not to be handed over to the Russians or to anyone else for that matter.

Chapter 2

General Abercromby and his Army

The road to Egypt, whither the army was shortly bound, was a long and sometimes painful one for the British Army. Notoriously, it did not enjoy a great reputation at this time and it is a commonplace that in Sir Henry Bunbury's eminently quotable and damning words the army was 'lax in discipline, entirely without system, and very weak in numbers. Each Colonel of a regiment managed it according to his own notions, or neglected it altogether. Professional pride was rare; professional knowledge still more so.'[1]

The reality was, of course, rather more complex, and Sir Ralph Abercromby's career is itself instructive, for despite his Wolseley-like status at this time as 'our only general', his own pre-war experience was surprisingly limited, and although he had proved himself to be both sensible and dependable, at 66 he was also getting rather old to be commanding an army destined for a harsh climate. Not the least of his deficiencies was that by now he was functionally blind; requiring both a telescope to see the enemy and someone to point it in the right direction for him!

He could, however, count on an extensive web of family connections, influence and political patronage. One of the Abercrombys of Tullibody, near Alloa, he belonged to a typical Scottish landed family of the day; one that was all too keenly aware of the need to go out and earn a living. Born on 7 October 1734, he was originally intended for a career in the law, but instead he opted for the army and so became a cornet in Bland's 3rd Dragoon Guards on 23 March 1756. Serving in Germany during the Seven Years' War, he shared in the frustrations of the battle of Minden, before becoming a lieutenant in the same regiment in February 1760 and serving as aide-de-camp to Sir William Augustus Pitt. In April 1762 he purchased a captaincy in the 3rd Horse, and as his new regiment was quartered in Ireland, he was destined not to hear another shot fired in anger for over thirty years! The well-known story that when the American Revolution came, he declined to serve there as a matter of conscience, loses some of its power when it is realised that his regiment was not only a heavy cavalry one, and so unsuited for service in North America, but was also a permanent fixture in the Irish garrison. There was therefore never any question of his being required or even expected to serve in America. In any case, having risen peacefully through the system first to the rank of major in 1770 and then lieutenant colonel of the regiment in May 1773, he was given letters of service to raise and command his own 103rd King's Irish Regiment on 3 November 1781. He had already found himself routinely promoted to the full rank of colonel by brevet a year earlier, but the ending of the war meant the reduction of his unblooded regiment in March 1784, and his own transfer on to half-pay. Nevertheless, seniority in the *Army List* alone saw him continue to rise effortlessly to the rank of major general on 28 September 1787 and he was also successively appointed to be colonel of the 69th Regiment in 1790 and then of the 6th Regiment in April 1792, but in practical terms he remained unemployed until volunteering for service in Flanders on the outbreak of war with France in 1793.

As a 'Scotch cousin' of Harry Dundas, the Secretary of State for War, and also connected to him by marriage, Abercromby had no difficulty at all in obtaining the command of a brigade comprising the 14th, 37th and 53rd Regiments. As a political gentleman, Dundas had absolutely no business at all in making military appointments of this kind, but such was his ascendancy in the government that he rather made a habit of it.

In this case, the brigade given to Abercromby was far from being a plum and all three of his regiments were in a very sorry state, having been hastily brought up to something like their proper wartime establishment with the usual rubbish gathered in by the Independent Companies.[2] The combination of an elderly, half-blind officer with no command experience whatsoever and a brigade of 'undisciplined and raw recruits' ought to have been the proverbial recipe for disaster. Nevertheless, although a popular officer with the ability to inspire confidence and the trust of his men, Abercromby was also something of a martinet and somehow he not only managed to knock them into shape, but emerged from the campaign with the reputation of being a dependable officer who could look after his men. Bunbury, for example, admiringly remembered him as a 'noble chieftain' who was: 'Mild in manner, resolute in mind, frank, unassuming, just, inflexible in what he believed to be right … An honest, fearless, straightforward man;

16

and withal sagacious and well-skilled in his business as a soldier. As he looked out from under his thick, shaggy eyebrows, he gave one the idea of a very good-natured lion, and he was respected and beloved by all who served under his command.'[3]

At any event, his solid performance in Flanders justified his subsequent appointment to command two relatively successful expeditions to the West Indies in 1796 and 1797 before being rewarded with the post of Commander in Chief in Ireland in December of that year. Despite his many years of service in that country and his very deep familiarity with the arcane politics of the notoriously corrupt regime in Dublin Castle, he almost immediately issued a thoroughly splenetic general order, deploring the abysmal want of order and discipline in the Irish garrison, which rendered it 'formidable to everyone but the enemy' (by which he meant the French rather than the anticipated Irish insurgents) – and so was forced to resign within a matter of months. Nevertheless, this did his career no harm, for he thereby not only avoided any involvement in the bloody debacle of the 1798 rebellion that followed, but in a mark of the King's continued confidence, he was appointed to be Commander in Chief Scotland instead. Then, in the following year he was also given command of the advance guard in the landings at the Helder in northern Holland. Despite some initial tactical successes, the unlikely Anglo-Russian expedition eventually proved a failure, but while its Royal commander, the Duke of York, afterwards returned to his desk at the Horse Guards, Abercromby retained the confidence of his cousin and in May of the following year he was appointed commander-in-chief of all the troops in the Mediterranean.

As was his privilege, Abercromby nominated his second-in-command without reference to anyone else and a surprising choice it was, too. Major General John Hely Hutchinson was a 43-year-old Irishman with no previous command experience and seemingly nothing to commend him beyond Abercromby's patronage. We shall encounter him properly later in the story, but at this early stage he was to be well-nigh invisible.

Fortunately, the two generals were supported by a competent and hard-working staff and brigadiers.

The adjutant general was Colonel John Hope, the son and heir of the Earl of Hopetoun. Originally a dashing young cavalryman, he was major in 2/1st (Royal) Regiment in 1792 and lieutenant colonel of the 25th Regiment in the following year. He then went to the West Indies in February 1795, but although invalided home almost immediately, he went out there again under Abercromby and had again served under the old man at the Helder.

The quartermaster-general (responsible for moving the army and quartering it), Colonel Robert Anstruther, was another Scot, born in 1768. He started off as an ensign in the 3rd Footguards at the age of 20, then served in Flanders as a lieutenant and captain (the Footguards had a system of double ranks – a lieutenant in the regiment ranked as a captain in the army), then transferred first to the 66th Regiment as a major in 1797 and to the 68th as a lieutenant colonel in August that year. He served under Abercromby in the Trinidad and Puerto Rico operations, and then exchanged back into 3rd Footguards as a captain and lieutenant colonel in order to go on the staff at the Helder in 1799. He still held this rank when accompanying Abercromby to the Mediterranean as his Quartermaster General.

Unsurprisingly, both their deputies were also Scots. Sir Ralph's second son, Colonel John Abercromby, served as deputy adjutant general (DAG), having begun his less than stellar career at the tender age of 12 as a cornet in the 5th Dragoons in 1784 and reached the brevet rank of colonel on 1 January 1800 despite never having done a single day's regimental soldiering in his life. Instead, from the outset he had served continuously as aide-de-camp to his father at home and in Flanders, the West Indies and Ireland, and ultimately acted as his military secretary on the Helder expedition in 1799. As deputy adjutant general, in Egypt he would be reporting directly not to his father but to Hutchinson, with whom he was also long acquainted.[4]

The deputy quartermaster general, on the other hand, was a very different individual and in contrast to young Abercromby's pampered existence, Lieutenant Colonel George Murray had already crammed a great deal of service into his career. The second son of Sir William Murray of Ochtertyre, in Perthshire, he too was born in 1772 but his first commission, which he obtained at the rather more respectable age of 17, was as an ensign in the 71st Highlanders. The regiment was serving in India at the time so he transferred to the 34th Regiment three months later and then to the 3rd Footguards in the following year. By January of 1794 he was a lieutenant and captain in the regiment[5] and served with it in Flanders and Holland before going to Quiberon Bay and then the West Indies as aide-de-camp to Major General Alexander Campbell of Monzie.[6] In 1799, however, he went to the Helder, and, tutored by Robert Anstruther, he served in the quartermaster general's department, before being picked to go to the Mediterranean as deputy quartermaster general (DQMG) under Anstruther.[7]

As we have seen, Abercromby's initial instructions laid down four objectives. The first was to strengthen the British troops at Malta by two or three battalions, in order to hasten the surrender of Valletta and so release the blockading squadron for service elsewhere. Secondly, after allowing 3,000 to 4,000 men as an adequate garrison for Minorca, he and the Royal Navy were to go to the assistance of the Austrian army in Italy. Thirdly, in the event of the Austrians being forced on to the defensive in northern Italy, he was to instead employ his forces in rendering assistance to Naples and Portugal, should either of their territories be threatened or invaded by the enemy, and seemingly at one and the same time, he also was authorised to co-operate with any pro-Royalist uprising in the southern provinces of France.

The latter suggestion was more delusional than realistic, especially after the Austrian defeat at Marengo, while a doomed defence of Naples was likewise swiftly avoided. Portugal it seems was never considered, since there was already a small British Army there, and so Abercromby retired to Minorca and while he waited to learn what else his political masters might have in mind, he occupied himself by embarking on an unprecedented intensive training programme.

This was a fateful decision and merits some discussion to understand its real significance. Bunbury's statement that 'There was no uniformity of movement,' was an unfortunate one; at once damning and yet wholly misleading, for it is quite untrue to claim that there was no standardised system of drill at the beginning of the war. Successive sets of official rules and regulations had been promulgated and more or less effectively enforced throughout the eighteenth century, charting the steady evolution of infantry fighting tactics.[8] When the war began in 1793 all infantry regiments were being required to conduct themselves in accordance with the then current 1792 *Rules and Regulations for the Formations, Field Exercise and Movements of His Majesty's Forces*. Those rules and regulations were very comprehensive, well thought out and clearly explained, but there were two major issues.

On the one hand, although they were popularly criticised for condensing the military art into just eighteen manoeuvres, in reality the opposite was true. Major General David Dundas' rather chunky set of regulations actually contained a great many other manoeuvres, which were capable of being combined and used to fit nearly every eventuality; of which the infamous Eighteen were no more than a standard proficiency test to be performed by battalions before inspecting generals at their annual review.[9] Consequently, commanders in the field, including General Abercromby, although bound to adhere to the regulations, were also prone to simplifying their tactical repertoire in order to concentrate upon those manoeuvres thought to be most appropriate to the situation

19

they were likely to face. It may have perhaps been this sensible tendency for individual commanders to concentrate on particular aspects of the regulations at the expense of others that led to Bunbury's remarks, but there was also a more fundamental conflict at work.

British infantrymen had claimed to enjoy a formidable reputation in the eighteenth century based on their mastery of weapon handling and the consequent ability to deliver a very rapid rate of fire, first by the cumbersome 'Platoon Firing' and then by the simpler Alternate system.[10] Both systems required well-aligned and tightly closed up linear formations, ideally drawn up in three ranks. However, that was in northern Europe, and service in North America had offered a completely different tactical doctrine based on the use of 'volley and bayonet' tactics, which essentially meant that instead of engaging in a static firefight, units were encouraged to manoeuvre swiftly in just two ranks, fire a single volley at close range and immediately close with the bayonet. This proved very successful against American insurgents but on the other hand it encouraged what was derided at home as 'loose files and American scramble' and engendered a heated debate between the so-called American and German schools, in which the latter looked to the Prussian practice of Frederick the Great, and argued the necessity of traditional linear formations allied to the solidity and regular movements neglected by the Americans, but which were considered vital in the face of numerous cavalry on European battlefields. The argument culminated in what appeared to be the complete victory of the German school, when the then Colonel David Dundas published his famous *Principles of Military Movement* in 1788. This system of drill and tactical manoeuvres was field-tested extensively on Dublin's Phoenix Park, attracting widespread admiration (including the approbation and encouragement of Major General Abercromby) and achieving official adoption in 1792; before proving unexpectedly inadequate when the Army actually went to war.

Dundas had produced a splendid drill book fit for a Frederician battlefield, but it was soon discovered that the art of war had moved on since *Alte Fritz*' day. French military thinkers had long favoured the use of swift movement in tactical columns rather than in unwieldy lines and amid the hurried expansion of their army in the wake of the Revolution they had married these tactics to loose screens or clouds of *tirailleurs* or sharpshooters that were very much more substantial than had ever been attempted under the *Ancien Regime*. Initially, to a large extent this reflected the inability of their hastily raised and unstable levies to assimilate or rather achieve proficiency in more formal tactics, but serendipitously these early campaigns were largely conducted in Flanders, a closely hedged area that was ideally suited to skirmishing tactics, but far from accommodating for linear ones – or for cavalry.

Similarly, in the extended campaigns in the West Indies, and on the Mediterranean islands, which followed, both sides saw little scope for large formations practising linear tactics and, of course, there was correspondingly little incentive for those serving there to invest time and effort in training for hypothetical Frederician encounters. Arguably, that changed with the Helder campaign in 1799, although even there it is telling that the chief criticism of the Army's fighting tactics related to its weakness in skirmishing, for the soldiers according to at least one critic were 'perfectly unacquainted with the system of sharpshooting (and it is impossible not to lament the want of that species of warfare in our army)'.[11]

David Dundas had only paid very cursory attention to the skirmishing tactics that were now such a necessary accompaniment to European warfare and barely mentioned them. It is hard to avoid the impression that he deliberately avoided the subject and may even have seen it as subversive. In fact, a very grudging total of just eleven out of 458 pages in the 1792 *Rules and Regulations* mentioned light infantry at all. Far from his drill book curing the want of 'uniformity of drill or movement' deplored by Bunbury, it was actually Dundas' own failure to address the requirement for skirmishing tactics that forced commanders in the field to devise their own unregulated ones and to question some of the limitations of the '18 Manoeuvres'.

The second and more urgent problem, and the one addressed now by Abercromby, centred around the actual implementation of the manoeuvres. Even in peacetime there were limited opportunities for meaningful training in the Georgian army. Prior to the 1790s, barracks were all but non-existent, except in some parts of Scotland and Ireland. Instead most soldiers were scattered in ad hoc 'quarters' and very rarely sufficiently concentrated to enable more than the most basic training. Undertaking battalion-level training was obviously even more problematic and brigade-level manoeuvres all but unknown – simply because there was no opportunity to bring battalions together on sufficiently broad ground on which to practise those manoeuvres, except in occasional wartime camps, or on Dublin's famous Phoenix Park. Crucially, once the frenetic expansion of the Army got under way after the outbreak of war, effective training was further hampered first by a shortage of competent instructors since those available were obviously spread very thin indeed – just as they would be when

21

Kitchener's New Army was created in similar circumstances in 1914.[12] Secondly, of course, urgent operational requirements all too often saw newly raised or rebuilt battalions comprised of raw recruits bundled overseas long before they were properly fit for service. If the Army's operational problems in the mid-1790s can indeed be attributed to inadequate training it was not for want of a common drill book but rather for a lack of opportunity to become thoroughly familiar with the one it already had – and to work around its tactical inadequacies.

Hence Abercromby's decision on arriving on Minorca on 2 August 1800 to commence an intensive training programme. Brigading his regiments into two divisions each of two brigades, under Major Generals Hutchinson and Moore he worked them relentlessly in order to bring them up to a state of efficiency that would both astonish and delight their officers when they arrived in Egypt. This programme ended, or rather paused, when Abercromby sailed westward on the last day of the month, having received fresh instructions from the government.

He was now ordered to transfer his forces from Minorca to Gibraltar, where he would be joined by Lieutenant General Sir James Pulteney with another 11,000 men, namely; five companies of artillery and fifteen battalions of infantry, who had just been engaged in an abortive attempt on Ferrol. The intention was nothing less than to seize the Spanish port of Cadiz and after Admiral Lord Keith was called into consultation, the whole lot passed through the Straits of Gibraltar on 3 October and anchored off Cadiz the next day. Rather predictably, at this point Abercromby had very little reliable intelligence anent the conditions at Cadiz, but what was known was hardly calculated to encourage him. That the Spaniards had been expecting a British attack for some time was only to be expected, but the news that yellow fever was raging in the city with unusual malignity was a nasty surprise.

Otherwise the strategic situation was not dissimilar to that which would later be faced at Alexandria, in that the city was situated on the end of a long narrow spit of land enclosing the inner harbour and part of the outer one. The plan sketched out before sailing was to land a force on the northern (landward) shore of the Outer harbour, capture the batteries and Fort St Catherine that commanded the bay from that side, and so gain a secure anchorage for the fleet while the land operations proceeded. Keith, however, on consulting with some of his officers who were better acquainted with the coast than himself, became doubtful whether this anchorage would be secure in a south-westerly gale. As Major General Moore commented dryly. 'It is regretted that this was not said at Gibraltar.' Nevertheless, Keith declined to take any responsibility for calling it off, and on 7 October the signal was thrown out to prepare for landing.

Moore thereupon went aboard HMS *Ajax*. Captain Alexander Cochrane was in charge of the boats and had offered to carry him ashore in his own launch. However, Moore recalled:

> I found the different captains, who under Captain Cochrane were to superintend the landing, all on board the Ajax asking for directions. Captain Cochrane was extremely busy, but confessed he was as ignorant as themselves. The fleet was all this time under way, seven or eight miles from the shore. Many flat boats were assembled alongside and astern of the Ajax full of troops, but not near the number that were expected. I begged of Captain Cochrane to go to the Foudroyant and mention to Lord Keith the great deficiency of boats; the necessity of their rendezvousing round some ship anchored inshore, &c. &c. Captain Cochrane returned soon afterwards, but apparently not better informed than when he went. The signal was made to know if we were ready to land. We answered from the Ajax 'No,' I told Captain Cochrane that my orders were to land with my whole brigade (the Reserve) and Guards: in all about 5000 men. As boats had come sufficient to hold 2500 or 3000 only, I could not take upon me to land without particular orders from Sir Ralph; the more so as the fleet was still under way so far from the shore, and there was no probability of the boats, after landing the 1st Division, being able to return and to land a second division before night. Sir Ralph had left the Foudroyant soon after the first signal was made to prepare to land, and had gone inshore to the Phaeton frigate. I went to the Foudroyant to explain to Lord Keith the situation we were in. I found him all confusion, blaming everybody and everything, but attempting to remedy nothing.

Amid the growing acrimony, Abercromby decided to abort the landing for that day and although an order was circulated to prepare to land at daylight, about 1.00 am directions were given to hoist in the flat boats and launches. Soon afterwards it began to rain and blow from the south-west right on shore and at daylight a signal was made to cancel the landing, and to be ready to weigh. Looking at the state of the surf, this order was received with some relief, and the officers on Moore's ship confirmed to him that if he had indeed landed with the Reserve the previous day, the worsening weather meant it would have been impossible to have

23

supported them. Later that day, everyone headed back to Gibraltar and the whole sorry business was summed up by Moore's comment that: 'The figure we have cut is truly ridiculous, but the shortest follies are the best, and it is lucky we did not land.'[13]

This was emphasised all too clearly when the Army and Fleet returned to Gibraltar and was promptly struck by a sudden hurricane on 13 October, which quite literally blew many of the ships out of Tetuan Bay on the African side and scattered them into the Atlantic. Fortunately, when the fleet reassembled five days later, the ships were all of them more or less battered, but none had been lost, but had the landing at Cadiz actually gone ahead, the storm would have turned a debacle into a disaster. The whole affair had been, in effect, been a masterclass in how not to conduct a combined operation and amphibious landing and it remained to be seen whether the lessons would be taken to heart, for even as the fleet rather shakily regrouped at Gibraltar, fresh orders were already coming south and reached Abercromby on 24 October.

The first of Dundas's latest set of instructions related to Portugal, which, shrewdly anticipating a Spanish invasion, had begged that the British expeditionary force already serving in that country should be raised to 15,000 men, and Abercromby was therefore directed to send 8,000 men to Lisbon. His Britannic Majesty's Army in Portugal was then to be commanded by Sir James Pulteney. On the one hand this appointment was only sensible in that, after Abercromby, he was the senior officer on the spot. On the other hand, however, there was also an element of underhand dealing at work here in that on being appointed Commander in Chief in the Mediterranean, Abercromby had nominated his own protégé, John Hely Hutchinson, to be his second in command. However, Lieutenant General Pulteney outranked Major General Hutchinson and so needed to be shuffled out of the way before Abercromby sailed eastwards.[14]

The next orders concerned Malta, which of course had just recently surrendered. The earlier policy reversal, declining to hand it back to the Knights of St John, was now reinforced by an absolute instruction to exclude Russian troops by every measure short of actual hostilities, and upon no account to admit them to any of the principal fortresses or works. Lip service was being paid to the rights of the Maltese people, but having gained possession of the island fortress, Britain now had no intention of letting it go – especially as the Kingdom of the two Sicilies was always regarded as a very doubtful proposition, and worse still, the ongoing conversion of the Tsar to friendship with France had altered the entire situation.[15] If the First Consul should succeed in forming a hostile confederacy of the Northern powers against Britain (as the League of Armed Neutrality) then it might be necessary to withdraw part of the British fleet from the Mediterranean. In that case Bonaparte was certain to seize the opportunity of reinforcing his troops in Egypt. Furthermore, it was easy to see that in the longer term an alliance between France and Russia would give those powers the opportunity to dismember the Ottoman Empire to their mutual benefit, Russia in the Balkans (which would also bridle Austria) and France in Egypt with all that implied for the Levant trade and for India. Therefore, the third batch of instructions definitively ordered Abercromby to embark 15,000 infantry, take them to some suitable port at Cyprus, Crete, Rhodes, or the coast of Asia Minor, and there to concert operations with the *Grand Seignor*'s officers for a landing in Egypt and the reduction of Alexandria.

So far it had been in the Allies' interest that a substantial part of the French army remained harmlessly marooned in Egypt. But to all intents and purposes the war was now over in Europe, so that no longer mattered. On the other hand, if the imminent peace settlement left France in possession of Egypt then the threat it posed to the East India Company would remain indefinitely. At least the Tippoo Sultan was now conveniently dead, slain in the storming of his capital, Seringapatnam, on 4 May 1799, but there were other Indian rulers aplenty who might welcome a French army emerging from the Red Sea.

Harry Dundas, who also held the post of chairman of the government's Board of Control that oversaw the East India Company, recognised that fact, but the rest of the Cabinet were still reluctant to sanction an uncertain campaign so far from home just as the war was drawing to a close. The risks were undoubtedly enormous and William Windham, the influential Secretary at War, sneered with some justice that having lost one army to yellow fever in the West Indies, Dundas was now proposing to lose another one to the plagues of Egypt. The King too was unhappy, but on 3 October 1799 the Cabinet finally gave way.

Dundas, far too optimistically, calculated the French force in Egypt at 13,000 men, of which 3,000 men formed the garrison of Alexandria, and assumed most of the remainder were scattered to different posts in Upper Egypt and Syria. What was more, a number of letters from French officers, both before and after the departure of Bonaparte from Alexandria, had been intercepted and published in England, all of them including one in particular from the late General Kleber, painting the condition and prospects of the French army in the gloomiest colours and suggesting that its soldiers were very anxious to return home. Consequently, Abercromby was authorised by Dundas to offer a guarantee to transport the troops in Alexandria and the other posts direct to France in return for their surrender, and if this offer were to be rejected by the French commander, he was to take care that it should become known to the French rank and file. While it is easy to sneer at Dundas' eager and uncritical acceptance of that assessment – and this part of his instructions might have seemed absurdly unrealistic – they were in fact not too far off the mark, and while the French resisted strongly at the outset, most of them, as we shall see in due course, were indeed sick of soldiering in Egypt and the offer of repatriation would time and again hasten the collapse of French resistance.

In the meantime, any advance into the plague-ridden interior of the country after the capture of Alexandria and the other sea ports, although not absolutely prohibited by Dundas, was firmly discouraged except with the limited object of facilitating a passage to the Turkish army.

On the other hand, on a cheerier note, Dundas reassuringly added that in order to 'straiten the resources of the enemy to the utmost', 5,000 troops had been ordered to sail from India for the capture of Suez and all the other posts occupied by the French army on the Red Sea.[16] The whole Egyptian operation was, after all, ultimately intended to protect the East India Company's hold on the subcontinent, and having just defeated the Tippoo Sultan, its own forces were not only available for service in Egypt, but were far better acclimatised than any European troops. On paper it was a splendid idea, but co-ordinating the arrival of two quite separate forces starting out some 5,000 miles and a whole continent apart was going to be all but impossible.

Next, although a British military mission under Colonel Georg Koehler of the Royal Artillery had for some months been attached to the Turkish army at Jaffa in order to improve its training and discipline, the Grand Vizier was asking for 5,000 British troops to join them. Indeed, without that support, Koehler reported, the Turks could never drive the French from Egypt. Moreover, it was plain that Bonaparte himself was anxious about the army in Egypt and was keen to rescue it if he could. He had already tried to create an opportunity to do so by inviting Great Britain to join in the suspension of arms that had been initiated by Austria after Hohenlinden. However, William Grenville, the Foreign Secretary, insisted upon excepting Malta and Egypt from the truce, and so the negotiations collapsed.

The instructions that Abercromby thus received to take his army to Egypt cannot have been unexpected, but a great deal of preparation and indeed a drastic last-minute reorganisation still remained to be carried out before he could sail eastwards. This was not least due to the need to sort out a contingent to go to Portugal under Pulteney. A supplementary instruction at least reduced the number required from 8,000 to 5,000, but although Abercromby reckoned they were 'of the worst description', paradoxically the choice of which of the battalions were to go to Portugal was primarily compelled by one of the government's rare successes; an Act of Parliament that encouraged the recruitment of militiamen into the regular army. On one level this had been a surprisingly effective measure and helped to bring in no fewer than an astonishing 41,316 trained volunteers in 1799 alone. Indeed, arguably the Helder expedition could not have been mounted otherwise. However, those men volunteering from English militia regiments were enlisted only for limited service (no such restriction was placed on volunteers from Irish units), which meant that the regiments designated to receive these recruits and so able to temporarily form second battalions could not then be sent outside Europe. Hence the diversion of the limited service regiments to Portugal instead of Egypt.

On the whole, the remaining battalions fell into two categories. First, there were those units that had come down with Pulteney after that futile series of coastal enterprises. These battalions were decidedly variable in quality. In fact, quite apart from anything else, whatever their origin, all of them were more or less debilitated and physically unfit as a result of having been crammed aboard transports for months on end. The two battalions of Footguards, who came direct from Ireland, were good of course, and some of the battalions who had been at the Helder such as the 92nd [late 100th] Highlanders came away from there with a swaggering reputation. Others, on the other hand, like the 13th Regiment and the 23rd Fusiliers had only recently been rebuilt with Irish militia volunteers after debilitating service in the West Indies, followed by heavy losses at the Helder,[17] while the two battalions of the 27th Regiment, although also filled up with recruits from the Irish militia, were so sickly that they were quite literally unfit for service. All but three companies of 2/27th had to be sent north to the hospital at Lisbon, while the remainder of both battalions later had to be set ashore on Malta.

In marked contrast to this mixed bag, the real hard men in Abercromby's army were the Mediterranean regiments that were trained so intensively at Gibraltar or on Minorca and had their ranks still substantially filled with pre-war regulars. As a result, they were widely judged 'aguerri',[18] and included among them were a number of foreign regiments. Most eighteenth-century armies enthusiastically recruited outside their own borders and Britain was no exception. Early in the war, most of the foreign regiments were recruited from French

Royalist or other emigres, and sponsored by the British treasury to form the nucleus of counter-revolutionary forces, but they did not survive long and by the eve of the Egyptian campaign the surviving foreign regiments were all unashamedly mercenary ones, largely drawn from Germany, Switzerland and Italy, albeit with a preponderance of French officers. Often, they were employed as 'light troops' rather than placed in the regular firing line. Some indeed were specifically raised as skirmishers and riflemen by way of making good the regular army's deficiency in that arm, but in Egypt they would all demonstrate that they were not only *aguerri* but just as capable of standing in the battle line as any other British soldiers.

As it was finally set ashore in Egypt, Abercromby's army mustered a final total of 16,570 men, exclusive of officers, organised into seven infantry brigades. Divided, purely for the sake of the Navy's convenience, into three divisions, Abercromby and his men began sailing from Gibraltar in the last week of October, but the continued poor state of so many of the ships compelled some to put into Minorca for repairs before they were all reunited on Malta by 1 December 1800. The strategic value of the newly acquired island was already very apparent and for more than two weeks the expeditionary force remained there while last-minute rearrangements were made, more urgent repairs were carried out to the sadly battered transports and the troops were as far as possible set ashore for fresh air and exercise.

The sick, including what remained of the 27th Regiment, were also disembarked there and left behind when the voyage resumed – together with most of the women and children accompanying the troops. Only three women per company were allowed to go on to Egypt rather than the official six, however, many other unofficial ones might also have got themselves aboard the transports. Notwithstanding their traditional (and very necessary) supporting roles as cooks, laundresses and nurses, and their even carrying water and ammunition right up into the firing line, Abercromby intended to travel light. Just how light was yet to be revealed, but already he was aware of his complete want of any means of transport and that was just one more reason why, on leaving Malta, he was not heading directly to Egypt, but to Makre (modern Fethiye) on the southern coast of Asia Minor, where he intended to establish some proper co-ordination with the Turks and obtain the hundreds of horses and mules that would be required to mount his cavalry, draw his guns and carry all his supplies. In the event, contrary winds compelled him to go ashore in Marmaris Bay, 50 miles further east, and there, to his dismay, he would remain for a frustrating seven weeks.

Chapter 3

The Iliad and the Odyssey

The Ottoman Empire had officially been an ally of Great Britain since January 1799, but despite the appropriate expressions of goodwill from the Porte and the attachment of a British military mission, it had been difficult to achieve anything concrete. Even Sidney Smith's freelancing had been limited in its effect, and often counter productive, especially after his involvement in the abortive Convention of El Arish in January of the previous year. In talks partly brokered by Smith, the then French commander General Kleber had successfully negotiated the evacuation of his forces from Egypt. However, at that point the British government was opposed to their being given free passage home, and Smith's rather testy superior, Admiral Keith, repudiated Smith's tenuous authority to negotiate with anyone and insisted that the French be treated as prisoners of war. This proved fatal. In the ordinary way of things, this ought to have meant that they still would have been transported home but would have been forbidden to serve again until exchanged for an equal number of Allied prisoners. Somehow, and Smith seems to have been blamed for the confusion, this was misconstrued to the French as meaning their being turned over to the Turks. This horrific prospect, of course, was totally unacceptable and Kleber not only refused but then proceeded to inflict a crushing defeat on the Grand Vizier and his forces at the battle of Heliopolis on 20 March 1800.

This time, establishing some effective co-ordination with the Turks was going to be essential and so before leaving Gibraltar, Abercromby dispatched his quartermaster general, Colonel Robert Anstruther, to Rhodes, in order to herald his arrival and to set in train the necessary arrangements to receive victuals and support the British expeditionary force.

Aside from agreeing some kind of a joint plan and the co-ordination of military operations, Abercromby's most pressing need at this stage was for an adequate supply of horses. All of his cavalry needed mounting, but more urgently, sufficient draught horses also had to be found to pull Abercromby's guns and to carry his supplies and ammunition once the expedition was set ashore in Egypt. His Commander Royal Artillery (CRA), Brigadier General Robert Lawson, had assembled a good and sufficient train of cannon and mortars of all sizes, but it would be useless if it could not be moved. The British Ambassador in Constantinople, Thomas Bruce, Lord Elgin (later of Marbles fame) was accordingly tasked with purchasing upwards of 600 animals for the army – a figure that suddenly had to be more than doubled after the arrival of two horseless regiments of Light Dragoons from Portugal.

'It was not taken into consideration that this expedition could only last a few months, and that if cavalry could be at all of use it must be in the beginning, and, therefore, if the expense was what prevented the horses from being sent, it would have been better,' complained Moore, 'to have saved the whole and not even sent the men. Lord Elgin had been asked to purchase horses for the cavalry and staff officers, and he accordingly did send 300 or 400, but his Lordship must have been miserably deceived by those he employed, for the horses he sent were the worst possible.'[1]

The debacle amply justified Abercromby's pithy observation that 'there are risks in a British warfare unknown in any other service'.[2] Having established himself not on Rhodes, but at Marmaris Bay on the coast of Anatolia, he impatiently awaited the arrival of the horses, but when they did eventually turn up, Captain Thomas Walsh reported soberly: 'No idea can be formed of the wretched and motley assemblage of horses, with which we were furnished. They were of all colours and sizes, and their backs and feet in miserable condition,' while that engaging rogue Robert Wilson rather more colourfully recalled that:

The horses for the cavalry at length arrived, and expectation was raised with eager hope to receive some of that species for which Turkey is so celebrated; but the mortification was excessive, to see animals naturally so bad, and in such a wretched condition, as to make the dragoons feel humiliation in being ordered to take charge of them. Every commanding officer solicited rather to serve with his corps as infantry; but the nature of the service the army was about to be employed on, rendered even such more desirable than none. However, out of several hundred horses, finally only two hundred were left for the cavalry, about fifty for the artillery, and the remainder shot, or sold for a dollar apiece. Miserable indeed would have been the state of the cavalry, had it not been amended by the horses purchased in the neighbourhood; but this supply was small, since it was a measure not pressed vigorously till too late; previously adopted it would have rendered the whole of the dragoons an effective force, and saved an enormous expense.[3]

In all fairness to Elgin, who prided himself on being a good judge of horseflesh, suitable horses for the artillery were simply not to be had anywhere in Anatolia. The Turks themselves generally had very little use for draught animals and relied on oxen rather than horses for moving guns or other heavy loads by land. There was also a suspicion that those horses actually purchased by Elgin may even have been exchanged for sorrier beasts en route, but whether this was true or not, the army was stuck with them.

As to the artillery, Lawson grudgingly reckoned about 130 animals were just about strong enough and tractable enough to train up in order to form no more than a dozen gun teams. This failure must have been particularly galling to him personally, since a few years earlier he had been the officer responsible for forming and training the very first troop of Royal Horse Artillery. Nevertheless, he also persevered with alternative expedients, including improvising means of carrying ammunition on stretchers and handcarts, and borrowing a number of carronades from the Navy. These large but stubby guns lacked the range and accuracy of ordinary cannon, but were very much lighter in relation to the weight of shot that they could throw at walls of wood or stone, and yet they were powerful enough to be popularly nicknamed 'Smashers'. These carronades, rather than the heavy battering pieces shipped by the Board of Ordnance, were intended to form Abercromby's siege train, but they would also play a crucial role in the battle of Alexandria.

Local purchasing by the cavalry officers themselves eventually proved reasonably effective, and although Walsh complained that the Turks 'were particularly exorbitant in their demands for their horses ...', he also conceded that: 'All these horses were stallions, low, but strong limbed, and altogether very serviceable.'[4] Nevertheless, as Moore grumbled, 'cavalry so badly mounted, and upon horses not trained, could not cope with the French, and they could therefore be employed only as patrols and videttes'.[5]

As we saw, Abercromby's original force had undertaken an intensive period of training on Minorca. Of those, however, only the general service battalions had subsequently come east, while the battalions brought by Pulteney obviously needed bringing up to speed, especially

31

after their long sojourn on shipboard. And so, the training programme started all over again, as Moore recalled:

> The Commander inspected the regiments and brigades separately. He gave praise where it was due, and was severe in his animadversions wherever he observed carelessness or inattention. He became thus acquainted with the state of every corps and the character of its commander. Discipline was improved and emulation excited. Corps were landed daily for exercise. The men were warned of the importance of preserving invariably their order in an open country exposed to the attacks of cavalry; and the attention of the general officers was called to adopt the simplest and most speedy modes of forming from the column of march columns to resist the shocks of cavalry. The troops, particularly those intended for the disembarkation, were placed in the boats in which they were intended to disembark, and arranged with the guns in their proper order, and the landing was practised several times in the order in which it was afterwards executed.[6]

And there were other, more mundane duties, too. '... two regiments were daily employed in cutting wood for gabions and fascines, of which a great number were made by a large party of artificers, selected from the different corps. A great quantity of wood, to serve as fuel for the fleet, was also felled by the soldiers and sailors.'[7] The army was painfully aware that it was going to fight in a desert and that it would need to carry everything it required for its sustenance. Most important, once they landed, would be a supply of water and Walsh rather blandly mentioned that: 'Strict orders were issued, to be extremely careful of water, as it was apprehended we should find great difficulty in obtaining any in the country ...'[8]

But all of this activity would be useless if the landing was 'bitched' as the Cadiz fiasco had been. Both Abercromby and Lord Keith were each in their own way and in their proper element great men, but there was a whole world of difference between fighting a fleet action and conducting a battle on land, and neither of them displayed a perfect understanding of the other's capabilities – and more importantly their limitations – in managing the extremely difficult interface between the two worlds. It was not going to be sufficient to sail to the desired spot and throw the troops ashore hugger-mugger as quickly as possible. They all needed to arrive on the beach at the same time and in the right place, able to immediately form up on the beach not just by battalions, but by brigades and all of them in their proper order of battle. While that might appear straightforward enough, accomplishing it was more difficult than it looked and, like most of his colleagues, Abercromby did not fully appreciate the real technical difficulties involved. Very sensibly therefore, rather than rehearse old arguments of Cadiz, the general and the admiral delegated the task jointly to the senior Naval captain, Alexander Cochrane,[9] and to the quartermaster general, Robert Anstruther.

Once a plan had been worked out between the two it then had to be practised – another radical innovation that seemingly had never been done before! Two brigades took part in the initial exercise on 21 January. Adjustments were then made to the plan and three brigades were involved in the second exercise twelve days later. The second one does not seem to have been regarded as successful as the first, but whatever the nature of the problem or problems, the experience was still regarded as invaluable and while the battalions continued to practise getting in and out of boats and manoeuvring once they were ashore, negotiations were under way to secure some more active Turkish co-operation.

When Anstruther came east he was accompanied by his Deputy Quartermaster General (DQMG), Lieutenant Colonel George Murray, who was tasked with proceeding directly to Palestine. There he was instructed to make contact with the Turkish Army, which was understood to be encamped outside Jaffa under the command of Kör Yusuf Ziyaüddin Pasha, the Turkish Grand Vizier.[10] His army was by all accounts still in a dreadful state after its defeat at Heliopolis back in March. Arriving on 3 December, Murray cannot have expected to find a disciplined European-style force, but what he did encounter was neither exotic nor romantic, but a squalid, disease-ridden horror. Walsh wrote:

> A Turkish camp may not unaptly be compared to a confused and crowded fair, in which every person whether officer or soldier, pitches his tent where he thinks fit. No police, no cleanliness are maintained; dead camels and horses, with offal and filth of every kind, are heaped up in every place and corner. No guards, no piquets, are mounted even in the face of an enemy; no duty is done; in fine, each person lives and forages for himself. And pays no attention to any other concern.
>
> The strength of a Turkish army can never be ascertained, as all the authority of the grand vizier cannot compel them to be mustered. Several revolts have been the consequence of such

attempts. In times of prosperity and success, the army increases in proportion with the hope of plunder; but should it experience a defeat, the general is entirely deserted, and left to seek his safety in flight.[11]

On this occasion Yusuf Pasha claimed to Murray that he had some 35,000 men under his command, but the head of the British military mission travelling with the army, Brigadier General Georg Koehler,[12] more realistically reckoned that there were only 7,000 to 8,000 of them. Nor did their appearance inspire any confidence and a three-day review laid on for Murray by the Vizier rather misleadingly suggested that their tactical repertoire was limited to straggling forward in a disorderly mass before turning around and repeating the exercise in the opposite direction. It was positively frightening and, worse still, with a horrid inevitability, plague was raging amidst the utter squalor of the camp. It was said that 100 men were dying each day and their corpses were simply tumbled into shallow scrapes promiscuously scattered around the camp, which only added to the already appalling stench.

Knowing that Abercromby required a thorough report, Murray bravely stuck it out for ten days before heading back to meet the general, who was still having doubts as to exactly where he was going. As he was operating so far from home, Abercromby's instructions from the government were necessarily 'conditional', and to a degree were contradictory, but ultimately they did give him considerable freedom of action. As we have seen, the primary objective laid down for him by Dundas was to take Alexandria, but now he was being advised (wrongly as it turned out) that no drinking water was available on the Aboukir Peninsula, his proposed landing place just to the east of the city. That might mean that unless he could take Alexandria by some kind of a *coup de main*, as Bonaparte had done two years earlier, he might find the whole operation to be impractical.

Instead, at this point Abercromby was now leaning strongly towards the much more ambitious option of landing at Damietta over on the east side of the Nile Delta. This was still far from ideal since the sea off the beach there was so shallow that it would mean the fleet launching its boats from as far out as 12 miles offshore, and it was obviously nowhere near to Alexandria. On the other hand, drinking water was understood to be readily available there and access via Damietta to the virtually undefended eastern branch of the Nile would allow him to disregard Dundas' strictures and strike inland directly at Cairo with the aim of forcing the French to fight a decisive battle. However, this plan

34

was going to require active Turkish co-operation, both in the form of a Turkish army operating out on his right flank and ideally providing a contingent of Turkish cavalry under his immediate command in order to make good his own deficiencies in that arm.

However, Murray's report and his verbal observations on the Grand Vizier's far from numerous host raised very serious doubts as to whether such a joint operation with the Turks was feasible. The issue was far too important to rest on the assessment of a single junior staff officer. Abercromby decided he needed a second opinion from a more senior officer before committing himself, and so Major General John Moore was sent off on 3 January with a remit to discuss specific proposals for joint operations with the Vizier as soon as Ramadan was over (it was due to begin about 18 January); suggesting that the British should land at Damietta while the Vizier crossed the Sinai to join with them at about Salahieh and then proceed together to Cairo. A bare agreement, however heartily entered into, was not going to be enough. Just as importantly, Abercromby also needed to know whether the Turks were actually capable of mounting such an operation and turning up to the proposed rendezvous on time and with sufficient men and supplies.

It took six days to reach Jaffa, where Moore was immediately met by a Royal Engineers officer, Lieutenant Colonel Charles Holloway,[13] bringing the news that General Koehler and his wife were both dead from a putrid fever (typhus) and that two other members of the military mission had died of the plague. Understandably enough, the survivors had promptly burned the bedding and clothing of the deceased, and seemingly even Koehler's papers as well, bequeathing Moore no detailed information on either the Turkish army or whatever magazines of food and ammunition it might possess. He was going to have to start from scratch. Three days of talks at least produced agreement to Abercromby's plan, and Yusuf Pasha now admitted to a more realistic estimate of 7,500 good but irregular cavalry and perhaps the same number of infantry, but he was dependent on receiving supplies of barley before he could move. Moore remained unimpressed. He wrote:

The Vizier's army is not composed of professional soldiers. The Janissaries are the only troops they have of that description. Even these, being generally resident in the same districts and having no parades or exercises, follow trades and other occupations. The Bashaws of the districts through which the Vizier passes are ordered to attend him, each with a certain number of followers. Those are the inhabitants of the country, who have all arms of their own and attend on foot or horseback according to their means. They are in general a stout, active, and hardy people, and are allowed to be individually brave. They are certainly material of which excellent soldiers might be formed; but under a Turkish Government everything becomes debased.

While individually the Turkish soldier could be imposing, he concluded, in the aggregate they were 'a wild, ungovernable mob'. They were also dying off faster than ever from the plague, and in any case there appeared to be insufficient supplies stockpiled to see them across the desert. In short, advised Moore, it was 'vain to expect any co-operation'.[14]

It would turn out in the end that he had underestimated both Yusuf Pasha and his men, but damning though Moore's assessment was. It would seem that Abercromby had already made his mind up on that score, for no sooner did he report back to Marmaris on 23 January than Sir Ralph informed him there and then that having consulted with those who reckoned to know the Egyptian coast, the operation would be directed not against Damietta, but directly on Alexandria after all.

By then things were at last starting to move and the long-expected *Kapūdān Pasha*, or second in command of the Turkish Navy, arrived two days earlier on 21 January. Küçük Hüseyin Pasha came as a stark and surprising contrast to most of the Ottoman commanders the British had to deal with. Almost inevitably, he was actually a Georgian and had come up from the ranks, but unlike most of his colleagues he was still a youngish man of only 43, and he was efficient. His forces also included a contingent of *Nizan I-Cedid* or regular infantry – disciplined Anatolian peasant soldiers trained and equipped in European fashion – rather than the usual unruly collection of Balkan irregulars who usually provided most of the infantry complement of a Turkish army. Basing himself at Makre, all of 50 miles away, this was not yet close co-operation but the *Kapūdān Pasha* did finally expedite the provision of gunboats and other small craft to assist in the landing and in any subsequent operations up the Nile. And above all, he expedited the arrival of the all-important horse transports, which finally turned up from Smyrna on 16 February.

Next day, Abercromby hosted a conference for all his staff officers and regimental commanders at which he confirmed that the intended landing place would be Aboukir Bay near Alexandria. Then, on the following morning, the embarkation began. It took four days to complete, but at 7.00 am on 22 February the signal was given to weigh anchor and the adventure at last began.

Abercromby, as it happens, was one of those unfortunates who were seemingly incapable of putting out to sea without encountering bad weather, which in this case not only scattered the fleet but forced the horse transports, gunboats and other small craft to run for the shelter of Cyprus. Although the larger ships soon reassembled when the storm abated on 28 February, very few of the smaller craft including the horse transports had turned up by the time landfall on the Egyptian coast was made on 1 March. Next day, Keith pushed his ships as far into Aboukir Bay as he dared, before anchoring amid the shoals.[15] The sea, unfortunately, was still considered far too rough to even attempt a landing and so they remained there sitting quietly in full view of the French as the days wore on without any abatement of the surf.

Bizarrely, it was all to the good in the end.

Shortly after his victory over the Turks at Heliopolis in March 1800 and his subsequent campaign in Upper Egypt, forcing the *Mamlūk* leader Murād Bey to acknowledge French authority, General Kleber was assassinated by a Muslim fanatic. Command of the French army then passed by simple seniority to the very much less imposing figure of *General de Division* Abdallah Jacques-François de Menou.

While the no-nonsense soldier Kleber had been all-too keen to extricate his army from Egypt as soon as he possibly could, Menou on the other hand was one of those seduced by the vision of turning it into a rich French colony. Already he had gone so far as to convert to Islam (hence adopting the name Abdallah) and to marry one Zobeida El Bawab, the daughter of a rich merchant (or as some unkindly claimed, a bath house keeper) in Rosetta. Unlike Kleber, he intended to stay put in Egypt, but not only was this determination to become a *Colon* not shared by many of his subordinates, at the best of times he had an unfortunate knack for falling out with them. In part this reflected his background. While many of them had come up from the ranks in the turmoil of the Revolution, he was a minor member of the nobility from Touraine and sometime commander of a cavalry regiment under the *Ancien Regime.* He had once been a good soldier and his survival during the years of Revolutionary fervour and murderous anarchy due to sheer ability does him credit. Unfortunately, his subordinates regarded him with varying degrees of contempt, both for his going native and in general because they reckoned that he was now getting past it. Aside from the destructive internal politics that became rife in the closed society of the upper echelons of the army, this atmosphere of reluctant subordination was to go a long way to compromise his defence of Egypt.

At least on paper Menou had enough men with which to conduct that defence; providing that he employed them effectively. It is one of the minor mysteries surrounding this campaign that the Turks apparently had no proper network of spies within their own dominions, or at least that if they did, they were not sharing crucial information with their allies. To all intents and purposes, as he lay offshore Abercromby was relying on little more than guesswork in contemplating his foes, and that guesswork turned out to be just about as wrong as it was possible to be. In an arcane combination of intercepted (but inaccurate) correspondence, speculative mathematics and sheer wishful thinking, London had advised Sir Ralph that the 40,000 odd men who had sailed east under General Bonaparte over two years earlier were by now so reduced by casualties, disease and desertion that they probably numbered no more than about 13,000! Furthermore, it was also reasoned that having been abandoned by their general in a foreign land, this homesick remnant of the *Armée d'Orient* was sickly, demoralised and very likely to surrender at the earliest opportunity. To a degree all of these things were true, but Abercromby was sensible that no matter what their condition, the French were veteran soldiers and that initially at least they were indeed going to fight. On the other hand, he allowed himself to be consoled with the thought that the French were so few in numbers and their defensive commitments were so extensive that they would be unable to concentrate a substantial force against him.

In actual fact, notwithstanding its losses, a subsequent analysis by the British staff would compute that the active part of the French army was actually some 20,950 strong at the outset of the campaign and that once second-line and garrison troops were added Abercromby's 14,967-strong expeditionary force was blithely launched against an army double its size. [16]

The French General Reynier, who might reasonably be expected to know what he was talking about, reckoned that the troops actually capable of taking the field amounted to 13,372 infantry and 1,661 cavalry, for a total of 15,022 privates on 1 March 1800. He did add a caveat that this figure included the 348 artillerymen manning the two light guns attached to each demi-brigade, although he evidently did not include the gunners and other personnel belonging to the artillery companies that were manning the heavier guns in garrisons and in the divisional field artillery companies, which each had four 8-pounders and two howitzers. [17]

Many of the individual French units, it is true, were by now reduced by as much as a third or more of their initial strength, and Thomas Walsh, after enumerating all fifteen demi-brigades, stated that they were 'very unequal in strength, some having recruited blacks from Africa'. One of the latter was the *21e Légére* out in Upper Egypt, whose ranks were said to have been partially rebuilt by Kleber through the somewhat unusual expedient of purchasing about 200 slaves from Abyssinian dealers.[18] No doubt there were others, but while it is suggested that some of the weaker demi-brigades consolidated their regulation three battalions into two, the actual situation was more complicated in that it was common to find units fielding two battalions for operations,[19] while the third battalion was employed on garrison duties, and the grenadier companies were also detached to serve as skirmishers, either by themselves or joining with the companies drawn from other units in order to form consolidated battalions.

Similarly, while the French cavalry had inevitably suffered a great deal of wastage in horses, they too made good much of their losses by acquiring remounts locally and although each regiment still perforce mustered a dismounted squadron,[20] they nevertheless very noticeably outnumbered Abercromby's little cavalry brigade.

What was more, although Walsh's analysis included 10,000 'non-combatants', that latter term is itself rather misleading, for it was not confined to the customary rabble of administrative and support services, camp followers, and the inevitable sick and convalescents. It also included a good many second-line units who might not be ranked with the remaining veterans of Italy or considered fit to stand alongside them in the firing line, but whose personnel were still perfectly capable of shouldering a musket and manning a fortified position or carrying out the multitude of ordinary garrison, policing and escort duties that would otherwise distract the regulars.

Among them there were also some 3,000 or more survivors from the late Admiral Brueys' fleet, who were formed into a substantial *Legion Nautique*, comprising both gunners and infantry, and largely employed as part of the garrison of Alexandria. There were also various units raised from among the local Coptic Christian and 'Greek' communities – although both were filled up to a degree with anyone else who could be induced to enlist irrespective of their real nationality. For the most part they were employed on internal security duties but the most notable of them were the *Grenadiers Grecs*, who were to fight in the front line at the battle of Alexandria/Canope. There were even a sizeable number of Syrian and *Mamlūk* mercenaries; although the short-lived *Legion Maltaise* had disappeared from the list by the time the British arrived, seemingly having been disbanded in the wake of the revolt on the island. An elite *Regiment des Dromadaires* on the other hand, while extremely useful, was formed of volunteers from regular units and so did not therefore add to the total.

Be that as it may, General Menou was therefore still in possession of a substantial army, but as Abercromby consoled himself, he also had extensive defensive commitments. Inevitably, it was necessary to establish a wide perimeter around French Egypt, which was broken down into four sectors, three of which were each the responsibility of a general de division. However, in all three cases a substantial number of their men were actually held back at Cairo, in order to create a substantial central reserve that could be quickly marched to whichever sector was actually threatened.

Menou's plan or rather defensive concept reflected his own total lack of reliable intelligence. It has been suggested that tactically he would have done better to place his central reserve in the Delta at Ramanieh, just as General Kleber did before defeating the Grand Vizier at Heliopolis. He would thus have been able to respond faster to a landing wherever it occurred, but Menou was mindful that Kleber had also faced down a revolt in Cairo when the Grand Vizier came knocking in March. As a *Colon* or colonist he may have been more sensitive to the possibility of another rising in the city than the ruthless Kleber, but there was a far more fundamental problem in that both Menou and Friant, the sector commander at Alexandria, were not unreasonably convinced the British would land further to the east, over on the other side of the Delta, or even beyond, in order to be able to link up with the Turks.

The first intimation to the French that Aboukir was indeed the likely landing place had in fact come on the night of 24 February when two Royal Engineers officers, Major William McKerras and Captain Richard Fletcher, attempted a clandestine reconnaissance of the bay. Using a small pinnace, the two officers sounded the approaches close inshore and then daringly ventured on to the beach itself. Perhaps inevitably, they were detected. A French gunboat came out to investigate and intercepted them as they tried to get away. In a brief fight, McKerras was shot through the head and Fletcher captured, but surprisingly nothing much seems to have come of the incident.[21]

Then of course, a few days later the fleet arrived, but notwithstanding that earlier incident, the French reaction was restrained. Messengers were promptly despatched to Cairo, where Menou responded by dissolving most of his central reserve! Instead of hurrying their troops to Aboukir, both Reynier and Rampon were ordered to close up to their allotted sectors on the east side of the Nile, but otherwise stay put. Reynier, for one, furiously protested that they would thereby be marching away from the point of danger, but as Menou saw it, the reverse might turn out to be the case. What made him suspicious was the British failure to land immediately. While he must have been told of the present rough sea state off Alexandria, he also knew that Bonaparte's landing two years earlier was successfully carried out in less than ideal conditions – so why were the British waiting? What Menou feared was the possibility that this was only a feint and that as soon as he rushed all of his reserves up to the Alexandria area, the British would simply weigh anchor again and sail off eastwards, leaving him flat-footed. The longer the British remained sitting quietly offshore, the more that suspicion deepened.

In any case, Friant, the general actually on the spot, seems to have been unduly confident both of his chosen fighting position and his numbers. He had only 2,000 men immediately under his hand, but they were deployed on a narrow front with plenty of artillery covering the beach. He was convinced that he could defeat the British by himself and only requested the assistance of just a single regiment of cavalry by way of reinforcement. General Menou duly obliged by sending up the 230 men of *22e Chasseur a Cheval*, and ordered Lanusse's infantry division to follow as well on 5 March. Then he dithered. Reynier passed on reliable intelligence that the Grand Vizier (who was still on the other side of the Sinai Desert) had not yet marched and nor was he expected to do so for a couple more weeks. Menou may have been wary of this news since Reynier was still insisting that the correct course of action was to first concentrate against the British and then turn on the Turks – if they ever appeared. Instead, the lack of movement by the Vizier only confirmed Menou's conviction that the British appearance off Alexandria was merely a diversion and that they would eventually sail east to join him. General Lanusse was therefore ordered to halt at Ramanieh and only one of his four demi-brigades was allowed to continue forward to join Friant. As to the other three, two of them were to await events there, albeit Friant was still authorised to call on them if need be, but the fourth was recalled to Cairo!

Unfortunately for Menou, not only was he completely wrong about Abercromby's intentions, but by now the sea was growing calmer. Most of the horse transports carrying the cavalry horses were still missing, but Abercromby had waited long enough.

John Moore in his diary:

Upon the 7th March the wind abated and the weather promising well, orders were given in the afternoon for the troops of the reserve. Brigade of Guards and two regiments of Major-General

Coote's Brigade, to get into the flat boats and launches at two in the morning. As the ships which contained them were all troopships, and were anchored six or seven miles from the shore, two small vessels were anchored in the evening near the shore; the one to mark the right of the landing, the other an intermediate point on the same line; the boats, as they received the troops, were directed to rendezvous alongside these two vessels, where the captains of men-of-war who, under Captain Cochrane, had the direction of the landing, arranged the boats of their respective divisions in accordance with an order previously settled, which was that of Brigades, of Regiments, and of Companies, agreeable to the order of battle of the army.

At 1.00 am the next morning the first wave began getting into the boats, and an hour later, exactly on time, a single signal rocket burst high over the fleet.

Chapter 4

Aboukir Bay

'Each flat-bottomed boat,'[1] explained Captain Walsh, 'contained about fifty men, exclusive of the sailors employed in rowing. The soldiers were ordered to sit down on the bottom, holding their firelocks between their knees. All the boats of the fleet were engaged either in towing the flats, or carrying troops. They might have contained in all near five thousand men. Six thousand had been intended for landing, but above a thousand remained in the ships, from the want of means to convey them.'

Even after the boats belonging to the hired merchant ships were pressed into service, there was still insufficient capacity to put the whole of the first wave ashore in a single lift, let alone the whole army. Instead, the beachhead was going to have to be secured with just three brigades; the Reserve under Moore, Ludlow's Guardsmen and the greater part (but not all) of Coote's 1st Brigade.

The problem of getting the men ashore was compounded by the fact that the shallow depth of Aboukir Bay forced the larger ships to anchor some 7 miles out from the beach. This meant that, as at Cadiz, there might be a dangerously long interval between setting the initial lift ashore and then fetching the second lift to support them.

The answer worked out by Arbuthnot and Cochrane was to range the warships and transports in two lines. The troops of the second lift were transferred in the evening from the large ships in the outer road to others drawing less water. These anchored further in for the purpose of supporting the first disembarkation 'more expeditiously'. Then, when the signal rocket was fired at 2.00 am, all the available boats were employed in carrying the first lift forwards and straight through this inner line of transports, in order to deposit it straight on to the beach, before rowing back the relatively short distance to collect the second wave.

In contrast to the rough seas of the preceding week, the bay now presented a flat calm, 'as smooth as glass' recalled Captain Stewart, and the carefully rehearsed operation went like clockwork. 'The moment was awful,' declared Walsh,[2] rather sententiously, 'and the most solemn silence prevailed, as the boats pulled to the rendezvous, a distance of about five miles. Nothing was heard but the hollow and dismal sound of the oars, as they dipped into the water.'

Soon after daylight, the majority of the boats arrived at the rendezvous, and while in Moore's view it took a considerable time to arrange them, by a little after 8.00 am they were all in position, formed in 'as correct a line as possible' and the beachmaster, Captain Cochrane, hoisted the signal to commence the final run in. Ahead of them lay an open beach stretching in a very gentle arc for some 5,000 m, running more or less due south from a promontory tipped by Aboukir Castle. Firm and hard at the water's edge, the strand quickly rose into a line of softer dunes, in the centre of which was a near-perpendicular sand hill known by the French as the *Monticule du Puits* from some nearby wells (*puits*) and estimated by Major Wilson to be about 60 m high. Formidable as it appeared, it was obviously the key to the French position.

Moore explained:

I was in the boat with Captain Cochrane and the reserve upon the right was directed upon the centre of the high sand hill. The rest of the boats were to dress by them. The high sand hill commanded the ground on each side; it was the left flank of the enemy's position or it was his centre. In either case it was desirable to possess it, and I was determined to gain it with the regiments of the right of the reserve as soon as possible. Just as the signal was about to be made for the boats to advance, General Hope came to me from Sir Ralph, who was with Lord Keith on one of the bomb-vessels, to say that if the fire from the enemy was so great that the men could not bear it he would make the signal to retire, and therefore desired Captain Cochrane and me to look occasionally to the ship he was in. General Hope then said that Sir Ralph wished to know if I was still of the same opinion with respect to the point of landing on the right, or if I did not think it would be better to extend a little more that way towards the bottom of the hill, as the latter appeared to be very steep in front. I said that I did not think a change necessary; that the steepness was not such as to prevent our ascending and was therefore rather favourable.[3]

Every oar was instantly in motion, pulling eagerly toward the shore. In order to protect our approach, the Tartarus and Fury bomb vessels commenced throwing shells as we passed them. Two gunboats, and three armed launches, kept up a constant firing for the same purpose, though with little effect.[4] We continued to advance unmolested, and not a Frenchman was to be seen, either on the sand hills, or on the strand; when suddenly, as we got within reach, they opened a tremendous and well-supported fire from fifteen pieces of artillery, which had been disposed on the hills that lined the beach, and from the guns of Aboukir Castle. Shot and shells now fell in profusion, striking the water all round the boats, and dashing it upon us. This, however, was comparatively but a feeble opposition. On our nearer approach, we were assailed with such a terrible shower of grape shot and langrage,[5] as was never before probably directed against so small a point, and could be compared only to the effects of a violent hail storm upon the water.

Never was there a more trying moment. Our troops penned up so close, as to be unable to move, and exposed to a galling and destructive fire, without the power of returning it, or taking any measures of defence. Two boats were sunk. Close to that in which I was embarked, a flat, conveying part of the Coldstream guards, was struck in the middle by a shell, which, bursting at the same instant, killed and dreadfully wounded numbers; the rest went to the bottom. Many were picked up, but in such a state as to be insensible of the obligation …

Captain David Stewart with the 42nd Highlanders similarly confirmed that:

With the sea as smooth as glass, and nothing to interrupt the aim of those who fired; and a line of musketry so numerous, that the soldiers compared the fall of the bullets on the water to boys throwing handfuls of pebbles into a mill-pond; and although the spray raised by the cannon-shot, when they struck the water, wet the soldiers in the boats, very few were hurt of the whole landing force; of the 42nd one man only was killed, and Colonel James Stewart and a few soldiers wounded.

It was nearly 9.00 am when the first boats actually grounded on the beach. Until that point the French infantry had remained concealed behind the dunes, not least because they were badly outnumbered. Despite his earlier confidence, when it came to the test Friant had only about 2,500 men and fifteen guns: 'The 67th demi-brigade with one twelve-pounder, two howitzers, and their two four-pounders, with their right towards the beginning of the dyke of Lake Maadieh; the 18th regiment of dragoons to the left of that demi-brigade and the 20th of dragoons and the 75th, to the rear of the height of the Wells. The detachments of the 25th and of the 51st, with two eight-pounders and a howitzer, formed a reserve between this last corps and the fort of Aboukir.'[6]

Half a dozen battalions were always going to be hard pressed to hold such a broad position, but Friant also had a handful of cavalry, which he intended to fling against the invaders while they were still in the surf and before they had a chance to form themselves up on the beach.

However, he was undone by Moore's unexpected decision to assault the tall sand hill head on. The Reserve were first ashore, and just as they had practised, they quickly formed up with Brent Spencer's little Flank Battalion comprised of the grenadier and light companies of the 40th Regiment covering the right of the line. Then came the 23rd Royal Welch Fusiliers, the 28th, the 42nd Royal Highland Regiment and the 58th Regiment, with the left flank of the brigade being covered by Major Hudson Lowe's Corsican Rangers. The sand hill towering above them as they dressed their lines was a daunting obstacle, but it was also so high and so steep that they were in dead ground, safe from artillery fire and indeed largely unseen by the French infantry, identified by Walsh as the two battalions of the *61e Ligne*. As soon as they were formed, Moore, unhesitating, led his men forward and straight up the slope, and Abercromby's official report duly confirms that: 'The troops that ascended the hill were the 23rd and the four flank companies of the 40th, under the command of Colonel Spencer, whose coolness and good conduct Major General Moore has mentioned to me in the highest terms of approbation.' However, Abercromby also added that: 'It is impossible to pass over the good order in which the 28th and 42nd landed, under the command of Brigadier General Oakes, who was attached to the reserve under Major General Moore ...'

The hardest fighting that morning may in fact have been done by the 42nd, for they lost far more casualties than any other battalion in the landing force, and Stewart recounted how:

The ascent was steep, and so deeply covered with loose sand, that the soldiers, every step they advanced, sunk back half a pace ... about halfway up came in sight of the enemy, who were prepared with their pieces levelled. Their fire being so close, was of course very effective; eleven men of my company fell by this volley, when the soldiers doubled their exertions, and reached the top of the

46

precipice before those drawn up there had loaded; but instead of making use of the bayonet, against men exhausted and breathless, the enemy turned their backs and fled in the utmost confusion.[7]

It might have been a famous victory but it was also an expensive one, for at the end of the day the Black Watch returned a total of twenty-one men killed and no fewer than 156 wounded, including eight officers.[8] By contrast, the 40th flank companies reported only Ensign Frederick Meade and fifteen others killed and another thirty-three wounded, while the 23rd Fusiliers had a modest six rank and file killed and forty wounded, and the 28th returned only five men killed and thirty-four wounded.

While the sand hill was being stormed, the rest of the first wave was still landing. In the centre of the attacking line were 1/Coldstream and 1/3rd Guards under Ludlow, and then Coote's brigade forming the left wing with 2/Royals, and both battalions of the 54th, albeit only 200 men of 2/54th came ashore in the first lift.[9]

The intention, obviously, had been for all of them to land at the same moment, but due to various factors both Ludlow and then Coote were very slightly delayed in getting ashore and so by arriving *en echelon* quite inadvertently scuppered Friant's intended counterattack.

Sensibly enough, the French general had concealed most of his cavalry in a large hollow between the rear of the sand hill and another row of dunes that lay behind it. Then, as the boats carrying Ludlow's brigade grounded and the guardsmen jumped out, Friant ordered his cavalry to charge. Riding down the skirmishers of the Corsican Rangers, who were covering the left flank of the Reserve, they killed four of them and wounded another twenty-five, including a Captain Panatini, but their real target was the Footguards and as Moore and the other chroniclers tactfully conceded, there was at first some confusion in the Coldstream ranks as they cleared the boats and started to form up. Fortunately, the sand hill masked the fact that the 58th Regiment, belonging to the Reserve, had already landed and formed up just minutes before and so were able to come immediately to the beleaguered Guardsmen's assistance, enabling them to present a front and drive off the French cavalry, who suffered 'a very considerable loss'. For their part, by the end of the day the Coldstream had lost Ensign George Warren and seventeen men killed, and reported another seventy-four wounded and six missing.[10]

Meanwhile, a second counterattack was being launched against Ludlow's men. This time a column of 'six hundred infantry was advancing with fixed bayonets through a hollow against the left flank of the Guards'. This was presumably Friant's only other major unit, the two battalions of 75e Ligne, but once again their timing was awry and this time the situation was saved by 2/1st Royals and 1/54th, who 'from being in transport boats (ie not in flat-bottomed landing craft) had not reached the shore so soon as the others.'[11] Their slightly delayed arrival meant that when they did splash on to the beach, they fortuitously found themselves coming in on the flank of Friant's counterattack. Despite the absence of the Gordons and a part of 2/54th, Coote still had about 1,600 men in his brigade at this point in time and a brief, but evidently vicious, exchange of fire followed, in which the Royals lost twelve killed and forty-seven wounded, and 1/3rd Footguards had five killed and forty wounded, before the French recoiled in confusion.[12]

The sight of the French turning their backs was an uncommon one in those days and there seems to have been some surprise in the British ranks that they gave up so easily. 'This moment of exultation cannot be described,' crowed Wilson, echoing a general feeling of unexpected triumph, 'but the most callous mind must be sensible to its effect.'

Although violent, the battle was to all intents and purposes all over within those first twenty minutes, albeit there was no pursuit and the French simply fell back to the inner line of sand dunes and maintained a scattered fire for about another hour and a half while the British concentrated on getting the rest of their men ashore.

In the circumstances, British losses were relatively high. Aside from naval personnel,[13] a total of four army officers were reported to have been killed and twenty-six wounded along with ninety-nine NCOs and men killed and another 579 wounded. In addition, twenty-one men were returned as missing (including fourteen Guardsmen) – who were presumably lost when their boats were sunk on the run in.[14] Walsh optimistically announced French losses 'at a very moderate computation' to be 400 killed, wounded and captured, along with six pieces of artillery and a howitzer. Wilson, less ambitiously, put them at about 300, while Captain Stewart sagely commented that, 'The loss of the French did not exceed one-half of that of the British, and, considering the relative situations of both, the difference might have been even more in their favour.' In all fairness, once his two major combat units, the 61e and 75e Ligne, were defeated, Friant only had other rather weak infantry battalion unengaged. The British, by contrast, as the afternoon wore on were reinforcing fast.

Impetuous as ever, and no doubt anxious to get close enough to be able to see what was actually happening, Abercromby had himself rowed ashore directly in the wake of Moore's assault on the sand hill. Meanwhile, the boats, having delivered the first wave on to the beach, were already turning around to collect the rest of the army. Some of the ships' longboats and launches hoisted sail and set off all the way back to fetch the rest of Coote's brigade, but the slower landing craft concentrated on running a shuttle service between the beach and the inner line of transports, evacuating the wounded and returning with units of the second division. Next came the rest of the field artillery, supplies of ammunition and as the day went on, even some horses as well. By the end of the day the first phase of the operation was complete and the British Army stood entire on the Egyptian sand. It was time now to think of Alexandria, but taking that objective was going to be by no means as straightforward as it had once seemed.

General Friant defiantly remained in position among the sand hills just to the west of the beach until about 11.00 am, then, having first detached a single company of *51e Demi brigade* to hold Aboukir Castle, he quietly started to withdraw along the narrow corridor of sand between Lake Maadje and the sea.

For a time he halted at the post of Mandara, a small redoubt built on a height in the narrowest part of the defile, about 4 miles from the landing place, but as soon as the French were finally gone, the Navy dragged some of their armed launches over the beach and into Lake Maadje (or Lake Aboukir)[15] and began preparations for using this fortuitously located body of water as a supply route to support the advance on Alexandria. Indeed, this salt water lake was to be of absolutely crucial importance, as Walsh admirably describes at some length:

> This lake is of a very modern date, having been formed by an irruption of the sea so late as 1778. A stone dyke, the greater part of which is to this day standing, was the only barrier, which kept out the sea from a plain much below its level. This was broken down by the fury of the waves in a violent gale, and the water, rushing in with impetuosity, destroyed several villages, and formed the present extensive inundation. The kalisch or canal of Alexandria divides it from the site of Lake Mareotis, which was almost everywhere dry, having no communication with the sea.
>
> Lake Aboukir is navigable in most parts for boats and small craft: it also abounds in excellent fish of different kinds, especially mullet, which afforded a welcome and plentiful supply to our army; the Arabs being glad to find so good and ready a market. The advantages which we derived from this lake were great

indeed; and to the accommodation it afforded us in many respects, we are in some degree indebted for our success. All our provisions, ammunition, guns, and stores of every description, were brought up to us with the greatest facility in boats; but had we been without this mode of conveyance, our means of land carriage were so feeble, that the moment of action would probably have been lost, before supplies could arrive. Two or three hundred miserable horses or mules could afford very little effective assistance in the heavy sands of the peninsula.

By affording a harbour for our gunboats, the lake was also of the greatest service; these boats, exclusive of other advantages, were no small security to our left flank. It is rather unaccountable, that the French, so long masters of this country, did not keep a strong force of armed boats on this lake, which would have annoyed us materially on our landing, or in any future movements.[16]

As to those movements, once the second division was landed and had closed up on the first, Abercromby began to cautiously feel his way towards Alexandria. Due to the restricted frontage between the sea and the lake, the army began moving forward by brigades, with each battalion formed in open column of companies. The Reserve (or at least most of it), was still acting as the advance guard, followed closely by Ludlow's Guardsmen, then Coote's, Cradock's and Cavan's brigades in succession behind them.

Only a part of Stuart's and Doyle's brigades were brought ashore in the course of the first day, and were temporarily assigned to a blocking position in front of Aboukir Castle, but then about seventy mounted and 200 dismounted cavalrymen also came on shore in the evening. The mounted men were immediately pushed to the front to act as vedettes at the head of the advance, while the rest remained near Aboukir and joined the forces blockading the castle.

Moore wrote:

On the morning of the 9th March I went forward with Lieutenant-Colonel Anstruther, the Quartermaster-General, who was going to look for a new position. We took with us some cavalry, the Corsicans, and the 92nd Regiment. We posted the latter about two miles in front, and proceeded a couple of miles further with the Dragoons. We then met a strong patrol of the enemy, which induced us to retire. The country which we had seen was uneven; sandy and thickly interspersed with palm and date trees. At the place where the 92nd had been posted, whilst we went forward with the cavalry, there was a small redoubt and flagstaff; and the sea and Lake of Madie, running in on each side, narrowed the ground at this spot more than at any other, either in front or in rear of it. Upon its being represented to Sir Ralph as a favourable point to possess, he directed me to take post upon it with the reserve. I reached it about twelve o'clock, and, after posting my outposts, I went with a patrol in front until I saw the enemy's cavalry.

On the 10th at daylight I advanced in front of the picquets with the Dragoons and Corsican Rangers to feel what was in my front. We very soon met the advanced guard of a considerable body of cavalry, who endeavoured to push us back; but, as we were but a little way from our picquets, and as the ground was favourable to infantry, the Corsicans were directed to disperse and post themselves.

By this means they forced the advanced guard of the cavalry back; but, instead of being satisfied with this and keeping their stations, they followed the enemy, who led them close to their main body, and then turned upon them, wounded several, and took an officer [Lieutenant Guiterra], a surgeon, and ten men prisoners. It appeared afterwards that it was only a strong escort of cavalry for the purpose of reconnoitring.

Many officers who by their dress and attendants appeared to be officers of rank were observed. The skirmishing which took place at first still continued, but, as it answered no purpose, I ordered our people to remain fixed and not to fire unless fired upon. By this means the firing was stopped. The main body of this detachment of the enemy remained in our neighbourhood until the afternoon, when they disappeared, leaving in our front common picquets and videttes only. All the afternoon I observed officers reconnoitring my front and flanks, so much so that I suspected they had some design. I however considered my position so strong that I did not apprehend a direct attack on my post. I thought they might endeavour to carry off a picquet. I reinforced the picquets, particularly those on the flanks at night. Nothing happened during the night.

Next morning Abercromby himself came up and explained that resumption of bad weather had delayed the landing of stores and provisions and that in turn was preventing an immediate advance, but at least, notwithstanding the concerns which had once so exercised the planners, water was soon found not to be a problem for a 'very tolerable supply of good water,' was found by digging about 4ft down. 'We were like-wise convinced,' commented Walsh wryly, 'that it sometimes rains in Egypt, for we had a smart shower.'[17]

That evening a more or less recovered 2/27th Regiment also came ashore and caught up with the army, and the following morning they accompanied Stuart's and Doyle's brigades up to the front, while the Brigade of Guards moved forward and took post in Moore's rear, about halfway between his position and the army. That left the Earl of Dalhousie with only the 2nd (Queen's) Regiment, and the dismounted dragoons, to maintain the blockade of the castle, but in the meantime the Navy had also been reconnoitring the lake to satisfy themselves of the feasibility of its carrying supplies. On receiving their confirmation, three days' provisions were issued to the troops, and in the evening, orders were issued for a resumption of the advance next morning.

Nevertheless, for some reason it was not until 10.00 am, with the sun high in the sky, that the march got properly under way again. The army moved off from its right in two columns, each corresponding to one wing. The reserve, formed in two columns, once again provided the advanced guard to each wing, with Moore leading on the right and Brigadier Oakes on the left. By way of guiding the advance, Moore 'had for object a square tower and flagstaff'; this was the tower of Mandara, which was to give the coming battle its name.

The French cavalry had in the meantime been reinforced by the 230 men of the *22e Chasseurs a Cheval* and, as Moore related:

The enemy's cavalry retired before us, skirmishing as we advanced. The country was sand interspersed with palm trees, and the ground not so uneven as to prevent the columns generally from seeing each other. The tower was evacuated, and the heads of the columns were there halted. From the top of it a body of infantry was seen advancing upon us, and some ground, a quarter of a mile in front, being considered as more favourable, we were ordered to form line and advance to it. The formation was made quickly and with correctness, and, though the ground over which the reserve marched was broken and intersected by brushwood and old ruins which obliged the companies frequently to file round, yet the general line was preserved, and the movement made with such steadiness that when we were halted upon the new ground there was hardly any correction necessary. I gave the object of march to the colours of the 23rd Regiment upon the right by which the whole was directed.

Encouragingly, on seeing that the British were advancing in earnest the French first halted and then began to retire. At first it was a matter of harmless bickering, and Walsh commented that: 'We continued to advance without meeting any serious opposition, as the enemy's force, which consisted chiefly in cavalry, retreated regularly as we came up with them, after exchanging a few shots.'

Moore was certainly having a good day and exulted that: 'The regularity and coolness with which they moved was the more creditable as it was in the face of the enemy, whose main body was posted upon heights which terminated at the distance of about a mile and a half!'

Walsh added:

At half past one we arrived upon our ground and formed in two lines, extending from the sea to the lake. The French were drawn up in our front, occupying a very strong position along a range of hills, with their left supported by an old ruin. A short time after we had halted, they opened a smart fire on us, from two pieces of cannon, which killed two men, one of the third regiment of guards, and one of the royals, and wounded two more. We were not long in returning the salute, and it is presumed we must have occasioned some loss on their side, as their fire was immediately silenced. The advanced posts and cavalry vedettes continued skirmishing till dusk, without doing each other any material injury.

In fact, he continued: 'Our loss in the course of this day was very trifling, compared to the extent and advantage of the ground we gained. It consisted in two men killed, one lieutenant, four privates, and four horses wounded.' [18]

Accompanying the army was a civilian gentleman named George Baldwin, who had formerly been the British consul at Alexandria, and was summoned from Sicily to join the expedition as a species of local guide. As it very soon turned out, he was not as knowledgeable about the geography outside Alexandria as had been hoped, but he did advise Abercromby that the defences of the city were dominated on its western side by an escarpment known as the Heights of Nicopolis. Not knowing the ground, it seems likely that Abercromby and his officers may have been inadvertently encouraged by Baldwin to think the army was closer to Alexandria than was actually the case and that the low range of hills that the French were currently occupying and the Heights of Nicopolis were one and the same.

What was more, the French position appeared vulnerable to a full-scale assault. While the British had now reached the head of Lake Maadje, the defile ahead continued to be defined along its southern flank by the elevated banks of the Alexandria Canal and beyond it the bed of Lake Mareotis, both of which were dried up at that time of year. The escarpment occupied by the French petered out before reaching the lake and Abercromby decided to pin Friant with his right, while his left wing under his second-in-command Major General Hutchinson swung around against the southern end of the escarpment to turn the position. However, for now his as yet unacclimatised troops needed to be rested and supplies and ammunition brought up.

The attack would therefore wait until next morning, and until then Moore was ordered to establish a picquet line. In view of what happened next, his arrangements are not without interest.

Moore said:

Their advanced posts were immediately in our front. We lay upon our arms where we halted, and I was ordered to take the advanced posts and cover the front of the army with the 90th and 92nd Regiments.[19]

The reserve had been fagged for several days before. As it was therefore desirable to give them rest, the 90th and 92nd, though belonging to other brigades, were put under my command for the night. I divided these two regiments each into three bodies, separated at such distances as to cover the front of the army, and I ordered each body to throw forward one-third of their numbers, with the officers belonging to it, as sentries in front. This formed a strong chain, which was relieved every hour by one of the thirds in reserve. The enemy was so close to us that it was evident that neither army could move without bringing on an action.

Chapter 5

Mandara

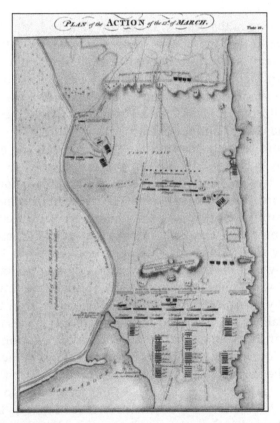

Mandara [Walsh]: This map drawn or sourced by Captain Thomas Walsh actually depicts two discrete actions; first the advance to contact in the morning against the escarpment, with Roman fort at the north end, and secondly; an unsuccessful push westwards from the escarpment in the late afternoon towards the second French position on the Nicopolis escarpment.

Standing behind Moore's picquet line, on the left, was Lord Cavan's brigade, comprising just three battalions, each drawn up in columns of companies; the 50th Regiment stood on the right of the brigade, the 79th Highlanders in the centre and Colonel Walter Smith's scratch battalion of marines on the left. In Cavan's immediate support was Stuart's Foreign Brigade, again with three battalions, and then further back still was Doyle's brigade, headed by the dismounted 12th Light Dragoons. Cradock's 2nd Brigade took the lead in the centre, with the remainder of Coote's 1st Brigade following immediately behind, 'to support him in case of necessity,' and finally the Guards were in rear of all, all under the command of Major General Hutchinson, who had finally come ashore after declaring himself too unwell to participate in the initial landing.

The right wing of the army was slightly detached. Marching parallel with the front of the Guards was Major General Hon. Edward Finch's cavalry 'brigade', still mustering only a single squadron apiece of the 26th and 12th Light Dragoons, while the Reserve was formed in two columns, one standing behind the other; the head of the first column was level with the front of Cradock's brigade while the second was level with the Guards and the cavalry.

Rather more sensibly than on the previous day, the advance was scheduled to begin at 5.00 am on the morning of 13 March. The necessary orders had duly been issued the evening before, but some 'untoward circumstances' still delayed its commencement by over an hour. It turned out that no orders had been forwarded to the 90th and 92nd, probably because their parent brigades assumed, not unreasonably, that Moore was looking after them, while Moore's staff just as blithely presumed that their own brigade majors would attend to the matter. It was a pretty common mistake and the present upshot was that, blissfully unaware that they were intended to head the advance, the two battalions had returned to their parent brigades at first light, thinking their duty done, only to have to be turned around and sent straight back out again, grumbling. It was therefore another hour and a half before the army actually began to move off at 6.30 am.

The delay gave the French ample time to prepare to meet them. Unbeknown to Abercromby, *General de Division* Francois Lanusse had arrived in Alexandria three days earlier, superseding Friant and adding three fresh demi-brigades to the army as well as some more cavalry and guns. In total, including Friant's division, Lanusse had an estimated 3,950 infantry, 520 cavalry and nineteen cannon and three howitzers.[1] Initially he deployed them along the sandy escarpment by the ruins, for while he was obviously outnumbered, he still felt obliged to fight. General Menou was also approaching the city, as he himself had done by following the line of the Alexandria Canal from Damanhūr. However, to keep that route open for his general, Lanusse needed to hold the escarpment. If it fell, the British would reach the canal and Menou would instead be obliged to undertake a lengthy detour away out to the west around the far end of Lake Mareotis, which although notionally dry, was assumed by both sides at this stage to be impassable.

Friant's Division was therefore deployed out on the right with *61e Ligne* posted near the canal, then *25e Ligne* and *75e Ligne* reaching into the centre. Lanusse's own division then continued the battle line northwards with *4e Ligne* and *18e Ligne* standing together and *69e Ligne* slightly detached to the left by the ruins, separated from the rest of the army by a shallow valley, through which passed the Aboukir road. Posted behind this valley and ready to debouch from it when called for, were his cavalry; the 230-strong *22e Chasseurs a Cheval* and various detachments of *3e, 18e* and *20e Dragoons*.

As the British infantry belatedly got itself going, the French horse artillery commenced a very uncomfortable fire, enfilading the advancing columns and causing some havoc in the ranks. In response, Abercromby ordered most of the regiments to deploy into line by companies on the left, which they carried out with a facility and precision that delighted everyone who watched it.[2] As the British extended their formations, Lanusse at once recognised the developing threat to his right flank, and aggressively responded by counterattacking. Unfortunately, while his instincts were good, as soon as he left the crest of the escarpment, his view of the battlefield became obscured both by its low sand hills and by the scrub and groves of date palms scattered across it, and according to his friend Reynier he seems to have conceived the notion that there was a large gap opening up between the two wings of Abercromby's army. Seizing the moment, as he thought, he directed his cavalry to come forward through the valley and attack the open flank of Hutchinson's supposedly isolated left wing.[3]

Instead the bold plan all came apart almost at once as about 380 men of the *22e Chasseurs a Cheval* and *3e Dragoons* collided with the 90th Perthshire Volunteers, who were unexpectedly emerging from a grove of date palms. The Scots, who Moore complained had got too far ahead, were equally surprised. As mentioned earlier, although not formally designated as such, the 90th were a very unusual unit in that they had been trained from their very inception as light infantry. At this point, acting as the advance guard, they were very properly deployed with the light company forward and spread out in a skirmish line, under Captain John McNair, who was in turn properly backed up with supports comprising three formed but widely separated companies, including the grenadiers under Major Kenneth MacKenzie,[4] and then finally the remaining six companies were following further back in reserve. It would shortly become a textbook deployment.

In keeping with their wholly unofficial status as a light corps, the regiment's officers sported dashing cavalry-style Tarleton helmets, while the rank and file may have had the same (or very similar-looking fur-crested round hats) rather than the cylindrical caps adopted by most regiments. As a result, a well-established legend holds that the French now mistook them for dismounted cavalry and therefore reckoned them easy game. However, instead of dutifully scattering before the French *Chasseurs*, McNair's light company hastily formed in little knots of men, standing back to back, presenting their bayonets as they retired on their supports. After the battle he reported a total of twenty-nine killed and wounded from his company, but made a point of remarking that only five of the men were wounded by sabres and none of them fatally.[5]

The supports themselves at the same time promptly closed up to the left with the steadiness of veterans and then, as the rest of the battalion came up, they all got off a rolling volley 'like a rattling peel of thunder'. Realising their mistake, the disordered cavalrymen immediately pulled up and veered away to their left, only to find themselves galloping across the front of the 8th and 18th Regiments, who had just deployed into line and so delivered a well-timed volley, which Walsh smugly declared 'brought great numbers of them to the ground'.

The French infantry were equally unsuccessful. While the Perthshire Volunteers were so peremptorily seeing off the unwary cavalrymen, the other advance guard battalion, the 92nd Gordon Highlanders, who were properly closed up in line on the extreme left, found themselves confronted by the rapidly approaching *61e Ligne*, and at the same time coming under a heavy fire from its attached pair of 4-pounders. The two units may have been fairly evenly matched in numbers, for the Gordons, who had not yet been engaged, came ashore with 529 rank and file, while *61e Ligne* had, according to Reynier's list, begun the campaign with some 680 men – although that was before they were tumbled off the big sand hill at Aboukir. Partially covered by a slight crest, the French now deployed into line about 200m short of the Gordons and then as they came forward again, they were hit by a battalion volley as soon as their feet became visible. That immediately stopped them. The two units were still sufficiently far apart to discourage either of them from trying to settle the business with a gallant rush and so instead they stood their ground and engaged in an intense firefight that soon became shrouded in impenetrable thick smoke. As always, the initial regular volleys soon gave way to an independent fire or *feu a billebaude*, with everyone blazing away blindly into the murk. Two British guns arrived at some point in the fight but quickly fell silent when their ammunition supply failed. Next Colonel Smith's Marine battalion came straggling up on the Gordons' right. Unfortunately, although the marines were game enough and their weapon handling was no doubt good, they had received none of the intensive training in manoeuvring that distinguished the army units. As a result, the battalion was jostling about in some confusion and proving more of a hindrance than help. Finally, however, three companies of Dillon's Regiment from Stuart's Foreign Brigade arrived on the Gordons' left and that settled the business, forcing the French to pull back, and abandon their two curricle guns. The 92nd, however, was in no state to pursue them, having lost their commanding officer, Lieutenant Colonel Charles Erskine, and no fewer than ten other officers and ninety-nine men killed and wounded in the space of what could only have been a few minutes.[6]

By now, however, the rest of Lord Cavan's brigade had also got into the fight along with Cradock's brigade, and the action became general. A little predictably, it also descended into a scrambling affair with each of the battalions engaged in in its own individual struggle amidst the scrub and low hills, against individual French battalions. Reynier certainly speaks of the French advance being covered by *tirailleurs*, but it rather seems that when they came into contact with the British the demi-brigades were first feeding their own skirmish line and then deploying (or perhaps even metamorphosing) into firing lines rather than aggressively thrusting forward through them. On the contrary, once checked they soon began to retire.

Moore related:

The action now became general along the whole front, the French, when forced back, retreated under the protection of a numerous artillery. They halted and fired whenever the ground favoured them. I kept the reserve in column, covering the right flank of the two lines. We advanced rapidly, exposed to a most heavy cannonade from the front, and of musketry from hussars and light infantry on the flank. The men, though mowed down by the cannon, never lost their order, and there was no period during the action or pursuit that I could not have halted the reserve and instantly wheeled to a flank without an interval.[7]

This scrambling, disorganised bickering saw the outnumbered French gradually pushed back to their original starting positions, until about 11.30 am, when Hutchinson finally got around the French right flank by the canal. At that point, Lanusse prudently called it a day and disengaged, pulling his men off the escarpment and swiftly withdrawing westwards. Although to some the French appeared to be retiring in confusion, Reynier insisted that they executed their retreat by echelons in good order and Wilson agreed, plausibly explaining the apparent scattering as being no more than the *tirailleurs* or sharpshooters deploying to cover the withdrawal.

Moore, whose Reserve had not been engaged and was still formed in column, stormed forward until he crested the northern end of the escarpment and saw that Alexandria was not lying on the other side of it after all. Instead there was another open, sandy plain stretching away to the actual heights, which were still nearly 2 miles away, and as: 'I observed that the right was in advance of the rest of the army, and that if we followed into the plain we should be under the guns of fortified heights in front of Alexandria, I begged of Major-General Cradock, whose brigade was next mine, to halt in this position, which was favourable, until the rest of the army came up. We should then perceive whether it was Sir Ralph's intention to pursue farther.'

This was sensible enough, but as the other brigades came up on their left, they showed no such restraint and simply continued advancing and so Cradock and Moore were obliged to shrug their shoulders and do the same. When, however, it was realised that the French were merely falling back on an even stronger position, the headlong advance ground to an awkward halt about the middle of the plain. Moore and the other brigade commanders then met with Sir Ralph and 'a consultation' was held. Discussion was seemingly hampered by Abercromby's inability to survey the battlefield, but once the situation was borne in on him, it was agreed that rather than quite literally pushing on blindly the army needed to halt and reorganise for a proper attack on the real Heights of Nicopolis, which were not only higher than the ridge that they had just swept over, but were crowned with a formidable looking set of fortifications and a considerable array of guns. In effect, to all intents and purposes there was going to have to be a second battle in one day, but at first there was still a hopeful feeling that if the momentum could be maintained, the French position could be bounced.

Nevertheless, rather than charge forward and assault it head on, it was decided that this time General Hutchinson, with part of the as yet unengaged second line, should once again mount an attack on the

French right, while the Reserve, supported by Ludlow's Guardsmen, should attack their left near the sea. However, as Hutchinson had some way to go, that meant Moore had to wait for him to get into position, and so at about 2.30 in the afternoon, Cavan's, Stuart's and Doyle's brigades worked their way forward to an 'advanced sand hill near the canal,' (which would later be facetiously referred to as 'The Green Hill') and probed forward to see if the attack was going to be practical, while the 44th Regiment even charged a French detachment with a howitzer on a bridge over the canal. It was immediately taken with the bayonet, but unsurprisingly the action provoked a tremendous fire from the guns up on the heights, which included some heavy 24-pounders. 'Near thirty pieces of cannon played upon this handful of men, and the earth was literally ploughed up all around them,' wrote an appalled Walsh.

Hutchinson, too, was dismayed by the violent reaction, especially as he could now look around the end of the Heights and see that they were in turn covered by the Alexandria defences behind and in particular by the elevated Forts Cretin and Cafferelli. 'When this column got round to the left, opposite to the ground it was intended to attack,' recorded Moore, 'it appeared to General Hutchinson so strongly defended by a numerous artillery, commanded by the guns of the fortified hills near Alexandria, that he halted and sent to Sir Ralph that the heights could not be carried without considerable loss, and if carried, as they were exposed to the fire of the fortified hills, it would be impossible to hold them without instantly entrenching themselves, of which they had not the means. He therefore demanded further orders.'

Abercromby, whose poor eyesight and consequent lack of control had contributed to the developing crisis, responded by first sending Brigadier General Hope, the adjutant general, across to have a look and give a second opinion as to the problem, and then, with impatience getting the better of him, he almost immediately afterwards followed him to try and see the situation for himself. In the meantime, the men were 'ordered to sit down', grumbled Walsh, 'uncertain whether we should attempt to force them from this new position, rendered formidable by nature, and defended by a powerful artillery'.

All the while the afternoon was slipping away and the day was getting late. Another probe, this time by Moore's reserve, was briefly meditated and quickly dismissed. The French, as Moore observed, had by now had time to recover their spirits and improve their position, and Walsh summed up the situation with his usual clarity.

'Our army, in the highest spirits, and elated by its recent success, was impatient to proceed; but Sir Ralph Abercromby, perceiving, that, if we drove the French from the heights, we could not retain them, as they appeared, on reconnoitring, to be commanded by forts Cafarelli and Cretin, deemed it improper to make an attempt, which must have been attended with a useless waste of blood.'

Instead, with more and more French guns being dragged into position on the top of the escarpment, Abercromby reluctantly ordered a retreat, and so at about 4.00 pm the army began to retire, with Coote and Cradock's brigades bringing up the rear as the redcoats fell back to the escarpment by the Roman ruins that the French had occupied that morning.

It was clear that tactically the morning phase of the battle had been a British victory, while the afternoon phase, although not actually a defeat, had not answered to expectations. It is hard to disagree with the criticism afterwards (on both sides) that British losses were unnecessarily high in that second phase of the battle because they were left sitting immobile under fire while the generals argued what to do next. Moore's critique of the battle was thoughtful and is worth recounting in full:

> Our loss this day amounted to 1300 killed and disabled; that of the enemy could not be near so great. His superiority in cavalry prevented our deriving that benefit from the defeat of his army which we might otherwise have done. His artillery was powerful, ours as nothing; for, as it had to be dragged by men through a sandy country, it could not keep pace with the infantry. We were therefore destroyed by his artillery without the power of retaliation. But the undaunted spirit of the troops made them constantly advance in spite of every loss, so that we gained ground, which is the great object in action. We drove the enemy back, though with loss superior to his. Every attempt the enemy made, either with their infantry or cavalry, was defeated, and at last the whole retired under cover of their artillery.
>
> The fault, if any, which we committed was the advancing beyond the position we afterwards took up before we had come to a determination to attack the heights. Halting to deliberate in the plain exposed us to the guns of the heights, and, when the attack was deemed imprudent, obliged us to a retrograde movement, which was mortifying to troops who had displayed such spirit, and who had been successful. It was made, however, with great order, and without any attempt of the enemy to impede it. I do believe that had we pursued the French over the plain without altering the disposition of the army, we might have driven them beyond the heights, even though their position had been prepared

and fortified; but, without cannon, ammunition, provisions, or the means of entrenching ourselves, I doubt if we could have held it. I therefore think we should have been satisfied with our first success, and remained upon the ground in which we first halted. At the time the attack was intended, it is probable it would have failed. The enemy had had time to recover himself, the position was strong and had been prepared.[8]

'The loss of the French,' declared Walsh with his usual optimism, 'may very safely be calculated at seven hundred men. General of division Lanusse was slightly wounded. We also took four pieces of cannon and one howitzer.' Reynier (and Wilson following him) offered a more modest 500 Frenchmen *hors de combat* during the two engagements, but significantly, Dr Larrey found some 600 wounded from both the Aboukir and Mandara battles lying in the Alexandria hospitals when he came up from Cairo on 19 March.

On the British side, in total, six officers, six sergeants, a drummer and 143 rank and file were killed outright, and no fewer than sixty-six officers, a quartermaster, sixty-one sergeants, seven drummers and 946 rank and file were wounded.[9]

Those 1,000-odd casualties to advance just 2 miles were simply unsustainable. The fact of the matter was that, while the army had performed splendidly, it was increasingly obvious that it was probably too weak and certainly under-resourced for the task being asked of it. As Walsh admitted:

Our force actually in the field was about fourteen thousand; that of the enemy nearly seven thousand. But though so much superior in point of numbers, we laboured under great disadvantages from our deficiency in cavalry and artillery; in both of which the French had a decided superiority. We had not two hundred and fifty cavalry mounted, and those so wretchedly, as to be scarcely able to act. They had upwards of six hundred mounted on excellent and remarkably well trained horses. In artillery their superiority was still more considerable; as they had in the field nearly forty pieces of cannon, and most of them curricle guns, while the few that we had were slowly and with difficulty dragged along by sailors and soldiers.[10]

Next morning the army found itself standing on the low escarpment running at right angles to the seashore, which had earlier been Lanusse's position at the commencement of the battle. Obviously enough, there was what turned out to be a crucial difference in that the position was now reversed in order to face towards the Heights of Nicopolis, and that in turn meant that a soon-to-be famous group of classical ruins lying at the northern end of the line no longer lay behind it, but now projected forward as a fortuitous bulwark. And there the army remained for the next week, while supplies were stockpiled for an assault in which no one had any confidence.

Moreover, even if the Heights could be stormed successfully without absolutely crippling losses, the job had still barely begun, for Abercromby then needed to establish his heavy artillery on top of it. And all of this was going to have to be accomplished not only in the teeth of the French artillery that opposed with more and probably heavier guns to his own, but also while contending against an aggressive field army based in the city. Little wonder then that there were severe doubts whether it could be done at all with the forces at his disposal. Yet if Abercromby attempted it and was repulsed, there would be no alternative but to retreat back to Aboukir and re-embark what remained of his army.

Reinforcements had already been requested, even before the landing, but they were unlikely to arrive any time soon, and in the meantime the decision was taken to dig in where they stood, while at the same time the Castle of Aboukir was completely invested. Five 24-pounders (probably naval carronades) and a few mortars were landed, and having been 'nearly converted into a heap of ruins', the fort surrendered on 17 March on the significant promise of the garrison being treated as British prisoners of war and not handed over to the Turks, who as it happened had just turned up in the person of the *Kapūdān Pasha*. Encouragingly, he had landed a small contingent of Turkish troops. So far there were only about 500 of them, and they turned out to be the usual rabble of Albanian *Arnauts* or *bashi-bazouks*, but at least there was a promise of more and better troops still to come. Even more welcome were the missing horse transports, which were also turning up at last, allowing more of the cavalry to be mounted.

However, by then, noted Walsh:

Various and contradictory reports of Menou's movements, in consequence of our successful landing, now reached us. Some accounts said that he had left Cairo on the 16th; while others reported that he had already arrived at Demanhour with eight thousand men. Very little credit, however, was given to these rumours; and still less apprehension entertained of his attacking

64

our position, which we had fortified with two redoubts, not yet finished, for they were still open in the rear, one on our right, in front of the old ruins of Kasr Kiasera, or the castle of the Caesars, mounting two twenty-four pounders; another along the canal on our left, with one twelve-pounder; and several small fleches, with one or two guns, disposed at intervals along the front of the line.

Nevertheless, any complacency on that score was disturbed by a couple of unfortunate incidents. The open ground between the two armies was a no man's land uncertainly covered by picquets from both sides. On the first two days after the battle, the French attempted to drive in the British ones, which brought on some skirmishing, in which the French had two or three men killed. These quite unnecessary deaths quieted things down a little and Sir Ralph, 'having occasion to write to the General commanding, expressed a wish not to aggravate the calamities of war by any acts which, without benefit to the general cause, tended only to distress individuals. He received a polite answer from General Friant, entering fully into Sir Ralph's sentiments.'[11] Unfortunately, on the night of 15 March, Colonel Arthur Brice of the Coldstream, whose turn it was to serve as field officer of the day, was shot and fatally injured when he accidentally tried to inspect a red-jacketed French guard post instead of a red-jacketed British one. Taken into Alexandria, he died the following day.

Then, at about three o'clock in the afternoon of 18 March, came a more serious affair entirely when a small body of French cavalry and infantry, seemingly about 150 strong, was observed reconnoitring along the canal of Alexandria near the village of Bedah. As they were also seen to be cutting up parties of locals who were bringing fresh provisions to the market that had been established in the camp, Lieutenant Colonel Mervyn Archdall of the 12th Light Dragoons promptly mounted up a mixed party of about sixty men from both cavalry regiments and went off enthusiastically chasing after them.

The best account of what happened next came from that other dashing cavalryman, Robert Wilson:

> … the major of brigade brought orders for the cavalry to turn out. As the greater part were gone to water, Colonel Archdale could only collect sixty men, with which he marched, but when he reached the picquet, he took that along with him, which increased his force to eighty men. With these he advanced briskly for about

three miles, till he came up with the enemy, who, according to General Reynier, consisted of a company of infantry and fifty hussars; their total number was about one hundred and fifty men (which they acknowledged themselves to be under the command of General D'Estin). Colonel Archdale, conceiving that he had orders to charge from General Finch, who was coming up, and who had sent his brigade major forwards, instantly detached Lieutenant Lewinson, with twelve men, to attack the left flank of the cavalry, while he charged in front with the main body. General D'Estin posted his infantry from the lake to the left of the canal, and drew up the hussars on the subsequently inundated ground, a little in the rear of his infantry. Colonel Archdale with his small detachment pressed on to the attack with the greatest ardour, and breaking through the infantry, who fired a volley, passed on to the hussars, who as immediately fled. The British cavalry pursued, killing and wounding several of them, but the main body, being better mounted, escaped. The dragoons were returning in file, with their horses blown, considerably reduced from the enemy's fire in the first attack, by which Colonel Archdale had lost his arm: imagining that the French infantry were prisoners, and forgetting that no guard had been left over them, since all had inconsiderately followed in the pursuit, they advanced within twenty yards of the French again, when General D'Estin ordered his men to fire, which they did with severe effect. The cavalry, thus surprised, instantly inclined away to their left, and halted out of the reach of the fire.[12]

A company of Stuart's Minorca regiment, commanded by Captain John McKinnon, was hurrying up to their rescue, but by the time they arrived on the scene, no fewer than thirty-three dragoons and forty-two horses were killed, wounded or captured, including Colonel Archdall, who lost an arm, so that the command of the 12th Dragoons devolved on Lieutenant Colonel Robert Browne.[13]

Disappointing as it was, this very minor cavalry skirmish hardly amounted to a real setback (arguably the horses were a more serious loss than the men) but yet there was an ominous aspect to it that was not at first fully appreciated. The very distinctively dressed French cavalry involved were not the Chasseurs encountered at Mandara but a detachment from the *7me (bis) Hussards*, and they were supported by a detachment of the blue-coated *21e Légère*, come all the way down from Upper Egypt. General Menou had arrived at last.[14]

Chapter 6

Kasr Kaisera

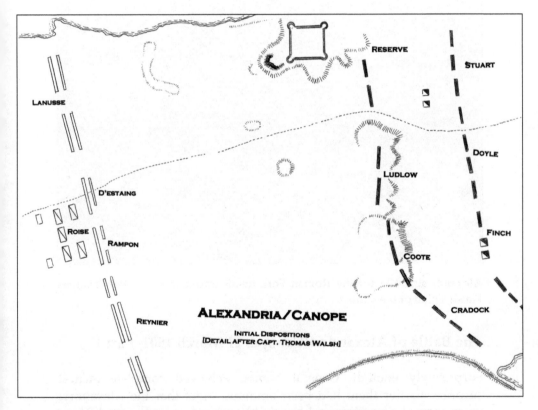

RESERVE

STUART

LANUSSE

DOYLE

LUDLOW

D'ESTAING

ROISE

RAMPON

FINCH

COOTE

CRADOCK

REYNIER

ALEXANDRIA/CANOPE

INITIAL DISPOSITIONS
[DETAIL AFTER CAPT. THOMAS WALSH]

Alexandria/Canope: Traced from Captain Thomas Walsh's plan of the pivotal battle on 21 March, but decluttered for the sake of clarity.

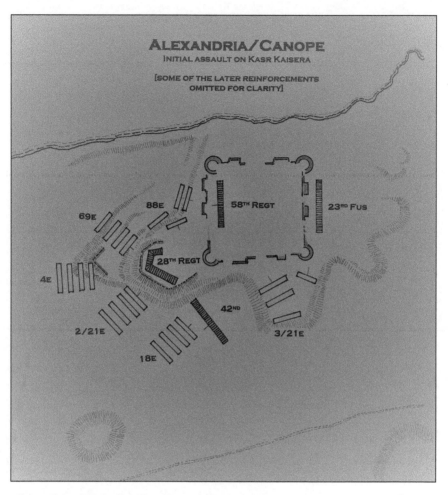

Alexandria: Battle for the Roman Fort: detail traced from Captain Thomas Walsh's plan of the battle

The Battle of Alexandria/Canope, 21 March 1801, Part 1[1]

Surprisingly enough, General Menou achieved complete tactical surprise. Earlier there had been ominous signs that the Alexandria garrison was being reinforced, had they been properly interpreted. There was d'Estaing's reconnaissance with an unfamiliar hussar regiment, and then a long column had later been seen making its way across the dry bed of Lake Mareotis, but the column was not only far distant but shrouded in a heat haze. Nevertheless, ignoring it was unwise. Abercromby, whose own lack of cavalry meant he was functionally as well as literally blind, ordered a heightened level of readiness, but otherwise he concentrated on his preparations for a difficult night assault on the Nicopolis Lines.

A route across the dry but spongy bed of Lake Mareotis, which was practicable for artillery, having been found, despite Lanusse's fears, Menou himself arrived in Alexandria on the evening of 18 March and when his infantry and artillery, swinging wide across the lake bed, came in a little less than forty-eight hours later, they were probably not very surprised to learn that they were about to launch a full-scale assault on Abercromby's forces in the early hours of the following morning. They were, after all, veterans of the *Armée d'Italie* and that was how they were accustomed to conduct the art of war.

Nevertheless, with time pressing, the tactical planning of the battle, according to Reynier, was largely delegated to General Lanusse, who was already on the spot and who knew the ground, having fought over it during the Mandara battle.[2]

The centrepiece of the position to be attacked was the long low escarpment running directly from north to south across most of the narrow spit of land between the sea in the north and the dried up basin of Lake Mareotis to the south. Unfortunately for Abercromby's men, the western face of the escarpment was the easier of the two, generally lacking the bluffs forming the eastern side. There was little to impede a French assault but by now the position was in the process of being garnished with various earthworks, including two unfinished redoubts, one at each end of the line and several small fleches with one or perhaps two heavy guns thrown up at intervals across the front.

To the left of the position there were some 500 m of low, open ground between the low southern end of the escarpment from the Alexandria Canal and the dry lake bed beyond, but Abercromby's line was refused here and the left flank proper was in any case well protected by the ditch and elevated dykes of the canal itself. This fortuitous defensive line was further improved by the erection of three small forts or fleches on top of the dykes to guard against any French attempt to infiltrate along the dry canal bed.[3]

The Guards and Coote's Brigades occupied the top of the escarpment with Doyle's Brigade behind them in support, while Cradock's Brigade, backed up by Cavan's Brigade, had the low ground between the south end of the ridge and the canal. Finch's little cavalry brigade was also posted in the centre of the second line, albeit still mustering only two squadrons of mounted men and on its right a small battalion formed from the dismounted troopers of the 12th Light Dragoons.[4]

At the northern end of the escarpment the Aboukir Road passed through a 300-metre-wide valley separating it from another group of low sand hills overlooking the sea. Sitting atop this slightly higher ground and projecting forward from the defensive line were a group of classical ruins. Although they had not actually featured in the earlier Mandara battle, and consequently seem to have been underestimated by the French, these ruins were not a random scattering of crumbled walls and shattered columns, but were to play a vital role in the coming battle – and with very good reason. At the heart of the ruins were the still substantial remains of a Roman fortress, *Kasr Kaisera*, or Caesar's camp,[5] standing four-square above the shore. Fortunately, although this once-formidable strongpoint is no longer extant, a rough series of plans indicating its size is provided by Walsh and astonishingly there was also a near contemporary and very detailed survey of the ruins carried out by celebrated Egyptologist Sir John Gardiner Wilkinson FSA:

About 2 miles beyond the French lines or 2½ from the Rosetta Gate, is a Roman station called *Caesar's* or the *Roman Camp*. It marks the site of *Nicopolis* or Juliopolis, where Augustus defeated the partisans of Anthony ... It is nearly square, measuring 291 paces by 266 within, the walls being 5 to 5½ paces thick, it had four entrances, one in the centre of each face, 15 paces wide and defended by round or semi-circular towers, 18 paces in diameter or 12 within. On each face were six towers distant from each other 33 paces; those of the doorway excepted which are only 15 paces apart. Those at the four corners were larger than the others, having a diameter of 22 paces. The whole was surrounded by a ditch, apparently filled from the sea, which is close to the N.W. face ... In the area within few traces of buildings can be perceived; and the walls themselves are very much decayed. The walls of the station were of stone, with the courses of flat bricks or tiles, at intervals, common in Roman buildings.[6]

As to how high the walls stood, Captain Stewart of the 42nd wrote how 'some parts of the ancient wall were from ten to twenty feet [3 to 6 m] high' and the ruins also appear, albeit somewhat indistinctly, as a rather substantial structure in a panoramic view of the battlefield published by Walsh.[7] Once the forward breaches or 'chasms' in the walls were blocked with rubble, the fort was a very formidable position indeed, especially as a large earthwork redoubt, intended to mount two guns, was constructed some 20-30 metres to its front, covering the south-western angle, while a small flotilla of gunboats, under Captain Maitland RN were positioned off the beach on the north-western side.

The defence of these ruins and the rest of the coastal sand hills was primarily assigned to Moore's Reserve, with Stuart's Foreign Brigade standing in its rear.

There is no surviving morning state for 20 March (and obviously no opportunity for one to be compiled on 21 March) but Wilson opined that the British forces were 10,000 strong that morning, including a total of 300 mounted cavalry. Walsh, on the other hand, reckoned that Abercromby disposed of a total of 11,759 rank and file, and his calculations are not without interest: 'Our effective strength on the 7th of March, as appears by the official returns was 14,697 rank and file,' he noted, but then subtracted from that number a total of 1,805 battle casualties between 8 March and 18 March; 530 marines left at Aboukir Castle and 'About 600 sick or convalescents [which] … reduces our force actually in the field on the 21st of March to 11,759.'[8]

There is a similar vagueness on the other side, but General Reynier reckoned the total strength of the French forces present at only 8,330 infantry and 1,380 cavalry, with forty-six pieces of artillery, albeit mostly of fairly small calibre. Menou's task therefore was to crack a partly entrenched position with a force that was inferior in numbers to the defenders.

His solution, as devised by Lanusse, was to set off at 3.00 am of 21 March and so pass the army across the intervening plain under cover of darkness, in order to arrive in front of the British position by 4.30 am, unseen and unharmed by artillery fire. The battle was then to be opened just before dawn by *General de Brigade* André François Bron with a diversionary force consisting of 300 light cavalry from the *7e (bis) Hussards* and *22e Chasseurs a Cheval* and some 200 mounted infantry belonging to the celebrated *Regiment des Dromadaires,* all of whom were operating out in the dried up wastes of Lake Mareotis to the south of the battlefield. Bron's task was to launch a noisy demonstration against the British picquet line along the canal, and so draw Abercromby's reserves away from the real attack, which was to be mounted against the right wing in the north.

This was to be begun by Lanusse himself, whose own division had been restored to its proper strength by the return of his fourth regiment, finally brought up from Cairo. This allowed him to deploy the division as two brigades; *4e Légére* and *18e Ligne* on his right under *General de Brigade* Pierre Louis François Sylly, and *69e* and *88e Ligne* on his left under *General de Brigade* Francois Valentin.

Lanusse's friend Reynier wrote:

Lanusse believed that the English redoubts might be easily carried by grenadiers, supported by the head of the columns. He marched his two brigades in close column, intending to form them beyond the main redoubt and the Roman Camp, and fall upon the right of the English army. The brigade of general Silly was to march directly against the redoubt; that of general Valentin to follow the shore, passing between the sea and the Roman Camp. The centre was to march close to the right of general Silly's brigade, following it as a second line; and on the first success vigorously to attack (along with the right wing) the position of redoubts of the enemy's centre.

Surprisingly, in the light of its purpose, the centre was a rather heterogenous collection of formations, but with no overall commander.

The senior officer present was *General de Division* Antoine-Guillaume Rampon, who had his own *32e Ligne* and the three *carabinier* (grenadier) companies of *2e Légére* – but unfortunately the rest of his men had been left behind in the Damietta area.

Then there was also a 'column' led by *General de Brigade* Jacques-Zacharie d'Estaing comprising two battalions of *21e Légére* under *Chef de Brigade* Hausser and a battalion of grenadiers under *Chef de Brigade* Eppler, in the form of the locally raised *Grenadiers Grecs* stiffened by two regular grenadier companies detached from *25e Ligne* and probably the two *carabinier* companies of *21e Légére*.[9] d'Estaing, however, for some unstated reason, was not formally placed under Rampon's command, and indeed his column was given an independent role as the army's advance guard.[10]

As Reynier also very rightly comments; '… the division of the French centre into two bodies, each with its separate commanding officer, and subdivided again by the detaching of its grenadiers, deprived it of that combined action necessary to the complete accomplishment of its orders.'[11] In broad daylight the commanding officers might have co-operated easily enough, but in the pre-dawn darkness it was only asking for trouble.

While the left and centre were mounting their attacks, the French right wing under *General de Division* Reynier was to pin down the rest of Abercromby's front line with two more divisions; namely his own one, temporarily under the command of François-Étienne de Damas, composed of the 13e and 85e Ligne, and Friant's Division with its by now rather battered three demi-brigades.[12]

72

The orders went on to optimistically declare that: 'When the positions of the enemy's right and centre are carried, and the whole of his front line overthrown, the French army must form anew with promptness, to march against the second line ... The object of this movement is, to endeavour to drive the English into Lake Maadie.'

As a final touch, the cavalry, amounting to most of no fewer than five regiments of dragoons and mustering about 900 men in total, under *General de Brigade* César Antoine Roize, were to avail themselves 'of every favourable circumstance, as well as of the moment for advancing and cutting down whatever has been shaken by the attacks of the infantry.'[13]

It was certainly a bold plan, but it was also a deeply flawed one for, aside from the fragmented command structure complained of by Reynier, the French were outnumbered, and had no reserves on the battlefield other than Roise's two cavalry brigades. That meant that Lanusse, Rampon and d'Estaing were going to struggle to achieve any local superiority and were going to have to rely on speed, aggression and above all close co-ordination, while at the same time counting on the British to co-operate by obligingly sitting still. It may have worked against the notoriously stolid and unimaginative Austrians, but it was asking for trouble against a British Army brim full of confidence in its training and its new-found ability to manoeuvre. In the circumstances it was perhaps unsurprising that the cunning plan not only went awry in its execution, but started to go wrong almost from the very beginning.

In accordance with Abercromby's standing orders, the British regiments had all slept fully accoutred and ready for action. This was an uncomfortable experience at the best of times, let alone when prolonged over a period of several nights, although one that would be all too familiar to their descendants on the Western Front a century later. Relief only came after the dawn stand-to, and so at 3.30 am on this particular morning, a full hour before daylight, the troops were already getting under arms in order of battle, when they heard the sound of musketry over on the left rear.[14]

This was, of course, the French diversionary force, under General Bron. Having successfully got into position unseen, unsuspected and on time, he moved against the British picquet line. The initial scattering of shots was at first attributed to nervous sentries but it soon grew in intensity. As the British picquet line fell back, some of the *Regiment des Dromadaires* followed it up so closely that they actually entered the eastern fleche, down by the head of Lake Maadje, along with some of the retiring sentries, and there killed or captured everyone inside and seized a 12-pounder gun, which they turned around and fired randomly into the British camp. Then, coming under fire themselves from another gun in the central fleche, they prudently melted back into the darkness again. They left behind an officer and four privates of their own killed, but successfully carried off all their wounded and no fewer than twenty-five prisoners, including three officers.[15] It was a good start and they no doubt considered themselves well satisfied with the excitement they had stirred up, as Bron's cavalrymen loudly spread themselves up and down the canal, continuing their noisy if mostly harmless fusillade with their short carbines. In response, either on the direct instructions of Abercromby, or of General Hutchinson who commanded on the left, Lord Cavan's 3rd Brigade, which had until now been refused, was now ordered to swing outwards instead, pivoting on its left, to line the canal and Stuart's Brigade also began moving across the rear of the army to reinforce them. The diversion was promising to be dramatically successful, but no one had time to actually move very far out of position before the French' real intentions were revealed.

Major General Moore, as it happens, was doing duty as major general of the day and recorded in his diary that:

After visiting the picquets I remained with the left picquet of the reserve until four in the morning of the 21st. The enemy had been perfectly quiet during the night. Nothing had been observed from them but some rockets, which it was not uncommon for them to throw. Imagining everything to be quiet, I left orders with the field officer to retire his posts at daylight, and I rode towards the left to give similar orders to the other picquets as I went along. When I reached the left picquet of the Guards I heard a fire of musketry on the left; but everything continuing so quiet on the right, I, from the style of the firing, suspected it was a false alarm.

Witheringly, he also added; 'I had observed a want of intelligence and confusion the evening before in the officer who commanded the picquets in that quarter. This confirmed my suspicion.'

This was a touch unfair, for it was not the unnamed officer's fault that Bron was enthusiastically doing his best to alarm everyone in sight. However, co-ordinating the movements of widely separated bodies of troops is notoriously difficult, especially in the dark, and Lanusse's orders apparently required him to take the noise of Bron's diversion as his own signal to advance.[16] 'On a sudden,' recalled Wilson, who was sitting in the rear of the Reserve at the head of his hussars, 'loud shouts

74

were heard in front of the right, which fully certified the enemy's intention; a roar of musquetry immediately succeeded, and the action there became general'[17]

Moore reacted to this new uproar at once: 'I was, however, trotting towards the left when a firing commenced from the picquets of the reserve. I immediately turned to my aide-de-camp. Captain [Robert] Sewell, and said, 'This is the real attack, let us gallop to the redoubt.'

They must have ridden straight across the front of the battle line for as they returned, they met all the picquets falling back, and by the time they reached the big redoubt in front of the Roman fort, the 28th Regiment were already under attack.

'My arrangements, in case of our being attacked, had been settled beforehand,' he recorded complacently. He and Brigadier-General Oakes, agreed that the redoubt and the fort in front of the right of the army, where he had posted the 28th and 58th Regiments, must be supported, and that the immediate area around the fort was the proper ground for the Reserve to fight upon. 'In fact,' he declared, unconsciously echoing the French plan, 'if carried by the enemy, it would have been impossible for our army to remain in their position.'[18]

Fortunately, the 28th Regiment, led by Colonel Edward Paget, was standing ready in front of their lines by the Aboukir Road. The Colonel had landed 587 rank and file on 8 March, of whom thirty-eight were killed and wounded during that first day, but his battalion had not been engaged again since then, so allowing for those on the sick list it must still have been over 500 strong. When the firing began on the left, Paget immediately ordered most of them forward to man the redoubt, which took the form of a slightly irregular lunette or half-moon, and looks from Walsh's map as if it was largely conformed to the local topography rather than to any known scientific principles. Although not explicitly referred to, the sandy nature of the soil compelled a fairly broad berm between the fort and the slope, and forward of the redoubt was a small fleche or redan situated on the projecting western tip of the sand hills, covering the dead ground. The outer face of the redoubt itself was immediately fronted by a substantial ditch, and the inner face boasted a wooden platform or fire-step, mounting one or two of the 24-pounder carronades or 'smashers', borrowed from the Navy.[19] As yet, however, it was unfinished and the gorge or rear face was still wide open, which would soon give rise to one of the battle's most famous incidents.

Unfortunately for Lanusse, in the opening minutes of the fight *General de Brigade* Sylly's assault was disrupted by the unexpected intrusion of another unit that had managed to go astray in the dark and blundered into his formation. While he himself was not an eyewitness to this particular incident, Reynier unhesitatingly declares the interloper was Rampon's *32e Ligne* and complains that as a result; 'The 18th, separated from the 4th, by the mistake of the 32nd, were unable to force the redoubt.' Thomas Walsh, however, rather more convincingly identifies the errant unit as one of the two battalions of *21e Légére* belonging to d'Estaing's column, which as we have seen had been ordered to 'march close to the right of general Silly's brigade, following it as a second line'.[20] However, they evidently marched rather too close and Walsh's invaluable map of the action actually shows how it forced its way in between Sylly's men. As a result, although the *carabiniers* of *4e Légére* successfully stormed the outer fleche, they were unable to get further forward. Indeed, a heavy fire directed from the redoubt into the open gorge of the redan quickly forced them to reverse the position, planting their colours in the parapet and taking cover on the outer face, albeit they then proceeded to hold on to it until very near the end of the battle.

Moore recorded:

We could feel the effect of the enemy's fire, but it was impossible as yet to see what he was about. His drums were beating the charge, and they were with their voices encouraging one another to advance. My horse was shot in the face, and became so unmanageable that I was obliged to dismount. Colonel Paget, whilst I was speaking to him on the platform of the redoubt, received a shot in the neck which knocked him down; he said he was killed, and I thought so; he, however, recovered a little, and he was put upon his horse.

Lieutenant Colonel William Chambers took over and then within moments the 58th Regiment too were heavily engaged as *General de Brigade* Valentin turned his men inwards to join in the fight.

The original plan, as devised by Lanusse, had called for Valentin to simply push past the fort, and help form a new battle-line in the rear, but he had evidently paid little attention to the fort during the Mandara battle. Not only had he failed to appreciate its strength, but he did not realise that there was insufficient space between the fort and the sea for a column of infantry to pass without getting their boots wet. Whether deterred by this, or by the presence of Spencer's 40th Regiment flank companies blocking the narrow passage, or simply by a recognition that Sylly needed supporting, Valentin turned south instead. While *88e Ligne* climbed directly up the slope towards the northern flank of the redoubt, *69e Ligne* pushed into the apparently open gap between the rear of the redoubt and the west wall of the fort.

Alas for Valentin's initiative, Colonel William Houston was waiting for him. The 58th Regiment had come ashore with 469 rank and file on 8 March, losing 50 killed and wounded in the process. Once again, some had no doubt fallen sick in the two weeks since then, but the battalion must still have been about 400 strong besides officers and NCOs on the morning of 21 March. As his piquets came running back, Houston lined the ancient walls, waited until the distinctive glazed leather caps worn by the French came into view in the darkness and then unleashed a point-blank volley which literally stopped them dead in their tracks.[21] Then to make matters worse, according to Walsh, 'Still attempting to force its way between [the ruins] and the redoubt, the sixty-ninth demibrigade was taken in flank by one of the twenty-four pounders loaded with grape shot and nearly exterminated. On this the remainder of the corps refused to advance; when General Lanusse, using his utmost efforts to rally them and bring them to the charge, had his thigh carried off by a cannon shot. Complete confusion then ensued, and a general dispersion of this column took place.'[22]

Nevertheless, there was no respite for the defenders, for Sylly's *18e Ligne* were at last finding their way into the attack. Having been forced by the intrusive *21e Légére* to swing around to the south of the redoubt, they were now fighting their way into the ditch and hoping to get around into its rear. Fortunately, they were momentarily stopped by the two reserve companies of the 28th Regiment which had been posted outside on the left.

The two companies alone could not have held them back for long, but help was close at hand. When the battle began, the 23rd Royal Welch Fusiliers and the 42nd Highlanders were both standing down in the valley, but as soon as the shooting began, Moore's second in command, Brigadier Oakes, had ordered the left wing of the Black Watch, commanded by Major James Stirling, to move up and take post alongside the 28th companies by the redoubt.

However, as the fight for the redoubt grew in intensity, Moore soon realised that the half battalion of the 42nd was not going to be sufficient by itself and sent his other ADC, Captain Paul Anderson, to fetch up Colonel Alexander Stewart with the right wing of the regiment. At the same time the 23rd Fusiliers, and the four flank companies of the 40th under Colonel Spencer (who were originally tasked with covering the beach), also seem to have been ordered to close up behind the ruins in order to support the 58th Regiment, perhaps by Oakes.

This meant that no one was covering the valley and, as a result, Moore next received an urgent report that a column of French had turned his left. At first the general dismissed the warning, for: 'I thought that in the dark they had mistaken the 42nd for the French, and said so. I could distinguish them forming exactly where I had ordered them; but Colonel Paget, who had not yet retired, rode up to me and said, "I assure you that the French have turned us, and are moving towards the ruins." I looked to where he pointed, and accordingly saw a battalion of French in column completely in our rear.'

The new arrivals belonged to d'Estaing's column. In the darkness one of his battalions, *2/21e Légére,* had already wandered so far off to their left as to blunder into Sylly's brigade in front of the redoubt, resulting, as Reynier rather delicately put it, in 'some disorder' [23] but now the other battalion, led by *Chef de Bataillon* Hausser, had fetched up all on its own in an unguarded part of the British front line. The summoning of both the Black Watch and Royal Welch Fusiliers from their original positions in the valley below the fort had, in fact, allowed General d'Estaing to blithely carry on down the Aboukir Road and penetrate right into the British front line without being detected. Given the darkness and confusion, he more than likely blundered in there inadvertently and it is far from certain that *2/21e Légére* ever caught up with him after tangling with Lanusse's men. Nor was there any sign at this point of General Rampon and his skeleton division to back him up, but with the furious musketry and cannon fire lighting up the darkness above him, it must have been obvious to d'Estaing where his duty lay and so he took the soldierly but fateful decision to pitch into Moore's rear. At first, accompanied by one of the two light field pieces attached to the demi-brigade and two pack camels laden with ammunition, all went well. However, as the French silently crept up the slope in the darkness, they were oblivious to the fact they were marching into an accidental trap.

Having come up in support of their regiment's left wing, the right wing of the 42nd was now standing parallel to it, but about 200 m further back, when one of Captain David Stewart's men came running up and urgently told him in a low tone of voice: 'I see a strong column of the enemy marching past our front; I know them by their large hats and white frocks.' In the pitch darkness, the French column had actually managed to inadvertently stumble between the two wings of the Black Watch, and creeping forward to verify the soldier's report, Stewart related almost with incredulity that: 'The air being now rendered much more obscure by the smoke, which there was not a breath of wind to dispel, this close column got well advanced between the two lines of the Highlanders before it was perceived.'[24]

'The right wing of the 42nd arrived at this instant,' agreed Moore rather confusedly. 'I ran to them, ordered them to face to the right about, and showed them the French completely in their power. Moore must in fact have run to the more advanced *left* wing of the regiment, under Major Stirling, for Captain Stewart confirmed that it was 'Lieutenant-Colonel Alexander Stewart with the right wing, [who] instantly charged to his proper front, while the rear-rank of Major Stirling's wing, facing to the right about, charged to the rear.'[25]

Both d'Estaing and Hausser went down in the confusion, the latter with his leg and thigh shot away, and the gun was abandoned, although history is silent as to the fate of the two camels.[26] Nevertheless, despite being assailed on both flanks 3/21e *Légére* still gamely struggled on to reach the ruins, and burst in through the gaps in the south wall. Inside the fort, Lieutenant Colonel John Crowgey,[27] commanding the left wing of the 58th, promptly swung two of his companies around to stop them just as the Black Watch came up behind. And then the 23rd Fusiliers pitched in as well. The latter's Lieutenant Jack Hill related how they had:

> ... mov'd up to the support of the 58 Regt. and halted about 60 paces from the front [ie east] wall of the ruin's Roman building, the Light company being in front; the Lieut. Colonels company was on the left flank; the head of a French column was observ'd entering through the broken wall on the left face, the dawn of day shewed their hats, on which I wheeled the company up in silence and gave orders to fire at about 35 yards distance, during the 2nd discharge Capn. [John George] Bradford brought up his company on the right and the late Colonel Sir Henry Ellis his on the left, when the word 'Charge' was given, the openings gain'd and about 340 prisoners made ... Our men attack'd like wolves, transfixing the Frenchmen with their bayonets against the walls of the building.[28]

Despite the best efforts of dramatic artists and popular writers, hand-to-hand fighting between two bodies of infantrymen, using bayonet, musket butt, sword, or even bare fists, was seldom encountered, but in and around that old Roman fort on that morning there was a struggle of appalling ferocity, which astonished and sickened some of the British officers who witnessed it. At least the fight was mercifully brief, and while Reynier admits that three companies of 3/21e, 'partly composed of Copts enlisted in Upper Egypt, and who were detached as sharpshooters, were compelled to lay down their arms' and claims that 'Thirty-seven who guarded the colours, refused to yield, and were all slain',[29] it appears that in all about 250 unwounded prisoners were rounded up and then marched down to the beach by Ensign Hillas of the 42nd.

Famously, the French battalion's colours were also taken. Far from describing a Spartan-like last stand around them, Captain Stewart simply related that they were surrendered by an unidentified French officer to Major Stirling of the 42nd, who in turn handed the flag over to Sergeant James Sinclair of the grenadier company, ordering him to guard both it and the captured gun.

It is unclear just how many French troops were involved in this action, for Reynier also asserts that most of 2/21e managed to escape, and adds that: 'Eppler, chief of brigade, who had marched a little more to the right, was wounded, and his grenadiers repulsed.' However, the latter statement is problematic, for while it sounds as if the *Grenadiers Grecs* and the other grenadier companies attacked alongside Hausser's *21e Légère*, none of the British accounts suggest that any other French unit was involved in this action.[30] On the contrary, they consistently speak only of a single French 'battalion', which suggests that neither 2/21e Légére nor the *Grenadiers* were involved in the debacle.[31]

Instead, both battalions may have taken part in Rampon's attack instead, which was only then starting to get under way, for even as the prisoners were being marshalled to be taken to the rear, the growing light revealed that more French infantry were advancing in great force, this time on the left of the redoubt, and all that seemingly stood in their way was the single rank of Highlanders left behind by Major Stirling.

Chapter 7

The Dawn's Early Light

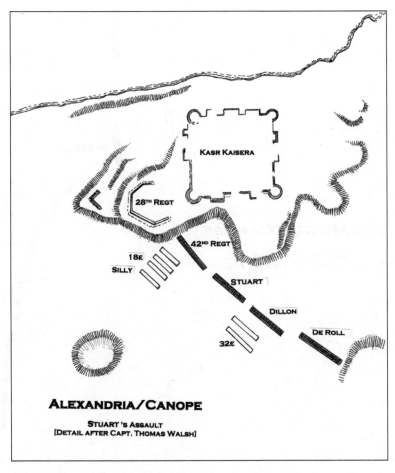

Alexandria: Stuart's Counterattack: detail traced from Captain Thomas Walsh's plan of the battle

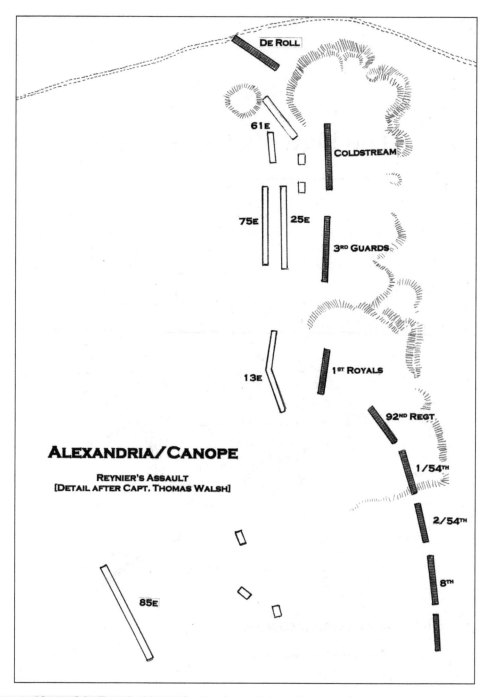

Alexandria. Reynier's Attack. detail traced from Captain Thomas Walsh's plan
of the battle

The Battle of Alexandria/Canope Part 2

This new attack coming down the Aboukir Road appears to have been a heterogenous collection of units. Walsh depicts the *18e Ligne* from Sylly's command coming up against the 42nd, and *General de Division* Antoine-Guillaume Rampon's *32e Ligne* attacking the centre of Stuart's brigade. However, Stuart had not come up yet, and the Black Watch had faced off against *18e Ligne* in the initial attack on the redoubt. The Highlanders, or at least a single rank of them, held them at bay during the fight for the fort, but now they were facing Rampon's Division rather as well as the *18e*, although it would be a complete misnomer to refer to Rampon's command as a division. Originally it had indeed mustered the usual two demi-brigades, but most of *2e Légère* remained behind to look after the Damietta area, and so only its three *carabinier* (grenadier) companies accompanied the general westwards, under *Captain-Adjutant* Sornet. Otherwise Rampon now had only his own *32e Ligne*, which he had personally commanded with some distinction in Italy, and which appears to have had two battalions with a combined total of only 542 men at the beginning of the month. Thus at best his 'division' was only the equivalent of a strong British battalion. Nevertheless, there must have been some other minor units accompanying the attack as well. Sornet and his *carabiniers* were certainly involved, and they may well have been joined by Eppler's *Grenadiers Grecs*, and perhaps even by the remaining battalion of *21e Légère* if it had managed to disentangle itself from the stalled fight for the redoubt by this time. At any rate, seeing them coming forward, Moore 'ordered the Highlanders out of the ruin, and directed them to form line in battalion on the flat on which Major Stirling had originally formed, with their right supported by the redoubt. This extension of the line enabled them to show a larger front to the enemy, who pressed forward so rapidly that it was necessary to check them even before the battalion had fully completed its formation in line.'[1]

Despite the rush to form up, the clash was a brief but bloody one and Rampon himself 'had his horse shot from under him, and his clothes pierced with balls. Sornet, adjutant commandant, was mortally wounded in advancing, and the grenadiers under his command could not penetrate the enemy's lines.'[2] On the other side, John Hope, the adjutant general, was wounded[3] and Moore was also shot in the leg during the exchange. While the wound did not at first appear to be serious, it may have been what convinced him to counterattack at once and drive off the French. As it happened, Sir Ralph himself also turned up at that point to find out what was happening and on being briefed by Moore he immediately concurred. 'Encouraging the troops in the language of which they always felt the force, he called out, "My brave Highlanders, remember your country, remember your forefathers." The Black Watch immediately charged forward and, along with the two companies of the 28th Regiment, drove the French tumbling back.

As they broke through to the road, however, the Highlanders immediately ran into unexpected trouble. Becoming all too aware of his wound, Moore borrowed a horse from Major Robert Honeyman,[4] and was no sooner mounted on it when he saw 'through the increasing clearness of the atmosphere' (as Captain Stewart rather quaintly phrased it) that they were now in the presence of a large body of French cavalry coming up behind Rampon's command. This was General Roise, rather reluctantly moving forward with his five regiments of dragoons.

In his original orders General Menou had somewhat pompously declared that: 'The general in Chief will be everywhere, to give orders according to the new circumstances that may arise.' Ubiquity, however, even for an officer far more dynamic than Menou, is difficult to achieve in pitch darkness, especially when his subordinates are falling at a frightening rate, and worse still he had no reserves of infantry to feed into the fighting. His offensive had stalled, and in Reynier's trenchant view:

> After the failure of this first attack the dispersion of the troops, and the loss of general Lanusse, further efforts were useless; because, before the action, every expectation of success had been founded on a first shock. Several of the principal officers being slain, three-fifths of the army that were dispersed could not rally and form again under the enemy's fire, to hazard any new attack. The right wing was too weak to make any attempt by itself on the enemy's centre, protected by the main redoubt, the Roman Camp, and their right wing. If the French had retired at this moment, their loss would not have been very great; the English would have considered this affair merely as a general reconnoitring; and the army would have remained strong enough to keep the field, and to attempt some new movement on the first favourable occasion.[5]

That opinion, however, was uttered in hindsight. On the actual day, Reynier was intending to cast himself as the hero of the hour and was busy shifting most of his men northwards in readiness to mount his own assault. He complains that he had sent message after message to Menou anent moving his division northwards, but received no response and so elected to march on his own initiative. In fact, Menou for his part was probably frustrated by the time Reynier was taking to get into action, for while the original plan had called for Reynier to come forward once Lanusse and Rampon were fully engaged, the battle had stalled. The British had not been pushed back but they were at least pinned down and the second phase of operation now depended on Reynier getting into the fight and assaulting the escarpment.

Notwithstanding the poor light, it is difficult to believe that Menou was ignorant of Reynier's approaching columns, but in the meantime, the only uncommitted troops available to him were Roise and his dragoons. Consequently, the general decided to turn to that traditional resource of French generals facing a crisis; the sacrificial cavalry charge. Far from being flung at the British in an impotent fit of pique, as Reynier alleges, the cavalry must have been ordered to charge precisely in order to buy time for the tardy Reynier to pitch in.

Roise, for his part, was understandably reluctant to send his men forward against what he presumed to be unbroken infantry, and according to Reynier protested vehemently 'that this was not the moment for a charge, and that they would be cut to pieces without rendering any service'.[6] Notwithstanding the general's remonstrances, Menou, with Reynier's division not yet up, must have felt that there was no alternative and had to twice repeat the order before Roise trotted forward to his doom.

Leading the way was *General de Brigade* Andre-Joseph Broussart with the *3e* and *14e Dragoons*, who according to Reynier's figures had mustered 225 and 195 troopers apiece on 1 March (exclusive of dismounted detachments), while Roise himself had the *15e*, *18e* and *20e Dragoons* mounting a further 397 troopers in his second line.

'It was doubtless a moment,' as the Black Watch's official account coyly admitted; 'in which a regiment, pressing close on a retreating enemy, cannot be supposed to be correctly in line.'[7] As soon as he saw the danger, Moore ordered the Highlanders to retreat to their original position, but it was already too late and 'owing to the noise of the firing, this order to fall back to the redoubt, although repeated by Colonel Stewart, was only partially heard ... the companies whom it distinctly reached retired; but those who did not hear it hesitated to follow; thus leaving considerable intervals between those companies who heard the orders to retire on the redoubt, and those who did not.'[8] It ought to have been a disaster, for the disorderly retreat of a straggling line of infantry was exactly the sight of which all cavalrymen dreamed.

Instead, what might have been a glorious charge never really happened. As they passed through or around the remains of Rampon's retreating troops, the French cavalry found themselves moving across what had earlier been the 28th Regiment's lines and discovered to their dismay that the ground was still covered not only with a tangled litter of collapsed tents and pegged ropes, but that a large number of pits were also dug into the sand, which Reynier indignantly referred to as *trous de loup* or wolf pits. Walsh, no doubt exaggerating, declares that they were 'between three and four feet deep', having been dug as 'conveniences to sleep in', before the arrival of proper camp equipage, while Stewart, rather more convincingly, refers to them as the pits that had been dug for the fires kindled under the camp kettles. At any rate, whatever their true purpose, the combination of pits, camp equipment and general debris were an awkward obstacle that forced the *14e Dragoons* to swing around the campsite while *3e* delicately picked through it. In tandem with the fact that the two sides were already so close when they discovered each other, this prevented Roise's leading brigade from going forward with any momentum and seemingly with precious little regularity either. As a result, just as had happened in the similar encounter a week earlier between the *Chasseurs a Cheval* and the 90th Regiment at Mandara, although the dragoons did get in among the ranks of the Black Watch, astonishingly little damage was done to the infantry. The scattered companies of Highlanders simply closed up tightly on themselves, each forming a compact little body, bristling with bayonets thrust in all directions. Only thirteen men, according to Stewart, were wounded by the sabre in this encounter; 'That they suffered so slightly was owing to the firmness with which the men stood, first endeavouring to bring down the horse, before the rider got within sword-length, and then dispatching him with the bayonet, before he had time to recover his legs from the fall of the horse.'[9]

As Moore rather more pithily recorded it: 'The cavalry were completely amongst us; but our men, though in disorder, rallied, and brought down with their fire so many men and horses that the rest were glad to get off.' One of the French casualties was the brigade commander, General Broussart, shot twice through the body,[10] but as soon as the wreckage of his first line cleared out of the way, Roise doggedly led forward his second line; the *15e, 18e* and *20e Dragoons,* in a second charge.

Again, the Black Watch held their ground. 'It was,' declared David Stewart, who was himself wounded in the action, 'a trial of personal firmness, and of individual courage, as indeed it nearly was in the former charge, every man fighting on his own ground, regardless how he was supported, facing his enemy wherever he presented himself, and maintaining his post while strength or life remained. But exertions like these could not have been long sustained.'[11] One of those who fell at this point was Sergeant Sinclair, still clutching the colours of 3/21 *Légére* and standing with them by the captured gun. A couple of dragoons knocked him down and snatched it back again,[12] but another and rather more notable casualty was General Abercromby himself, who was wounded and almost captured.

Stewart recalled how: 'Early in the day he had taken his station in front, and in a line between the right of the Highlanders and the left of the redoubt, so as to be clear of the fire of the 28th regiment who occupied it.' The result was perhaps inevitable, especially for a near blind man.

Moore lamented some days later:

Sir Ralph has always been accused of exposing his person too much, but I never knew him carry this so far as in the action of the 21st. When it was so dark that I could scarcely distinguish, I saw him close in the rear of the 42nd without any of his family [ie his personal staff]. He was afterwards joined by General Hope. When the French cavalry charged us a second time and our men were disordered, I called to him and waved with my hand to him to retire; but he was instantly surrounded by the hussars. He received a blow with a sabre on the breast which cut through his clothes and only grazed the flesh. He must have been taken or killed if a soldier had not shot the hussar …[13]

Moore himself could not help amidst the swirling melee, for: 'I was obliged to put spurs to my horse to get clear, and I galloped to the ruins to bring up from thence some of the troops which I knew were formed and in good order. The 28th Regiment, who were lining the parapet of the redoubt, without quitting their post turned round and killed the dragoons who had penetrated there.'[14]

The latter incident is, of course, a famous one and the origin of the regiment's celebrated 'back badge', but while there is no doubting that the action was a critical one and the distinction well-earned, it is also worth emphasising that, notwithstanding numerous paintings and other illustrations, the 28th were not standing out in the open at the time. Meanwhile, continued Moore, 'The 42nd, though broken, were individually fighting, and I ordered the flank companies of the 40th from the ruins to pour in a couple of volleys, though at the risk of hurting some of our own people.'

But now, in the very nick of time some more substantial help arrived and: 'Brigadier General Stewart, bringing up his brigade, at this critical moment, his own regiment gave the enemy a close and well-directed fire, which allowed time to the 42nd to join their efforts to those of the rest of the reserve and of the foreign brigade in repelling the cavalry.'[15] It is a pity that Stuart's well-timed charge, which Wilson believed with some truth had decided the action, is not better known, for it is clear that the Foreign Brigade did not trouble to form into the square formation prescribed by the drill book for opposing cavalry (and nor, of course, did anybody else that morning) but instead stormed forward in line to at least partially plug the yawning gap in the valley between the 42nd and the Footguards. Moore also saw Stuart's counterattack as the climax of the action and declared that: 'The field was instantly covered with men and horses, horses galloping without riders – in short, the cavalry were destroyed. Every attack the French had made had been repulsed with slaughter. In the dark some confusion was unavoidable, but our men, wherever the French appeared, had gone boldly up to them. Even the cavalry breaking in had not dismayed them.'

'General Roize was killed,' lamented Reynier and, 'a prodigious number of officers and privates shared his fate; and many others were wounded or dismounted. The broken corps of the cavalry retired in disorder; and, when they were again formed behind the infantry, there were not found the fourth of the number that had charged.'

Yet, even as the cavalry attack receded, the fight was still not over. Under cover of the action, General Sylly, who had rallied his shattered brigade and joined them to the remains of Rampon's men, was ordered by Menou to lead them all forward again in the wake of the cavalry. 'They made another effort with a line of infantry to attack the redoubt in front and on both flanks,' explained Moore. The earlier attempts to carry the position in a rush with heavy assault columns had failed, and the demi-brigades had dissolved into a thick band of *tirailleurs*, or skirmishers, on the lower slopes of the sand hills. Recognising the impossibility and even the futility of forming them into columns again, it was this substantial skirmish line, probably reinforced on the left with Valentin's men and with Rampon's 32e on the right, that Sylly was now bringing forward, The British were waiting for them, having patched together a proper battle line of their own. Stuart's regiment was now formed alongside the remnants of the Black Watch, while the '58th Regiment in the ruins allowed them to approach within sixty yards, and then gave their fire so effectually as to knock down a great number of them'.

General Sylly himself was among those shot down and the attack then withered like the others.[16] This was just as well, for while those attackers immediately in front of the ruins are said to have run off again, elsewhere the struggle was perhaps more bitter than British accounts liked to admit, and must have accounted for most of the near 350 casualties suffered by Stuart's brigade.[17] By now too, the 28th Regiment had quite literally run out of ammunition. Nevertheless, at first both sides grimly refused to let go and Wilson claimed that: 'The French on the right, during the want of ammunition amongst the British, had attempted to approach again close to the redoubt, and some of them also having exhausted theirs, absolutely pelted stones from the ditch at the 28th, who returned these unusual, yet not altogether harmless, instruments of violence, as a serjeant of the 28th was killed by one breaking through his forehead; but the grenadier company of the 40th moving out, the assailants ran away, the sharp shooters in front left the hollows they were covered by, and the battalion [ie the *carabiniers* of *4e Légére*] also evacuated the fleche.'[18]

The position had been held, but yet they still endured. Moore recalled:

Our cartridges were expended, and our guns for want of ammunition had not fired for some time. Daylight enabled us to get our men into order, and, as the enemy's artillery was galling us, I placed as many men under cover of the redoubt as I could. We were for an hour without a cartridge; the enemy during this time were pounding us with shot and shell, and distant musketry. Our artillery could not return a shot, and had their infantry again advanced we must have repelled them with the bayonet. Our fellows would have done it; I never saw men more determined to do their duty; but the French had suffered so severely that they could not get their men to make another attempt.

Unsurprisingly, he went on to grumble; 'Our artillery failed us as it did in Holland for want of arrangement; with the Reserve there were none but subalterns at the guns.[19] There were no captains or superior officers to superintend, and, when the ammunition contained in the boxes and the limbers was expended, there was no supply. The musketry ammunition was also too far to the rear, and it took hours to bring it up.' The criticism was unfair and certainly underestimated the sheer effort required to bring up the ammunition. There were no tumbrils or pack animals for the purpose and every artillery round and box or barrel of cartridges had to be carried up by hand over the soft sand by sailors and by Turkish auxiliaries, who according to Wilson, insisted on throwing themselves flat on the ground whenever a round came over.

Sheer exhaustion of both men and ammunition meant that the fight for the Roman Fort was finally over, but the wider battle was not yet finished.

Following the sequence of attacks in the various contemporary accounts of any battle is far from easy. This was never truer than of the battle of Alexandria/Canope, largely fought as it was in darkness, yet Moore at least was positive in writing of facing those three distinct French attacks; the first was, of course, General Lanusse's ill-fated assault on the Roman fort position at the very beginning. Then came General Rampon and behind him the cavalry, and finally there was Sylly's doomed effort.

Now, as dawn was breaking, came one last French offensive, this time directed not against Moore's exhausted men, but against the hitherto unengaged brigades on the main escarpment.

General Reynier's men arrived at last. He claims, as we have seen, to have several times sent to General Menou, advocating that instead of sitting uselessly facing the British left, he and his men should be switched to the other side of the battlefield, but answer came there none. In the end, writing in the third person, he says his frustration, impatience, and contempt for Menou drove him to act unilaterally in what he himself represented as an extraordinary (but justified) act of insubordination. 'As soon as general Reynier heard of the brave Lanusse's wound, and the disorder of the centre, he made his wing advance to their support, giving orders to General Damas to remain with the 13th, between the two lakes, to occupy the enemy's left, and to push some sharpshooters towards the canal.' Then he himself marched across with the rest of his command in order to renew the fight against the British right. 'Its success would have afforded an opportunity,' he claimed, 'to rally the scattered troops, and bring them again into action. While Friant's division and the 85th were in motion, to make this attack, and the light artillery advanced, by his order to silence the redoubts, General Reynier proceeded to some sand-hills not far from the main redoubt, the more perfectly to observe the enemy's movements, and discover what was best to be done, to attack them with some chance of success.'

To the considerable confusion of subsequent historians, despite Reynier's stated intention of attacking the British right, after carrying out this reconnaissance he actually ended up doing nothing of the sort. Viewing the battlefield from the vantage point of the sand hills soon convinced him 'that no new attack could be successfully made with the divisions of Lanusse and Rampon'. Instead, rather than reinforce failure, his own offensive was to be directed against the British positions on the escarpment.

Having made that decision, he headed back to his command, and to his professed surprise he then met the cavalry trotting forward and 'passing through the intervals of the 61e and 75e retarding their march and already under the fire of the enemy's infantry. It was too late to stop this ill-timed charge. The cavalry would have suffered almost as much in halting where they were, as in executing the charge.'[20] Making no attempt to co-ordinate his advance with Menou, far less with Sylly, he hurried forward the *25e, 61e* and *75e Ligne*, belonging to Friant's division, and his own *85e Ligne* to support the cavalry, but by the time he got them up, it was too late; General Baudot was fatally wounded at the head of *85e*, lamented Reynier[21] and 'scarcely had the 61st reached the foot of the redoubt, when the cavalry were already repulsed'.

The latter part of this statement at least is quite misleading, for as Walsh's map clearly shows, the redoubt fronted by the *61e Ligne* was *not* the one by the Roman Fort, but a quite different one, on the other side of the shallow valley, which was anchoring the northern end of the central escarpment, occupied by Ludlow's Brigade.[22] Moreover, Reynier's complaint that: 'Several of the commanding officers of corps were wounded, and the troops of the left and centre had no officer who might have taken advantage of their proximity to the enemy, when the cavalry threw their first line into disorder,' rather glosses over his own failure to intervene effectively.

It is easy to gain the impression from some narratives that this final attack in the centre began at an early hour, and Walsh for one claims that Rampon's earlier offensive had lapped along it as far the 92nd Highlanders, but Wilson is positive that the escarpment was not seriously attacked before dawn and a simple counting on fingers confirms this. All four demi-brigades of Lanusse's division were engaged from start to finish in the fight for the ruins. As to the two columns comprising the notional French centre, both battalions of *21e Légére* were sucked into the same fight, while Rampon's troops were smashed by the Black Watch and Stuart's brigade as they tried to push down the Aboukir Road. It is less easy to account for the *Grenadiers Grecs* and the other little detachments of grenadier companies, but they were minor satellites of Rampon's and d'Estaing's demi-brigades. Some skirmishers may well have engaged in sharpshooting but there were simply no unengaged major French units left available to attack the escarpment until dawn, when Reynier finally arrived on the scene.

Waiting for them, George Ludlow's Guardsmen were initially posted on the reverse slope, with the Coldstream very properly standing on the right of the line and the 3rd Footguards on their left. Immediately to their south the sand hills apparently rose quite appreciably, separating the Guards from Coote's brigade, which was posted on the higher ground with 2/1st Royal on the right, then came the rather attenuated 92nd Highlanders. Afflicted by a long sick-list and having been badly mauled at Mandara, the Gordons should never have been there at all. Now mustering little more than 150 effectives, they had actually been ordered to go back that morning to take over the garrison of Aboukir. How far they actually got on their journey is unclear, but having sensibly commenced their march well before daybreak, they were, according to Walsh, already 2 miles down the road when the firing began on the right. Notwithstanding, after a brief exchange with a then sceptical Abercromby himself, Major Alexander Napier promptly turned around and marched them straight back again and inserted the little battalion into its proper place in the centre of the brigade.[23]

There was plenty of time for them to do so, for thus far the two brigades had been no more than passive spectators as the battle literally blazed in the darkness around the Roman fort. Now as the fighting at last died down and as the sun rose over the battlefield, Reynier's men started to climb the escarpment and they were at last involved. Ludlow moved his Guardsmen a few metres forward to the military crest[24] and Wilson described what happened next:

> As soon as day dawned, a column of grenadiers had advanced, supported by a heavy line of infantry, to the assault of this part of the position. The Guards posted there at first threw out their flankers to oppose them, but these being driven in, when the column approached very near, General Ludlow directed the brigade to fire, which they did with the greatest precision. The French General, seeing the echelon formation, had advanced to turn the left flank of the guards, but the officer commanding there instantly wheeled back some companies, which checked their movement, and the advance of General Coote with his brigade compelled them to retreat.

There was a little more to it than that, of course. Walsh states that the French 'made an attack on the centre, extending as far towards the left as the ninety-second', but this could only have applied to the thick skirmish line that invariably preceded the demi-brigades, for the real effort was made to 'turn the left of the brigade of guards, which was a little advanced; but was received with so warm and well kept up a fire from the third regiment of guards, whose left was thrown back, and from the royals, as to be forced, after a sharp contest, to retreat with great loss.'[25] Evidently what happened was that Coote's brigade, already separated from the Guards by a combination of distance and elevation, was initially slow to conform to Ludlow's forward movement, which meant that the left flank of 1/3rd Footguards was for a very short time in the air. The French naturally attempted to take advantage of this by thrusting between the two brigades, but as Wilson notes, Colonel Samuel Dalrymple wheeled back some companies of Guardsmen to confront them and at the same time Lieutenant Colonel Peter Garden came up with 2/1st Royals.

Consequently, the French attack was not pressed. Having their commanding officer shot down before they had even started probably dampened the ardour of 85e, while Friant's three demi-brigades were by now getting used to defeat and in no mood to continue another lost battle. In the end, notwithstanding Reynier's bombast, it was all very half-hearted, and; 'Finding this effort ineffectual, they then dispersed as sharp shooters, and kept up a very destructive fire, at the same time that the French cannon played incessantly.'

No one, however, was in any doubt that by now the battle was drawing to an exhausted close. Walsh recorded:

After the last effort of the cavalry, the French army remained drawn up in order of battle, contenting itself with keeping up a heavy cannonade, which was warmly returned. By this cannonade our second line suffered very considerably, because, great part of the first line being disposed along a height, the French were obliged to give great elevation to their guns, so that the balls, clearing the height, fell in among the ranks of the second line posted behind it. The enemy seemed wavering and uncertain, whether to attempt another attack; and in this debate between prudence and courage, their troops lay completely under the fire of our guns, which caused a dreadful havock among them. Presently, however, two of their ammunition waggons blew up with a dreadful explosion, and their fire began considerably to slacken, most probably from a want of ammunition.[26]

At last, after two pointless hours of desultory firing, General Menou reluctantly recognised that it was all over and ordered a retreat – a decision that was greeted with considerable relief by both sides. Moore recalled:

> Amongst the last shots which were fired, one killed the horse Major Honeyman had lent me. The wound in my leg, which I received in the beginning of the action, had become painful and stiff towards nine, when the affair ended. General Oakes was also wounded about the same time, and nearly in the same part of the leg that I was, but we had both been able to continue to do our duty. The affair being ended, as soon as I could get a horse I desired Colonel Spencer to take the command of the reserve, and I returned with Oakes to our tents, where the surgeon dressed our wounds.[27]

There was no pursuit, save by the Turkish battalion that apparently at Sydney Smith's urging, and rather to the annoyance of everyone else, advanced a short distance out into the plain, but only as far as a small hill, with numerous flags fluttering triumphantly.

Moore commented afterwards that he had never seen a field thicker with dead than that around the redoubt and the Roman fort. All in all, Walsh and other British writers hopefully suggested that the total French losses in killed and wounded must have come to about 4,000; in addition to the 250 unwounded prisoners, two cannon and a colour belonging to *21e Légére* were also taken.[28] At any rate, the provost marshal, to whom fell the task of collecting and burying the bodies, dispassionately recorded that the French left 1,160 dead on the field, besides uncounted others lying on the out on the plain within their picquet line, and on the other side Dr Larrey, who certainly ought to have known, states that there were also 1,300 wounded, although this figure presumably only relates to those who were successfully evacuated back to Alexandria.[29]

For its part, later that morning the British Army reported the loss of a total of ten officers, nine sergeants, 224 rank and file and two horses killed, with another sixty officers, forty-eight sergeants, three drummers, 1,082 rank and file and three horses wounded.

The distribution of those casualties was obviously very uneven. With the exception of Stuart's brigade, those units standing in the second line, including the cavalry, escaped more or less unscathed, as did Cradock's brigade on the left of the front line. Only a few casualties were lost in those units to random artillery rounds falling in the rear of the army. Up on the ridge itself, 1/3rd Footguards reported 198 killed and wounded, including Ensign Lorne Campbell, said to have fallen while carrying the colours, and three captains were wounded, while the Coldstream had just sixty casualties. Similarly, in Coote's Brigade on the other side of 1/3rd Footguards, the Royals had a total of eighty-two casualties, with progressively fewer returned by the battalions going down the line.

The highest losses, for obvious reasons, were suffered in the fight for the sand hills. Thanks to the very substantial cover afforded to them by the earthwork redoubt and the stone walls of the Roman fort, some units escaped comparatively lightly. The 28th Regiment suffered only seventy-eight killed and wounded, including four officers wounded, including Colonel Paget, while the 58th Regiment ensconced inside the fort itself had just twenty-six casualties in total, and the 23rd Fusiliers boasted only twenty. The 42nd Highlanders on the other hand, standing out in the open and twice ridden over by the cavalry, lost no fewer than six officers and forty-eight men killed and another eight officers, six sergeants and 247 men wounded over the course of the morning. Similarly, the three battalions of Stuart's Foreign Brigade, who intervened so decisively against Roise's cavalry and Sylly's last attack, suffered a surprisingly high total of 342 casualties, 206 of them in the Minorca Regiment alone, including its commanding officer, Lieutenant Colonel Peter Dutens.[30]

Sir Ralph Abercromby himself, alas, was of course also among the wounded, and after being rescued from his would-be captors by Corporal Barker of the Black Watch, he was forced to dismount from his horse and then walk painfully up to the small battery at the north end of the ridge. Here he quietly awaited the end of the battle. Oblivious to the incoming artillery rounds, he gave no orders, or directions to bring up fresh troops and at first no one seems to have realised that he had been hurt, far less how seriously he was wounded. Eventually, having hung on until it was obvious the French were retreating, he became faint through loss of blood and delayed shock, and was at last carried down to the boats in Lake Maadje and evacuated. The sabre cut to his chest was only a slight wound and of no significance, but unbeknown to his officers at first, a musket ball had also entered his groin – perhaps in the same volley that felled Hope – and was lodged deep in the hip joint. It could not be extracted and a week later he was dead.

Appendix

Return of Killed, Wounded, and Missing, of the Army under the Command of General Sir Ralph Abercromby, K. B., in the Action near Alexandria, the 21st of March, 1801.

Cavalry. – 2 horses killed; 1 trumpeter, 13 rank and file, 3 horses wounded.

Artillery – 14 rank and file killed; 5 officers, 40 rank and file wounded; 1 rank and file missing.

Brigade of Guards. – 1 officer, 3 sergeants, 45 rank and file killed; 3 officers, 9 sergeants, 197 rank and file wounded.

1st Brigade. – 1 officer, 16 rank and file killed; 8 officers, 173 rank and file wounded.

2nd Brigade. – 1 rank and file killed; 6 rank and file wounded.

3rd Brigade. – 1 sergeant, 2 rank and file killed; 5 officers, 4 sergeants, 58 rank and file wounded.

4th Brigade. – 7 rank and file killed; 6 officers, 8 sergeants, 49 rank and file wounded.

5th Brigade. – 3 officers, 2 sergeants, 61 rank and file killed; 17 officers, 14 sergeants, 1 drummer, 235 rank and file wounded; 3 officers, 1 sergeant, 21 rank and file missing and taken prisoners.

Reserve. – 5 officers, 3 sergeants, 78 rank and file killed ; 16 officers, 12 sergeants, 1 drummer, 330 rank and file wounded; 6 rank and file missing.

Total. – 10 officers, 9 sergeants, 224 rank and file, 2 horses killed; 60 officers, 48 sergeants, 3 drummers, 1082 rank and file, 3 horses wounded; 3 officers, 1 sergeant, 28 rank and file missing.

Officers killed:

3rd Guards: Ensign (Lorne) Campbell. – 42nd: Major (Robert) Bissett; Lieutenants (Colin) Campbell, (Robert) Anderson, (Alexander) Stuart. – 58th: Lieutenant (Robert Salisbury) Joceljn. – Stuart's regiment: Colonel (Peter) Dutens, Lieutenants Duverger and Dejean. – 2nd battalion 54th: Captain (Godfrey) Gibson.

Officers wounded:

His Excellency Sir R. Abercromby, KB. Commander in Chief (since dead); Major General (John) Moore; Brigadier General (John) Hope, Adjutant General; Brigadier Generals (Hildebrand) Oakes and (Robert) Lawson; Majors of Brigade Doyle and St Pern (since dead); Captain (Paul) Anderson, Aide-de-camp to Major General Moore.

3rd Guards: Captains (Charles) Rooke, Ainslie, Doare. – Royals: Captain Gardner; Lieutenants (John) Gordon, (Charles) Johnson,

(John) M'Pherson (since dead). – Second 54th: Lieutenants (William) Conran and Predam. – 92nd: Captain (John) Cameron, Lieutenant Mathieson. – 50th: Captain (James) Ogilvie; Lieutenants Campbell, Tilsby; Ensign (Benjamin) Rowe. – 79th: Lieutenant Ross. – Queen's: Ensign Aliman. – 44th: Lieut. Colonel David Ogilvie (since dead). – 89th Captain (Dennis John) Blake, Lieutenant (Patrick) Agnew. – Stuart's Captains (Ernest) Mislett, Mahony, Richardson; Lieutenants (William) M'Carthy, (Matthew) Sutton, Hutton, F. Zehender, Loreg, (Louis) Girard, Ensign (Ernst) Olferman – De Roll's: Lieutenant Motzger, Adjutant la Ville. – Dillon's: Captains Dupont, Renaud, d'Heral; Lieutenants Laury, Daville. – 23rd: Lieutenant Cooke (since dead). – 28th: Colonel (Edward) Paget; Lieutenants (John Cathcart) Meacham, (Michael) Hearne, (John) Ford. – 1st; battalion 40th: Lieutenant Southwell. – 42nd: Major (James) Stirling; Captain (David) Stewart; Lieutenants (Hamilton) Rose, (Archibald) M'Nicholl (since dead), (Alexander) Donaldson (since dead), (J. Milford) Sutherland, (Maxwell) Grant, (A.M.) Cuningham, (Frederick) Campbell; Ensign (William) M'Kenzie. – 58th: Lieutenant Curry O'Toole. – Artillery: Lieutenants (Thomas) Gamble, Campbell, (Robert) Lawson, and (James) Burslem.

Chapter 8

Up the Nile

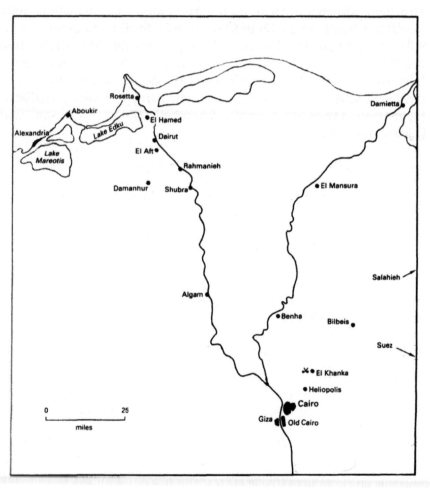

Lower Egypt: the seat of the war

As the firing faded to silence and Sir Ralph Abercromby was carried away to die aboard HMS *Foudroyant*, command of His Britannic Majesty's Army in Egypt passed, almost unobtrusively, to a 44-year-old Irishman; Major General John Hely Hutchinson.[1]

Seemingly a slovenly, unsociable man with a filthy temper, Hutchinson was little regarded by his contemporaries and is now pretty well forgotten. The son of a prominent judge and statesman, born in Dublin in 1757 and afforded a 'liberal' education, he entered the army as a cornet in Lord Drogheda's 18th Light Dragoons in 1774, was a lieutenant in December 1775, a captain in the 67th Foot by the following October and its major in 1781. Like Drogheda's Horse, the 67th Regiment was part of the Irish garrison and his swift rise in rank was entirely facilitated by the usual combination of hard cash and social and political influence rather than by any discernible military talents. Then, in March 1783, he took the odd step of purchasing the lieutenant colonelcy of another unit forming part of the Irish garrison; the 77th (Athole) Highlanders. The American war had just ended and having been specifically raised for the duration of the conflict, the regiment was about to be disbanded, which meant that Hutchinson was no sooner promoted than he retired straight on to the half-pay.[2] He had risen from cornet of dragoons to colonel of foot in less than ten years, while seeing precious little proper regimental soldiering in the meantime, but like Abercromby he was now to remain unemployed for the next decade. It was a pretty typical career in the Army's notoriously corrupt and lackadaisical Irish Establishment, but he did latterly at least spend some of his time afterwards in study at the French artillery academy in Strasbourg, then perhaps the most famous military school in Europe. Then, when war broke out between Revolutionary France on the one hand and most of the rest of the Continent on the other, he visited the armies on both sides as a self-proclaimed professional observer. His strong left-wing sympathies naturally inclined him towards the Revolution, but in 1793, when his friend Major General Abercromby received the command of a brigade in Flanders, Hutchinson had no hesitation in tagging along with him as an Extra ADC.[3] After that first campaign he then returned home to raise a short-lived regiment of his very own, and when that was reduced in order that its men could be transferred to needy veteran units, he effortlessly moved over to the Irish staff.

In the meantime, he had been routinely promoted through seniority alone to the wholly undeserved rank of major general in the brevet of 3 May 1796 and he was still ornamenting the Irish staff when the great rebellion broke out there two years later. The '98 was a bloody affair punctuated by appalling massacres on both sides, but by the summer's end when it was all but over a small French army turned up like the Devil at prayers. Landing in remote County Mayo of all places, it boldly advanced into the interior before finding itself confronted at Castlebar by an Anglo-Loyalist force commanded by Lord Lake and a certain Major General John Hely Hutchinson. And it was the latter, rather than Lake, who for some reason got the blame for the disaster that followed.[4] The French, against all the odds, won, and so speedily did Hutchinson and his colleagues run away that the battle was ever after celebrated as 'The Races of Castlebar'. After that chastening experience it probably came as a relief for him to go to the Helder in 1799, where having once again attached himself to Abercromby's staff as a volunteer, Hutchinson ended up by commanding a brigade after Lord Cavan was wounded in the closing stages of the operation. It also cost Hutchinson himself a creditable wound in the thigh, and may have cemented Abercromby's already close friendship, for soon afterwards the old man insisted on taking Hutchinson to the Mediterranean, not just on his staff, but as his second-in-command! As the anonymous author of the *Military Panorama* rather delicately put it, this was 'a measure which created some surprise at the time as the major general had not been employed on any previous occasion in the command of an army'.[5]

It was hardly for want of anyone better, and Sir James Pulteney, for one, was on the spot, having brought down the necessary reinforcements to enable Abercromby's Mediterranean operations. Indeed, he acted as second in command at Cadiz (which was, of course, on the Atlantic side of Gibraltar) and he was not only senior to Hutchinson, but was a very experienced officer who, as Sir James Murray (as he was before a fortunate legacy), had been chief of staff to the Duke of York in Flanders. Inevitably he too had his failings, but professionally he must have seemed infinitely preferable to Hutchinson, and yet Abercromby insisted on keeping the latter, and Pulteney went home via Portugal.

Exactly why Abercromby was willing to place so much faith in Hutchinson is very hard to discover, and it appears that the decision was primarily based on an unashamed cronyism, which at first sight appears wholly at odds with the general's posthumous reputation and ultimately reflects badly on his judgement. And yet it is entirely consistent with the blatant nepotism underpinning Abercromby's shameless facilitation of his own son John's less than distinguished military career, which was mostly spent in acting as the general's personal secretary, but which nevertheless saw the boy rise effortlessly from ensign to lieutenant colonel without spending a single day's regimental soldiering. Moreover, part of that rise had also been eased by Hutchinson! When the latter raised his short-lived 94th Regiment in 1794, he awarded the major's post to Abercromby's otherwise totally unqualified son, who then very soon afterwards proceeded to become lieutenant colonel of the equally ephemeral 112th Regiment, raised by none other than Hutchinson's elder brother, Viscount Donoughmore. The fact of the matter is that, notwithstanding his professional standing and near saintly posthumous reputation, Abercromby was at bottom very much a product of the corrupt old Irish Establishment in which he had spent most of his career, and his appointment of Hutchinson to be his second in command in the Mediterranean was, in that wonderfully expressive eighteenth-century phrase, a 'job'.

Notwithstanding, when it came to the touch, Hutchinson was soon turning out to be a sad disappointment to Abercromby. He had been 'sick' at Aboukir and then slow and uncertain at Mandara, and indeed in all their discussions from Marmaris onwards he had proven to be unduly pessimistic and lacking in energy. Reflecting on his performance at Mandara, Abercromby wrote to the Duke of York's formidably efficient military secretary, Colonel Robert Brownrigg, complaining that: 'General Hutchinson has bad health and does not like responsibility.' As the officer next in seniority, General Coote, was considered by Abercromby to be a reliable brigade commander but equally unfitted to command the army, he begged that another general be sent out who was up to the job of second in command.[6] Pulteney, if he learned of that, may have permitted himself a hollow laugh.

How this might have developed in the end is unknown, for those serious misgivings were cut short by Abercromby's wounding and ultimate death, and so Hutchinson, for good or ill, succeeded after all to the command and to all the problems attendant on it; not least the prospect of a renewed French attack, perhaps on a different part of the line.

Walsh wrote:

There being some reason to apprehend that the enemy intended to repeat their attack during the night, our troops remained under arms, and at their alarm posts, till morning. Had the French again tried our strength, however, they would have met even a warmer reception than they had received in the morning. Two additional twenty-four-pounders had been brought up, and placed on a commanding ground in the rear of the third regiment of guards; great abundance of ammunition of all kinds had been also conveyed from the depot to the lines, which had been strengthened by trous de loup, trenches, &c.[7]

Within hours too, Hutchinson was also sending off appeals to Pigot on Malta and Fox on Minorca, begging for reinforcements to at least make good what was already an unsustainable casualty rate.[8]

The battle on 21 March might have been won, albeit at painful cost, but despite the considerable moral victory and the irreplaceable casualties inflicted on the French, the strategic situation was actually now worse than before the battle. Alexandria still remained to be taken. The city's defences were just as formidable as before but the difficulties of overcoming them had now been vastly increased by the accession of the troops brought in by General Menou. The British Army was therefore facing the prospect of besieging a force more or less equal in number to itself, and comfortably ensconced in a well-fortified town that could not readily be cut off from the outside world and its plentiful supplies and reinforcements.

As if that were not enough, Admiral Keith took the opportunity to warn Hutchinson that under no circumstances could the fleet remain offshore beyond October and that he would obviously prefer to be gone long before then. That being said, no one could realistically have expected that the affair would drag on until October, for Keith and Hutchinson still faced an increasingly urgent political time problem. A general peace settlement was imminent and only an unequivocal victory in Egypt could stave off utter failure for Britain.

In all fairness, this was precisely the problem that had sent Abercromby and the British Army to Egypt in the first place, and on the other side of the plain General Menou was shaping his strategy accordingly. Alexandria was the key to Egypt and his primary task was to hold it until France's possession was acknowledged at the Peace. In the meantime, he was to dig in and wait for the substantial reinforcements that were coming from France aboard the Toulon fleet under Admiral Ganteume. Until they arrived, he ought not risk his position by doing anything adventurous. This cautious attitude naturally placed him wholly at odds with some of his subordinates, most notably, of course, *General de Division* Jean Louis Ebenezer Reynier, who claimed that:

The day after the affair ... general Reynier, perceiving that general Menou gave no orders for the army to take a stronger position than that of Nicopolis, and for such a disposition of the various corps scattered over Egypt as circumstances required, went to his quarters, and represented to him, that the heights of Nicopolis were too extensive to meet the English there, who with 15,000 men, might, by a vigorous attack, route the troops, and enter Alexandria with them; that a better position might be taken, by posting the right on the heights of Pompey's Pillar, the centre in the ancient works of the Arabs, and the left at Pharillon; but that important considerations gave the preference to more hardy measures. The junction of the troops at Alexandria wasted the magazines which were very inconsiderable. The visir's army and the troops from India must be on their march; the English might attempt to seize Rosetta, send a flotilla into the Nile, and attack Rahmanieh, which movements it was necessary to oppose. To conclude, the remainder of the army being dispersed in various untenable posts which were useless, and could no longer be succoured, these isolated detachments would be cut off one by one, unless these forts were dismantled, and their garrisons added to the main body of the army. To meet the various dangers which threatened the French, general Reynier proposed to leave sufficient garrisons in the citadel of Cairo, at Alexandria, and at forts Julian and Lesbeh; and to concentrate the army at Rahmanieh, to watch a favourable opportunity to engage the English, when they should quit their position to attack Alexandria or Rosetta; or, if circumstances should require, to march Against the visir as soon as he had passed the desert.

Reynier's proposal was certainly the more soldierly of the two, but far from realistic. All else aside, judging by the French army's subsequent performance it is doubtful whether it was actually still up to engaging the British with anything like the necessary elan. Some sense of this may in fact have been perceived by Hutchinson, for having carried out the immediate replenishment of his ammunition and sent off for reinforcements, his first positive action was to send Robert Wilson into Alexandria with an invitation to surrender. The French would have to give up their guns, their ships and their military stores, but the officers and men would be returned to France without exchange. Not knowing for certain who was actually in command on the French side, the proposal was prudently addressed simply to the commandant of Alexandria and Friant, still declining to admit that Menou was present, returned a suitably defiant reply, declaring that the proposals were inconsistent with the honour of the garrison.

Hutchinson's own response to that entirely predictable rebuff was uncharacteristically decisive. The government's instructions, which he inherited from Abercromby, required him to break the French hold on Egypt by capturing Alexandria and at the same time warned against risking the army by advancing into the pestilential interior. So far so good, but on the other hand, he had no desire to fling his rapidly dwindling forces against the Nicopolis defences, and so instead his thoughts turned to other ways of making life difficult for Menou. While he was in no position to close up on Alexandria while the French held the heights of Nicopolis – he had already abandoned Abercromby's desperate plan for a frontal assault – and it was impossible to properly invest or even throw a close cordon around the city, the French line of communications from the Nile was a long and tenuous one and surely vulnerable.

The return of the *Kapūdān Pasha* on 25 March with another 3,600 Turks provided the necessary impetus and, displaying some unwonted energy, Hutchinson decided as a first step to cautiously probe towards the town of Rosetta, at the mouth of the Nile. If the town was to be taken that would not only open up access into the Nile itself and so greatly ease his own supply situation but it would also open up communications both with the Grand Vizier's forces coming across the desert and the Indian contingent that he believed ought by now to have passed up the Red Sea.

The energetic Colonel Brent Spencer was accordingly tasked with carrying out what initially amounted to an armed reconnaissance with two infantry battalions; his own provisional one formed from the 40th Regiment flank companies, and the 58th Regiment. He was also given thirty mounted troopers of the Hompesch Hussars and three light guns.

Delayed by a sandstorm, Spencer did not set off eastwards from Aboukir until 6 April, having been reinforced at the last minute by a third battalion; the 2nd (Queen's) Regiment under Lord Dalhousie.[9] He was also rather flamboyantly accompanied by the *Kapūdān Pasha* and all 4,000 of his Turks, who 'kept by way of amusement firing constantly in the air with ball'.

A 'painful' two days' march across the desert followed, contending with extreme heat, 'where frequently in the hollows of the ground the air was so hot as to excite the sensation of the vertigo, and where from the mirage it seemed a lake of water, reflecting even the shade of the date trees; an extraordinary deception which no reasoning or strength of sight could remove.' This brought him in sight of Rosetta, where on the morning of 8 April and a little to the south of the town, Spencer found an estimated 800 French troops posted on a high sand hill at Aboumandour. The French had already evacuated the town just in

104

time and were passing most of the garrison and its dependents across to the safety of the right bank of the Nile. Once they were all over, the rearguard then fell back upstream to El Hamed.[10]

After pausing to bring up two guns and fire on those standing on the other side of the river, Spencer detached the Queen's Regiment with 500 *Arnauts* or Albanians to take possession of the town, and then pushed south to chase the French out of El Hamed as well and occupy what Major Wilson described as a 'remarkably strong' covering position with 'the right being on the lake (Edko), the left on the Nile, and the highest banks of a canal in Egypt running along the front'.

Thus securely planted, he then set about his main task of clearing the mouth of the Nile and this meant taking Fort Jullien, lying on the west or left bank of the river, a few miles downstream from Rosetta and in sight of the *boghuz* or bar.

Originally this fort had been a low, squat rectangular structure with a central blockhouse and a tower at each corner, and a French savant who visited it in 1799 noted that it was 'constructed of parts of old buildings; and that several of the stones of the embrasures were of the fine free-stone of Upper Egypt, and still covered with hieroglyphics' – one of them as it turned out being the celebrated Rosetta Stone. The fort then had been taken in hand and modernised by French engineers, who repaired the walls and replaced the old towers with modern bastions and repaired the stout wooden palisade on the glacis. They also renamed it Fort Jullien after one of General Bonaparte's favourite aides, Thomas Prosper Jullien, who had been ambushed and killed during the early days of the campaign. Its fourteen heavy guns now commanded the river, and its small harbour also served as a base for a little flotilla of gunboats. The garrison itself was a tough old collection of about 300 *Invalides* – veteran troops disabled by wounds, infirmities or general debility, but still perfectly capable of doing garrison duty – stiffened by a company of the *61e Ligne*. Unlike Rosetta, it was not going to fall without a fight and the taking of it required some heavy artillery.

While Lord Dalhousie, with his Queen's Regiment and the *Arnauts*, blockaded the fort, the CRA, Brigadier General Robert Lawson, was sent down from Aboukir to set about assembling an adequate siege train, including some gunboats of his own. Once again, the series of shallow lakes fringing the Egyptian shoreline provided the most obvious route and seven gunboats were sent along Lake Etko, although its eastern end turned out to be so shallow that they had to be dragged for some 3 miles over sand and mud before eventually launching them into the Nile. Similarly, some naval 24lb carronades were landed on the open beach and dragged inland to arm the siege batteries raised against the fort. Admiral Keith fretted the while about the delay in opening the river, but suddenly it all came together. The newly arrived gunboats forced their French counterparts to retreat under the guns of the fort and that in turn allowed more British and Turkish gunboats to cross the *boghuz* at the mouth of the river and so proceed to sink three of the French gunboats and blow up a fourth.

Shortage of ammunition compelled the British guns to fire slowly, but on 18 April Wilson reported:

> The wall of the salient angle exposed to the battery began to fall, and open the enemy's guns; but they still worked them, although the Turks, creeping within fifty yards of the works, covering themselves by the felled date trees which had formed the [palisade on the] glacis, maintained a constant fire of musquetry. Another French gunboat had been sunk, and now one was set on fire by a shell from the Turks, which blew up with a considerable explosion, sinking with her falling yards the fourth and last. In the evening Sir Sydney Smith, who had been actively employed in fitting out four captured *djermes* at Rosetta, sent them to attack the castle at the south-east front; after firing several rounds, the wood-work of the carronades broke from the recoil, and they were obliged to retire. Towards night a mortar battery which had been erected considerably to the right, within three hundred yards of the Nile, and nine hundred of the castle, under the directions of Captains Lemoine and Duncan, fired some shells with extraordinary accuracy; one of them pitched on the centre of the roof, and tore away the flag-staff and colours, which the French never dared to erect again.[11]

Instead, at 11.00 am on 19 April a white flag cautiously appeared above the ramparts and on Dalhousie granting the same terms earlier extended to the garrison of Aboukir (ie promising that they would not be handed over to the Turks) at 3.00 pm the French filed out and laid down their arms on the glacis.

The number of men taken was 268, of which 160 were well clothed and able soldiers, having recently come from France; the remainder were invalids, but all capable of service in a garrison. The garrison had forty-one killed and wounded, mainly due to mortar fire, during the short siege, while Dalhousie lost only Lieutenant Thomas Derisley ('unfortunately shot, through mistake, in the night, by one of his own centinels')[12] and two privates of the Queen's regiment killed. Whether any casualties were suffered by the Turks is unknown.

The Nile was now open and Hutchinson took his courage in both hands and, with a new-found decisiveness, resolved to join Spencer and push further up the Nile to take the vital crossroads at Ramanieh, thus cutting off Menou from the interior.

There was no question, however, of abandoning the position in front of Alexandria and the Aboukir depot, and that meant that if he was to divide his forces in order to create a mobile force that could march on Ramanieh, then the existing fortifications forward of Aboukir needed to be strengthened. Work had, of course, already begun on a series of redoubts and trenches along the escarpment line held during the battle, but something more radical was needed and this forced a decision on an earlier suggestion to flood Lake Mareotis by cutting the canal dyke separating the dry bed of the lake from the salt waters of Lake Maadje. There was some uncertainty as to the consequences and even the morality of doing so, but if successful this measure would not only secure the southern end of the defensive line covering Aboukir, but would also block the French from using the direct route across the dry lake bed into Alexandria.

Wilson explained:

The position which the army occupied required so large a force, that it was impossible to maintain it, and prosecute the new expedition. In General Roiz's pocket had been found a letter of General Menou's, anxiously expressing a fear that the English had cut the canal of Alexandria, and thus let the waters of the sea into Lake Mariotis. [The canal commences at Rhamanieh, and passes over fifteen or sixteen leagues of country; the bed of it is higher than the level of Egypt but the land which lay between it and Lake Mariotis was considerably lower than the level of Lake Maadje.] From that moment it had become the favourite object of the army, as, by securing the left and part of its front, the duty would be diminished, the French nearly cut off from the interior, and a new scene of operations opened. But there were very serious objections to the measure. First, the mischief it might do was incalculable. The Arabs could give no information where such a sea would be checked: the ruin of Alexandria was probably a consequence, and whilst it strengthened the British left, it secured the south front of the French position, except from a new landing; but the urgency of the present service at last superseded general philanthropy and more remote considerations. General Hutchinson reluctantly consented, whilst the army was in raptures; never did a working party labour with more zeal; every man would have volunteered with cheerfulness to assist. Four cuts were made, of six yards in breadth, and about ten from each other, a little in advance of the farthest redoubt, but only two could be opened the first night. At seven o'clock in the evening the last fascine was removed, and joy was universal. The water rushed in with a fall of six feet, and the pride and peculiar care of Egypt, the consolidation of ages, was in a few hours destroyed by the devastating hand of man. Two more cuts were finished the next day, and three more marked out; but the force of the water was so great, aided by the removal of a few banking stones worked out by the foot of an officer (who justly thought that these partial measures would not complete the inundation for months) as soon to break one into the other; and now an immense body of water rushed in, which continued entering for a month with considerable force; it then found nearly its level, but from the sand absorbing the water, there was always a fall of nine or twelve inches at the entrance. The first boat which floated on this sea was one belonging to Lord Cavan, whose efforts had contributed so much to its formation.[13]

The fact that there was a 10ft (3m) difference between the respective levels of the two lakes caused unintended problems, for, as Walsh complained: '... as the current flowed with tumultuous rapidity, it swept down large pieces of the canal into the inundation, which extended as far to the westward as the eye could reach. Lake Aboukir [Maadje] in consequence subsided considerably, as it emptied its water faster into the Mareotis than it was replenished by the sea, so that our boats repeatedly got aground in it.'[14]

That, however, was just a minor nuisance and with the Aboukir bridgehead now more secure thanks to the creation of what was ever afterwards referred to by everyone as 'The Inundation', Hutchinson immediately began to thin out the position in order to transfer himself and the seat of operations to the Nile. On 13 April the 18th, 79th and 90th Regiments, together with the detachment of the 11th Light Dragoons, marched east to support Spencer, and on 17 April the 30th and 89th Regiments followed. Then on the next day, Generals Craddock and Doyle were formally named to command brigades in the 'Rosetta division' and finally on 24 April, Major General John Hely Hutchinson rode east towards the Nile. Behind him Coote, who was now second-in-command of the army, was left in charge of the Aboukir position.

Although he was far from feeling well at this point, Hutchinson was growing in confidence and by the time he caught up with the Rosetta Division he was keen to move swiftly. As Walsh explained:

> The division of the army encamped at El Hamed, and commanded by major-general Hutchinson, marched thence in two columns; the right proceeding by the beach of lake Edko, under major-general Cradock; and the left by the road on the banks of the Nile, under the orders of brigadier-general Doyle.
>
> They took a position on the canals to the north of the village of Derout. The ground occupied by the body of Turks under the Capoutan Pacha was along a canal, about two miles in front of them; and the intervening ground was so bad that it would have been very difficult to move up to its support had it been attacked.
>
> Colonel Stewart of the eighty-ninth regiment was detached across the Nile with his own battalion and twelve hundred Albanians to keep parallel with our main body on that side of the river. The object of this was to prevent the enemy from passing at Fouah with a small force, to annoy our flank, or our gunboats, of which about fifty English and Turkish had entered the Nile, since the reduction of Fort Julien, and proceeded up the river on our left.[15]

They had all arrived unopposed at Dairut on 5 May and the next day the whole army was mustered and the British contingent enumerated as follows:[16]

Cradock's Brigade:	8th Regiment	
	18th Regiment	
	79th Highland Regiment	
	90th Regiment	(1650)
Doyle's Brigade:	2/1st (Royal) Regiment	
	30th Regiment	
	50th Regiment	
	92nd Highland Regiment	(1650)
Reserve (Spencer):	2nd (Queen's) Regiment	
	58th Regiment	
	40th Regiment Flank Companies	
	Corsican Rangers	(1150)

In addition to the three brigades, Colonel William Stewart with the 350-strong 89th Regiment and his *Arnauts* was set to marching parallel with the main body, but over on the east side of the Nile.

The cavalry was primarily comprised of the 350-strong 12th Light Dragoons, all of whom by now were mounted, reinforced by eighty men of the 26th Light Dragoons. In addition, there were still fifty men of the 11th Light Dragoons attached to the Reserve, and thirty more of the 12th with Colonel Stewart's column on the right bank. Hompesch' Hussars, however, were no longer present with the army. After three men had deserted to the enemy back on 8 April, the decision had been taken that the rest of them should be dismounted and ordered back to Aboukir, although Major Wilson himself remained with the army and would make himself thoroughly useful.[17]

In total the British contingent, exclusive of artillerymen, therefore amounted to 5,310 men, while the Turks were broken down as to 1,200 *Arnauts* or Albanians attached to Stewart's column, 1,100 *Nizan I-Cedid* regulars and 1,500 *Bashi-bazouks* all under the *Kapūdān Pasha*. By now, thanks to Colonel Lindenthal, who had been borrowed from Stuart's Regiment, the Turks had been weaned off their unsettling habit of firing off their muskets at random, but then, at the last moment a reinforcement of cavalry sent by the Grand Vizier unexpectedly turned up. This ought to have been vastly encouraging but, as Wilson grumbled, 'these troops were not real Turks, but Syrians, almost naked, many without arms, beyond belief miserably mounted, totally undisciplined, even to savage wildness. Such a reinforcement, and their force did not exceed 600 men, offered no great advantage, yet was not to be rejected. The Captain Pacha was vexed particularly at the defalcation of their numbers; and the alleged acts of pillage and oppression, which they had been guilty of in their march across the Delta, were objects of serious mortication to him.'[18]

That night, outflanked by Stewart's little column, the French evacuated their strongly fortified position at El Aft and withdrew further upstream. They tried to carry everything with them, although thirteen *djermes* (native boats) carrying rice and other supplies were intercepted by Stewart, along with five unfortunate Frenchmen whose heads were brought in by the Albanians. By now Hutchinson was only about 12 miles from Ramanieh, where General de Brigade Joseph Lagrange apparently commanded some 3,331 infantry, artillery and sappers and 600 cavalry, and was occupying a strong position with his left flank resting on the Nile and his front covered by the embankments of the Alexandria Canal.[19]

110

A straightforward frontal assault appeared to be called for and Hutchinson's initial plan was to move forward early on the morning of 9 May and close up on the French with a view to attacking Ramanieh on the day after. However, by 11.00 am that morning the general was close enough to have a look at the town for himself and got a nasty surprise. Lagrange was indeed dug in behind the canal, but not where he was expected. The first mile or so of the canal actually ran northwards parallel to the Nile, before making a sharp turn to the west and heading across country to Alexandria. Instead of lining up along that east–west alignment at right angles to the Nile and squarely facing Hutchinson's forces, Lagrange was dug in with his back to the river, on either side of the fortified depot, with no fewer than thirty-three field pieces and seventeen heavier guns. It was time to rethink the operation.

Although Hutchinson was still confident of taking Ramanieh, he was also more concerned to prevent Lagrange from making his escape westwards to Alexandria. The French were fast marchers and the fear was that if reinforced by Lagrange, Menou might counterattack, overwhelm Coote's Division and take the Aboukir depot long before Hutchinson could catch up. That would, of course, be disastrous and therefore Hutchinson's first priority was to manoeuvre his forces round so as to block any attempt by Lagrange to break out towards the west.

In the meantime, the detachment under Colonel Stewart had marched at 5.00 am, intending to attack the French at Dessoug, on the other side of the river, while the main army closed up on Rahmanieh. About 6.00 am he was spotted by a picquet of forty French cavalry on the west bank, who in turn sent a party of 300 to 400 men consisting of grenadiers, light artillery, and cavalry across the river, to attack the 89th Regiment. At that point the British battalion was Stewart's whole force, since the *Arnauts* had not yet come up in their usual shambolic fashion, and the gunboats, commanded by Captain Curry, were becalmed further downstream. Therefore, he halted and took up a position by the river to wait patiently for either of them to turn up. Eventually it was the *Arnauts* who arrived first and began skirmishing with the French, so Lieutenant Colonel Lord Blaney advanced with the grenadiers of the 89th Regiment and six light guns to take up a position along the Nile, within half-musket shot of the French batteries. The French immediately in their front resisted for about a quarter of an hour, then hastily fell back to their boats, covered by the fire of two heavy batteries on an island, commanding the entrance of the harbour of Ramanieh. Notwithstanding the constant

111

discharges of grapeshot whistling about them, the grenadiers of the 89th marched steadily on to the dyke running parallel to the Nile, behind where Stewart ordered them to lie down while Captain Adye of the Royal Artillery placed his guns and duelled with the French batteries for a time. Although Stewart eventually ordered him to cease firing and take cover as there was no sign of Hutchinson attacking, the French *djermes*, who had been trying to escape, were forced back into the harbour by the guns, and one of the gunboats was sunk. 'The Turks,' said Wilson, 'who had seen with admiration this advance, could scarce find expressions to explain their sense of such conduct. *"Bono John!"* was vociferated whenever any officer crossed over from the western bank, and *"Tieb!"* with the thumb raised, was re-echoed by the Arabs.'[20] After that, an irregular fire of musketry was kept up during the night, and another French gunboat, attempting to escape, was taken, with a quantity of powder on board.

While this bit of excitement was taking place on the east bank of the Nile, at about noon the French cavalry came forward on the west, so Hutchinson halted and drew up the army in order of battle. The Turks massed on the left next to the river, while Major-General Cradock's brigade constituted the right; and the Reserve, under Colonel Spencer, and Brigadier-General Doyle's brigade formed a second line. The Turks were rather advanced, and their right untidily spilled over the front of Craddock's brigade. The British cavalry was stationed in front of the right, that of the Syrians in front of the centre.

The line then advanced; with the French skirmishers at first being kept in check by the Syrian horsemen, but then the French brought forward a gun, and the Syrian irregulars promptly fell back and flatly refused to come forward again. The 12th Light Dragoons therefore came forward with two guns, but as soon as they unlimbered, the French opened fire, the first shot carrying off Captain Henry King's leg, and killing three horses. The second shot also struck in the squadron, forcing the cavalry to take ground to the right, but the Royal Artillery stayed where they were, gamely returning fire until ordered to retire. Otherwise, both sides banged away at each other for the rest of the day without displaying any inclination to close. Finally, late in the afternoon, Colonel Spencer was ordered forward to take the village of Mehallet Daoud on the Alexandria canal. The village itself was quickly occupied by the Corsican Rangers, backed up by the 11th Light Dragoons, and then everyone else moved up to line the canal.

Darkness coming on shortly afterwards eventually put a stop to the firing on both sides. It was all very unsatisfactory and Walsh was probably not alone in grumbling that the skirmishing was certainly not deserving of the name of a battle, but Hutchinson at least was satisfied. A full-dress assault on the Ramanieh position might be more glorious but it would cost him irreplaceable casualties. Instead, the general planned to use Stewart's detachment on the far bank of the Nile to flush the French out of their position next morning, for by holding the line of the canal he was now perfectly placed to intercept the French in the open as they tried to escape up the road to Damahur and Alexandria.

Chapter 9

The Heart of Darkness

Long before dawn on 10 May the British Army was astir and moving into position for the keenly anticipated battle, but rather to the chagrin of some, the rising sun revealed a white flag flying over the fort. Under cover of darkness, Lagrange had evacuated Ramanieh and quietly slipped away; but only after first tipping his heavy guns into the river, scuttling his remaining gunboats and reluctantly abandoning both the seventy-odd *djermes* trapped in the harbour and the very large quantities of supplies still stored in the magazines. These comprised biscuit, flour and aqua vitae, which would go far to provisioning the Allies. He also left behind his sick and wounded, together with a detachment of 110 men to protect them and ensure that they were safely able to surrender to the British.[1]

Otherwise he at first left no trace of his passing and the early assumption was that he had somehow stolen past the forces ranged along the canal and was now marching hard to re-join Menou at Alexandria. As the morning wore on, however, it became clear that Lagrange and his men had stood not upon the order of their going but had incontinently rushed off, leaving behind a variety of stray convoys and detachments who were as ignorant of his departure as everyone else. Shortly before noon, a Lieutenant William Drake took out a watering party of thirty cavalrymen. Hearing the sound of firing, he very properly went to investigate and discovered a fifty-strong detachment of the French *20e Dragoons* beset by a large predatory band of Bedouin, who had surrounded them and were steadily picking them off one by one.[2] On Drake's approach their officer, an unnamed captain, hastily waved a white handkerchief and surrendered the entire party to his outnumbered British saviours. He had been escorting an aide-de-camp with despatches from Alexandria, and, ignorant of the abandonment of

Ramanieh, had run into the Bedouin while detouring into the desert to avoid the Corsican Rangers unexpectedly found occupying Mehellet Daoud. While the despatches themselves turned out to contain little information of any significance, the captain and his men confirmed that they had not encountered Lagrange on the Alexandria road. Discomfited, Hutchinson sent Doyle off with the 12th Light Dragoons backed up by a battalion of infantry to confirm this, but it soon became obvious that, far from falling back on Alexandria, Lagrange was actually heading straight for Cairo – and with some speed.

This uncomfortable realisation presented Hutchinson with a terrible dilemma that was as unexpected as it was unwelcome and all the more so given his well-attested reluctance to exercise responsibility. His whole attention was focussed on taking Alexandria and the operations lately mounted against Rosetta and then Ramanieh had themselves been directed towards that aim.

His instructions warned against proceeding further into the interior and it was assumed Cairo and the other minor French garrisons in the interior could safely be left to the Grand Vizier, and to Major General David Baird's Indian army, especially as the *Mamlūks* were wavering in their allegiance. Murad Bey had died of the plague and his successor, Osman Bey, was already addressing overtures to Hutchinson, anent changing sides and adding the still formidable *Mamlūk* cavalry to the Allied forces in return for protection against the Turks.

However, if Lagrange and his men were allowed to reinforce the Cairo garrison the whole situation could change dramatically, for the city's governor, *General de Division* Augustin-Daniel Belliard, might then be strong enough to come out of the city's defences and face the Turks in the open. No one was in any doubt as to the outcome of such a battle and a Turkish defeat at this point would not only block Baird's approach but worse still would open the possibility of a future French counter-offensive down the Nile either to link up with Menou's army coming out of Alexandria or at the very least disrupt the forthcoming siege operations.

Wilson admirably summed up Hutchinson's dilemma thus:

Should he pursue to Cairo, or return to Alexandria, was the anxious alternative. On the one hand, he had to consider, what would be the probable consequences of exposing the Turks under the Grand Vizir to the attacks of the French, then not confined in their operations by any fear of the advance of the English. Whether the Mamelukes, who had as yet not openly avowed their alliance, would be friendly or hostile, if he did not move to their assistance, as Morad Bey had declared was necessary. Whether the Indian army would not be subjected to disaster, if he tamely allowed the French to oppose them with their whole force? Whether the junction with the Grand Vizir, the Mamelukes, and his army, did not ensure success at Grand Cairo? If, on the contrary. General Hutchinson returned to Alexandria, could he besiege the place? Had he men enough to defend the Nile, the entrenched camp before Alexandria, and to admit of his detaching a corps to the westward [of Alexandria], which was deemed absolutely necessary for the siege, and which corps would have not only to resist the sortie of the garrison, but any attack which General Belliard, with his army, might make from the side of the Desert?

Once upon a time that sort of behaviour would certainly have come as second nature to the old *Armee d'Italie*. Whether they still possessed the energy and even the will for such a bold and resolute course of action was beginning to look questionable, but this point in time it was a threat that Hutchinson could not ignore. He must pursue Lagrange up the river, as far as Cairo if need be. On the other hand, a number of Hutchinson's own senior officers still took the view that pushing further into the interior was foolhardy in the extreme and almost certain to end in disaster. There were no magazines prepared to support such a march and the likelihood of obtaining fresh supplies was considered uncertain and even doubtful. That aside, the multiple hazards of plague, dysentery, and ophthalmia awaited, and in addition the blistering heat, the sheer fatigue to be undergone, and even the want of shoes, were all predicted to bring about the ruin of the army. Finally, it was argued that even if the operation could be accomplished, the conquest of Cairo would achieve little so long as the French still retained Alexandria.

Nevertheless, the capture of the large fleet of *djermes* and the abundant supplies in the Ramanieh magazines that there had been no time to destroy provided Hutchinson with the immediate means to get up the Nile, and so notwithstanding the mutinous grumbling (which apparently was far worse than he appreciated), he turned over the Ramanieh fort to the *Kapūdān Pasha* and set off up the Nile early on the morning of 11 May. It proved a discouraging march in awful heat, justifying his numerous critics, and by the day's end Hutchinson too was minded to turn back to Rosetta after all. But then there was a complication.

Word was received from Rear Admiral John Blankett, in the Red Sea, that the French had evacuated Suez and that he had landed a garrison of his own there, in preparation for the arrival of General Baird's army coming from India! ³ At this point Hutchinson was exactly halfway between Ramanieh and Cairo. If Baird's advance guard was by now at Suez, the crossroads at Belbeis assumed crucial importance, for it was there that the caravan route from Suez emerged from the desert. Lose control of it and Baird's advance would be completely blocked.

Moore at this time was convalescing from his wound in Rosetta, but was in regular touch with Hutchinson, who seems to have used him as something of a sounding board. Now Moore recorded in his journal:

> … he [Hutchinson] at first had thoughts of going to Cairo, but he found it impossible. The troops from the heat were getting sickly, and from not being prepared for so distant a march, the army was unprovided with many essential articles. The General states that it is necessary to make a show of following the enemy in order to drive them into Cairo, and prevent their crossing into the Delta and attacking the Grand Vizier. He would therefore continue his march for a couple of days more, and would then return to this neighbourhood; he adds that he had sent to the Grand Vizier to retire to his entrenched camp at Salahih.⁴

The message to acquaint Yusuf Pasha of this decision was carried across the Delta by Hutchinson's principal ADC, Major Thomas Montresor.⁵ Depending on the outcome of his meeting with the Vizier, he was also given discretionary orders to proceed to Suez and make contact with Colonel Lloyd and the 86th Regiment.

In the meantime, the operation did not go well, for the army promptly ran into a suffocating *khamsin* or sandstorm, and at the same time the level of the river was falling, which delayed the boats, thus forcing the army to halt at Kafr Houdig throughout the next day.

This unlooked-for delay meant it was now Major Wilson's turn, and no doubt dashingly swathed in an Arab *burnoose* like generations of British military adventurers ever since, he set off across the Delta on the evening of 14 May to again warn the Grand Vizier of his increasing peril and the impossibility of helping him. However, Wilson arrived at Belbeis to find the crisis had already arrived. Having taken just four days to cover the 100 miles between Ramanieh and Cairo, Lagrange had joined with Belliard and the French were now out and coming on fast, intent on defeating the Turks before the British could arrive. Wilson, together with Colonel Charles Holloway and Captain Robert Hope of the Military Mission, all pressed Yusuf Pasha to withdraw at once, but instead, the stubborn old man refused. He had brought his men all the way across the desert only by holding out the glittering promise of the plunder that awaited them in Cairo. Already the decision to halt at Belbeis had aroused 'strong symptoms of discontent' and an order to retreat now would surely result in utter ruin, for his troops would disband in 'despondency and disgust'. Rather philosophically, he concluded with his usual fatalism that if the worst did come to the worst and defeat followed, the French would not be able to pursue the Turks very far.[6]

Next morning, while Wilson rode back to update Hutchinson, the Grand Vizier advanced to face the enemy head-on with an army that frankly horrified his British allies.

Wilson wrote:

The Grand Vizir's army presented a very different appearance to the Turks under the Captain Pacha. Here were no regularity, no trace of discipline; each corps encamped confusedly around its chieftain; horses and camels crowded all the intervals; tumbrils and cannon lay mixed amongst them, and the whole formed a most disgusting chaos, whilst the dirt and filth of the camp certainly were amply sufficient to generate the plague and every pestilential disease ...[7]

There were some Janissaries and other relics of imperial glory, but the only ones who counted were the *Arnauts* or Albanians; although even they would make a sergeant major blush; these comprised a body of *Bashi-bazouks* or irregular cavalry under Tahir Pasha and a large contingent of mounted infantry (those lacking horses capable of passing for cavalry mounts) commanded by Mehmet Ali Pasha.[8] Perhaps amounting to 7,000 in all, it was they who first encountered the French near the springs at El Khanka on the morning of 16 May.

In Cairo, General Belliard had at first viewed the Turkish advance with some concern, for he reckoned he simply did not possess enough men to defend the city and its various forts and depots against the twin threats of the Grand Vizier's army and the inevitable revolt that would break out on its arrival. All in all, even after he was joined by Donzelot with *1/21e Légére* from Upper Egypt he could muster only 3,000 men. As he gloomily contemplated the prospect of packing both soldiers and civilians into the mediaeval citadel and hoping for the best, everything appeared to change with the unexpected appearance of Lagrange and his men. Unaware that Hutchinson's advance was only a bluff, Belliard reckoned that he now had a narrow window of opportunity in which to move out and destroy the Turks before the British arrived.

Scraping together virtually every man capable of marching, he left Cairo at dawn on 15 May with a total of 4,600 infantry, 906 cavalry and twenty-four pieces of cannon. Behind him he left General Louis Alméras to hold the great city with a skeleton garrison made up of the remaining regular infantry, 500 Coptic and Greek security troops, and all the invalids, dismounted cavalry, and artillerymen capable of holding a firelock. This amounted in all to no more than 1,300 men, exclusive of another 900 sick in the hospitals, and the numerous civil and military rear area personnel.

Word of his do-or-die advance soon came in to Belbeis, and after dark that night, Tahir Pasha was sent forward with 3,000 *bashi bazouks* and three light field pieces with orders to do the French a mischief if he could and at the very least impede their advance. About 10.00 pm they ran into the French advance guards some 3 miles out and both sides lay on their arms until next morning. At first light, Tahir Pasha commenced his attack and was soon reinforced, first by another 1,500 cavalry and then by Mehemet Ali Pasha with 5,000 Albanian infantry. The French advance guard had by now taken up a position in a grove of date palms, where for three hours they maintained a sharp fire against the encroaching Turkish sharpshooters. Then, as the respective main bodies came up, Belliard tried to go on to the offensive. As he had previously arranged, he began by forming his infantry into two large squares, with a column of cavalry in the centre. As always, this reflected Austrian and Russian best practice for fighting the Turks, and up until now it had proved effective in Egypt, but to his dismay on 16 May Belliard found that the Turks, or rather the British, had changed the rules.

Hutchinson might be too far away to help, but the British Military Mission was still with the army and a now forgotten soldier, Colonel Holloway, successfully prevailed upon the Vizier to let him and his officers run the battle: 'The advanced guard was composed of a select body of cavalry, under Tahir Pacha, and of Albanian infantry under Mehemmed Pacha; the first accompanied by Captain [William] Leake, the second by Captain [Thomas] Lacey, each receiving their orders from Colonel Holloway, who remained near the person of the Vizier.'[9] Another member of the mission, Captain Robert Hope, cemented the British oversight of operations by taking charge of the Vizier's guns, which were themselves manned by twenty-nine regular gunners of the Royal Artillery.[10]

Restrained by their British advisers, instead of obligingly shattering themselves against the French squares, the Turks avoided any attempt by the French to close with them. At the same time, while using their numerous cavalry to deny Belliard the opportunity to deploy his own sharpshooters, the *bashi-bazouks* cheerfully swarmed around the French, shooting them up at a safe distance. For the French it was a frustrating and ultimately futile experience. In order to win the battle, Belliard needed to pin down the Grand Vizier's forces and destroy them, but instead, as Major Montresor complacently reported, 'he attempted to advance; but wherever he appeared, the Turks opened out, and assembled again on his flanks'.[11] Worse, as the hours went by and both ammunition and water began to run short, and as more and more of the Grand Vizier's army straggled up to join the fun, Belliard realised that the Turks were not only extending their front and outflanking him on the right, but that a substantial contingent of their cavalry had completely vanished from his front and might already be riding hard for Cairo. It was time to concede defeat and fall back in good order while he still could. The victorious Turks followed his retreat for some 7 miles before letting him go, but it is a measure of the strange nature of the battle that despite fighting all day, Belliard had lost only fifty killed and succeeded in bringing away all 300 of his wounded. The Turks by contrast admitted to 150 killed and wounded, while the small British contingent lost none at all. It might not have been a particularly glorious victory, and indeed Reynier optimistically tried to pass it off as having been no more than a reconnaissance in force, but for the first time a Turkish army had defeated a French one in the open field and it settled the campaign. Had Belliard been successful he might have saved Cairo and forced Hutchinson to retreat, but instead he was compelled to fall back on the city as the Allies closed in. It was the beginning of the end.

From the beginning, the Egyptian expedition was largely predicated on the British government's rather optimistic assessment that the *Armee l'Orient* was greatly depleted in numbers and badly demoralised by its long exile and seeming abandonment. At first, the fighting around Alexandria had suggested otherwise, but on the Nile, a succession of events now revealed that French morale was much more brittle than it once looked.

Immediately after the conference at Belbeis, Wilson headed back and found Hutchinson at Algam on the evening of 16 May. At that point the imminent prospect of a Turkish defeat meant that Hutchinson had to contemplate the prospect of taking the army across the Delta to recover Belbeis, but in the meantime, all he could do was await news of the outcome.

And while he waited, an extraordinary and significant event occurred. Lagrange's precipitate retreat had already strewn confusion

The archetypical British infantryman in Egypt; Private 28th Regiment of Foot in light field order 1801. (Copyright the Estate of Bob Marrion, image supplied courtesy of Partizan Press)

Lieutenant General
Sir Ralph Abercromby.
(Author's collection)

THE RIGHT HON: LORD HUTCHINSON.
LIEUTENANT GENERAL & K.B.

Lieutenant General
Sir John Hely Hutchinson.
(Anne S.K. Brown
University Collection)

Major General John Moore. (Anne S.K. Brown University Collection)

Major General John Francis Cradock. (Author's collection)

Sir Eyre Coote.

SIR EYRE COOTE.

Philip de Loutherberg, Battle of Alexandria. (Anne S.K. Brown University Collection)

Detail of Loutherbourg's Battle of Alexandria:
From Left to Right, front row: 1. Sergeant Sinclair 42nd Highlanders; 2. Private Anton Lutz, Stuart's Minorca Regiment; 3. Captain Sir Sidney Smith RN (with telescope); 4. Colonel John Abercromby; 5. Sir Ralph Abercromby (seated); 6. Captain Charles Sutton (ADC); 7. Sir Thomas Dyer (ADC); 8. John Hely Hutchinson: *Rear row mounted*: 9. Colonel Robert Anstruther (QMG); 10. Major General Ludlow; 11. Major General Coote; 12. Major General Moore.

Charles Orme's take on the battle of Alexandria repays close inspection, most notably in its depiction of the very substantial remains of the Roman Fort. (Anne S.K. Brown University Collection)

Officers of the 61st Regiment of Foot in Egypt after Private William Porter.
(Author)

Officer of Staff Corps; note single-breasted jacket. (Author)

Officer of 16th Regiment of Foot after William Loftie, depicting a service dress worn in Surinam in 1803, showing the continued use of the short single-breasted 1796 pattern jacket in hot climates.

Field officer, 1st Royal Regiment, in full dress, after William Loftie, 1801. One of this ancient regiment's distinctions was the privilege of gold embroidered buttonholes, for those who chose to afford them.

Highland piper, by William Pyne, 1805.

42nd and 92nd Highlanders by Charles Hamilton Smith. Although not published until 1812, the uniform had not changed in the intervening period.

Major of brigade after William Loftie. This staff officer is wearing the full-dress uniform and in Egypt would have worn a plain single-breasted coat and a round hat – see 10.

Officer 21st Royal North British Fusiliers after William Loftie. While this regiment did not serve in Egypt, the Tarleton-style helmet was a popular substitute for the bearskin cap among other fusilier officers at this time, including the 23rd. Lieutenant Jack Hill was certainly wearing one at the Helder in 1799. The same was also worn by officers of the 90th Perthshire Volunteers.

Light Dragoon from Warnery's *History of Cavalry*.

De Roll's Regiment. Note the crested round hats – similar ones were probably worn by the rank and file of the 90th Perthshire Volunteers.

Turkish infantry and cavalryman, probably serving with the Grand Vizier's army.

Turkish regular infantrymen of the kind brought by the Kapūdan Pasha.

A Mamaluke on Horseback, with a Patern, or Foot Mamaluke, and a Bedouin Arab Soldier.

Mamlūks.

French fusilier of the *85e Ligne*. (Copyright the Estate of Bob Marrion, image supplied courtesy of Partizan Press)

Regiment des Dromedaires, 1803.

JACQ. FRANC.ᵉ DE MENOU

Député du Département d'Indre et Loire,
élu Président à l'Assemblée Nationale,

Tour voir la liberté, dans la France, établie,
Ce loyal Chevalier n'épargne aucun moyen,
Intact, incorruptible, ardent pour sa patrie,
Le seul due, à ses yeux, est d'être citoyen.

Lutaine

General Menou.

in his wake. As we have seen, unaware he was gone, on 10 May a party coming up from Alexandria promptly surrendered to escape massacre by the Bedouin and two days out from the town on 14 May the army 'fell in' with a convoy of *djermes* coming down the river, also heading for Ramanieh in blissful ignorance that it had been abandoned. Already under attack by the local Bedouin, the escort, comprising some 150 men, mainly belonging to *25e Ligne*, were only too glad to surrender to Lieutenant Richard Diggins and his reconnoitring party from the 11th Dragoons. Then three days later on 17 May came a greater and even more significant coup.

Four days earlier Menou had sent out a large party from Alexandria led by the dashing *Chef de Brigade* Jacques Cavalier, of the celebrated *Regiment des Dromedaries*, with orders to forage the area around Damanhūr. Unfortunately, it soon became clear to him that the villages were deserted and there were no stocks of food to be had there so he decided to go all the way to Cairo instead and pick up supplies from its substantial depots. Ordinarily, this would have been a sensible enough decision, but he was unaware of the British advance and soon the Arabs were coming into Hutchinson's headquarters reporting that a substantial body of French troops were approaching the Nile at the point where the *Kapūdān Pasha*'s boats were lying up. Soon Küçük Hüseyin himself was also sending courier after courier with a running commentary on their progress as the French unwittingly camped just 4 miles away from the boats.

Eventually, Cavalier realised the danger and hurriedly veered off into the desert, but by then it was too late and what happened next is best related in the words of one of the principal actors, Major Robert Wilson, who had just returned from Belbeis:

> General Doyle, who had zealously urged and volunteered to pursue the convoy, was ordered to take out the 11th and a detachment of the 26th dragoons, amounting to 250 men; two field-pieces and his brigade of infantry was directed to follow him, whilst General Craddock, with a brigade, moved along the banks of the Nile.
>
> Colonel Abercromby and Major Wilson galloped on to find the enemy's column, which was not then perceptible, attended only by the wild Arabs who flocked from all parts of the Desert.
>
> When they had gone about seven miles, they came up with the convoy, and reconnoitring it attempted to make the Arabs attack their front and right flank, whilst Lieutenant [Matthew] Sutton of the Minorca regiment, an aid de camp to General Doyle, who then

also arrived, used his utmost exertions to effect the same service; but the French *tirailleurs* kept them completely at a distance. At length Major Wilson proposed to Colonel Abercromby that he might be allowed to offer the commandant of the convoy a capitulation, since the stratagem might succeed, and at all events the delay of the negotiation would give time for the arrival of the infantry. Colonel Abercromby consented, and Major Wilson, after some delay for a handkerchief, during which time General Doyle arrived with the cavalry, and approved of the measure, rode up with a white handkerchief on his sword, and approaching within twenty yards, demanded to speak with the commandant. Colonel Cavalier came forwards, and asked him what he required. He answered, that 'he was sent by the Commander in Chief to offer, before circumstances might render his submission useless, terms for the surrender of his convoy, which were, that the troops should lay down their arms, and be sent directly to France.' Colonel Cavalier violently cried out to him to retire instantly, for he scarcely knew whether he ought not to order his people to fire. Major Wilson answered, that it was the humanity of the general which induced him to offer these terms, and reminded Colonel Cavalier of the responsibility which now attached to him, and the sacrifice he was about to make. To this, Colonel Cavalier seemed to pay no attention, and Major Wilson was proceeding towards General Doyle, when an aid de camp from the French galloped after Major Wilson, and required him to return to Colonel Cavalier, who asked for the proposed conditions to he repeated, and then requested that he would wait the event of a consultation with his officers. An evident sensation of joy was perceptible in the troops, and their actions betrayed their inclinations; but the manner in which they were drawn up, presented a formidable resistance; a corps of infantry formed the front and rear line, whilst three divisions of the dromedary corps and heavy dragoons *en echellon* protected the flanks; in front of the right was a piece of cannon, and in the centre of the square were the baggage camels.

Colonel Cavalier suddenly came back, and said 'that it was the definitive resolve of his officers, that they could only agree to the surrender of their camels and horses, but that the troops must be sent into Cairo free'. Major Wilson replied, that he lamented this determination, which he must consider as a positive refusal, since plunder was not the object of the English General, but the capture or destruction of this corps of troops, therefore such terms would

122

be an insult to offer him. The Arabs began now to press on, and the uneasiness of the column became more and more apparent. At last Colonel Cavalier declared, 'that if he might lay down his arms at head-quarters, instead of in the Desert before the Bedouins; if the officers might retain their private property, and the men be sent directly to France, and on their arriving there be no longer considered as prisoners of war; if an officer might be sent to Cairo for the security of their baggage left in depot there, and Major Wilson remain as a hostage for their safe conduct to the British camp, he would agree to such terms.'

As these conditions all conformed with the instructions of General Hutchinson from government, and such had been offered to General Menou, Major Wilson accepted them, and was proceeding to General Doyle for his sanction, when General Hutchinson arriving in person, ratified them. The Arabs, some of whom had followed from the moment the convoy had left Alexandria, were thunderstruck at seeing the enemy thus quietly submit, and the event will remain recorded in their tribes for generations.[12]

In all 569 men; infantry, cavalry and artillery, including 120 of the elite Dromedaries, surrendered along with 550 pack camels and their Arab drivers. That night, word also came in from the Turks that the various French posts around Damietta on the eastern side of the Delta had been abandoned and their garrisons fled in small boats – and into the waiting arms of the Royal Navy.

It was, according to Wilson, the promise of repatriation to France that was decisive in persuading Cavalier's convoy to surrender without a fight. The government's rather hopeful assessment of French morale was turning out to be correct after all, but only as a direct result of Hutchinson's decision to move up the Nile. So long as military operations were stalled outside Alexandria, then French Egypt remained a reality with its network of garrisons, depots and supply routes, and above all the administration that held it all together, but now the outer crust was broken and the British Army had got in amongst the rear areas. No longer could outposts simply shut the gates if threatened and wait for a mobile column to turn up and disperse the insurgents. All the scattered posts and detachments, large and small, were now scrambling to find safety from the local Bedouin, from the Turks of various colours and even from the local Fellahin. Only the British offered protection from the imminent prospect of death or slavery – and the enticing prospect of prompt repatriation to France made the offer irresistible.

Next day the gathering sense of momentum was increased by the arrival of Major Montresor with news of the unlikely victory at El Khanka, and despite the broiling heat, Hutchinson immediately despatched Colonel Stewart with the 30th and 89th Regiments and a fifty-strong detachment of the 11th Light Dragoons to reinforce the Turks, and then took himself to Benerhassett (Benha) on the Nile, about 30 miles north of Cairo, there to meet the Grand Vizier on 22 May.

Amidst all the colourful festivities that followed, Hutchinson had to tread a difficult path. Between the *Kapūdān Pasha* and the Grand Vizier was a fierce rivalry verging on hatred, so their meeting was reluctant and required careful handling, although in the event both managed to behave towards each other with unaccustomed civility. The real problem, however, was the Vizier's insistence on marching on Cairo immediately, before his rapacious horde dissolved. There were now estimated to be some 15,000 of them and all of them were demanding to be let loose on the city.

On the other hand, only dire necessity had drawn Hutchinson so far up the Nile and he was anxious to delegate responsibility for the siege of Cairo to the Turks and to General Baird and his Indian army, while he himself returned to the north. Unfortunately, while Colonel Lloyd and a party of the 86th Foot were holding Suez in anticipation, Baird's army was still immobilised by contrary winds, and likely to be so for months. Hutchinson, however reluctantly, was going to have to push further up the Nile and tackle Cairo himself.

It was not a decision he took lightly, for the sickness of the troops under his immediate command was now increasing alarmingly. Soon a total of 1,122 would either be returned to Rosetta or sent to a hospital camp on the point of the Delta, while a further 346 were reported sick but still with their battalions. This left him just 4,000 ragged and often barefoot men of all arms fit for duty and so there was no alternative but to pare Coote's division at Aboukir to the very bone by summoning reinforcements, in the form of both the siege train, with 120 gunners, another sixty mounted cavalry and two more of Coote's precious infantry battalions; the 28th Regiment and the 42nd Highlanders, all in order to enable him to move forward.

Led by Brigadier Oakes, the reinforcement set off on 4 June, following the line of the Alexandria canal to Ramanieh and then up the Nile, but inevitably they would take some time to arrive. A more immediate reinforcement, however, came in the form of the *Mamlūks*. On the evening of 29 May an envoy came in from their *Culu Bey* (general) advising that their advance guard was close at hand, and so the ever-ubiquitous Major Wilson was sent out to 'congratulate him and assure him of protection'. Notwithstanding that assurance a transfer of allegiances is always a tricky business, and as Wilson explained:

> He appointed four o'clock in the morning, and a village in front of their army as the place of rendezvous, from whence he was to proceed to the English generals tent, but anxiously stipulated that the Captain Pacha was not to know of the time of his coming: however, so great was his dread of being betrayed by the Turks, who accompanied Major Wilson, that instead of keeping his appointment, he at three o'clock marched, and, striking into the Desert, came by the rear of the camp, after a considerable detour, to the general's tent, where he was assured by General Hutchinson in person of his protection, and that the Captain Pacha should confirm those stipulations he had in the name of the Grand Signor already pledged.[13]

For the moment though all was well and the various contingents headed up both sides of the Nile by short marches; Hutchinson on the west bank, flanked by the *Mamlūks* on his right and the *Kapūdān Pasha*'s Turks on his left, while parallel to him on the Damietta branch was the Grand Vizier's horde and Stewart's contingent. At length they all arrived near the village of Shubra on 16 June, from where they saw the towers and minarets of Cairo laid out before them, just 4 miles away.

Grand Cairo itself was by any standards a large city and occupied an irregular area measuring between 3 and 4 miles from north to south and nearly 2 miles across. On the south-east side was the imposing-looking citadel, but otherwise the old walls, with their fourteen towers, were of little military value and the real reliance was placed on an outer ring of forts hastily constructed by French engineers. Whether Belliard had sufficient strength to adequately hold the perimeter was also open to doubt, and Wilson comments that a *feu de joi*, in which all the batteries in the citadel and entrenched camp successively fired, woefully failed to impress the Allies. 'If the number of cannon awed,' he wrote, 'the vast extension of the line to be defended by the then estimated strength of the garrison counteracted the impression; and the opinion was universal, that if the object of the enemy was to inspire terror by the display of strength, the effect was diametrically opposite.'[14]

On the west side of the city, about a mile of flood plain separated Grand Cairo from the Nile, which broadened at this point to encompass three large islands, and on the east bank of the river a little to the south of the city was the entirely separate Old Cairo and on the opposite side was the fortified suburb of Giza. (See the appendix to this chapter.)

Hutchinson's natural instinct was to approach the city from the east, and so orders were given to cross the river on the morning of 20 June and combine with the Turks, but then a reconnaissance confirmed that there was a bridge of boats linking the city with Giza and that meant that before the siege could begin properly, it would have to be neutralised in order to prevent Belliard from either sortieing out to disrupt operations, or worse still making his escape.

The next day the battering train arrived and then on 21 June the two battalions summoned from Alexandria turned up as well. So too did Lloyd's 86th Regiment, which had made a dreadful march over the desert from Suez: 'Never were soldiers in a more pitiable condition; for in consequence of the plague, they had been obliged to burn all their uniforms, and on the march had lost their knapsacks, &c. but being uncommonly fine men, their appearance excited great interest.'[15]

These reinforcements required a partial reorganisation of the army, which saw Major General Cradock transferred across the river to take over from Stewart in command of a new brigade comprising all three British battalions serving alongside the Grand Vizier, while his own brigade was given to John Hope, who was in turn succeeded as Adjutant General by Abercromby's son.[16]

Then, while the Turks faced off against the northern defences of Cairo, everyone on the west bank closed in on Giza. Reversing the usual order of march, the three British brigades stood on the left, by the river, facing south, while the *Kapūdān Pasha*'s Turks and some of the *Mamlūks* formed the right wing. Forward of them, a mix of British, Turkish and *Mamlūk* detachments formed a semicircular picket line around the town to cover the establishment of the siege batteries in 120 degrees of heat. The guns were intended to be ready on 22 June and after that General Lawson was confident that four to five days would be sufficient to deal with Giza and cut off Belliard's escape. Once that was accomplished, the planned shift to the east bank could finally take place and then the siege would be little more than a mathematical exercise with a predictable result.

Belliard recognised this too and on 22 June, before the guns had a chance to open fire, an envoy rode out from the gates of Giza with a white flag and announced that the general wished to negotiate the terms of a surrender – to the British Army.

An armistice was immediately declared and, with the Grand Vizier's agreement, talks began next day between Colonel Hope on the one hand and Generals Donzelot and Morand on the other. Although a capitulation was not signed until 27 June, neither the outcome nor the terms were ever in doubt. Hutchinson was in a hurry and had no appetite for a lengthy siege, and Belliard, with the complete backing of his officers and men, was keen to oblige him – for a price. The French were to march out with their arms and cannon (less a matter of military punctilio in this case than prudent self-preservation) and all their baggage – interpreted in a surprisingly elastic fashion by Belliard to include all manner of public property and even not only the corpse of General Kleber, but the bones of his assassin as well! Having surrendered, they were then to be escorted to Rosetta and embarked for France at the Allies' expense. The sheer scale of the operation took some time to organise, of course. The 79th Highlanders took possession of the Giza Gate, and the 89th Regiment, Fort Sulkowsky on the same evening, but it was not until the night of 10 July that the French completed their evacuation of the city and assembled in Giza for the march north. Until that point Hutchinson and his officers had reckoned that they would be dealing with about 6,000 men, but rather to everyone's surprise there turned out to be nearly 14,000 of them besides an unknown number of women and children.[17] It was not until 9 August that the last of them were shipped to France and by then operations were once again getting under way against Alexandria.

Appendix: Colonel Wilson's description of the Cairo defences[18]

The circumference of the city of Cairo, including the suburb of Boulac, is six miles; and yet this place, till lately, was considered in the east, and partially through Europe, as the largest capital in the World ...

The military position of Cairo is not good; its citadel is commanded by the heights of Mokattam, which are perpendicularly elevated about a stone's throw from the works, and completely look into every battery, so that musquetry could play on any part. But to plant cannon on these heights would have been extremely difficult. The detour was very considerable to reach them, yet necessary, in order to avoid the forts, whilst the immense chasms and ravines in this part of the Desert, to go round which there was scarcely a camel track, rendered any attempt to bring heavy artillery almost impossible; and as the number of troops to maintain the post must have been proportioned to the strength of the garrison, the great want of water would have rendered its occupation nearly impracticable; yet if these obstacles could have been surmounted, the citadel was so weak, that a very slight battery would have crumbled the whole into dust.

The French, for the further defence of the town, constructed on the high hills of rubbish, which laid on the north and east fronts of it, small square stone towers, at such distances as to flank each other, and the line of each front was commanded by a principal fort, that to the north was called Fort Camin, that on the east Fort Dupuis.

All of these towers were bomb proof, a deep ditch surrounded them, and a gun from the upper story was worked out of a covered embrasure. (Each tower was intended to be manned with fifteen men it was such a tower as those which at Corsica resisted for three days several men of war, one of which was set on fire, and another dismasted; nor was it taken until a landing was made by some troops.) Each was provided with a cistern; the door was in the centre, and a moveable ladder the means of access: so fortified, they defied attack. It would have required the battering of heavy artillery, when they might have still resisted four or five days; but nevertheless, as they could be passed in an assault by night, they were to be considered rather as a strong chain of works to an entrenched camp, than the defences of a fortified city.

Behind these was a line of entrenchments, in front of which was dug a very deep ditch, and the Walls of Cairo formed the last line of defence.

The southern front was protected by an aqueduct (with the cavity of the arches built up), extending from the citadel to a large building, on the banks of the Nile, and in which were the works to throw up the water into the aqueduct, this building was converted into a fort by the French. In front were several small detached forts, and the remains of Old Cairo, which place was not fortified except by a few batteries on the bank of the Nile, open in the gorge, consequently not to be defended against an army which had crossed the river higher.

Fort Ibrahim Bey and Fort L'Institute formed the second line. This was the weakest side in regard of fortification, but strong from position, as the Nile was to be passed, and the front was very contracted.

The Western side is defended by the Nile and the island of Rhoda, on which were several heavy batteries, particularly at the northern point. At the dry season of the year, the interior channel, which runs by the farm of Ibrahim Bey, is fordable in several places, so that the Nile must be considered then as the only river to be forced.

The island of Rhoda is the prettiest spot in Egypt; very fine sycamore trees grow along its banks, affording the most gratifying shade, yet do not prove a sufficient barrier to the whirl-winds and clouds of dust, which, although having to pass the Nile, are still here intolerable.

On this island is the celebrated Meklas, by which the height of the Nile is ascertained; a redoubt, with six pieces of cannon, served as the tete du pont to the bridge, which connects Giza. Giza is a dirty village, which the French have improved by building half a dozen houses, and establishing in it their manufactories of arms, shot, &c. The chief ornament of the place is a palace of Morad Bey's, much in ruins; and an excellent coffee-house kept by a Frenchman, who remained behind, was acknowledged to be its most agreeable embellishment.

The works of Giza are very contemptible; a wall surrounds the whole, except on the northern front, where Morad Bey's house forms the defence. This wall is very thin, and not high enough to render an escalade difficult; but to delay the immediate approach, a chain of redoubts was thrown forwards about sixty yards; yet the whole resistance would have proved insignificant, if the strength of the garrison had not prevented an assault. Such were Cairo and its out-works. In this state, defended by ten thousand men, and with three hundred and sixty-three serviceable pieces of cannon, including the fifty removed by the French, did the whole surrender without the firing of a shot.

Chapter 10

Another Part of the Field:
The Fall of Alexandria

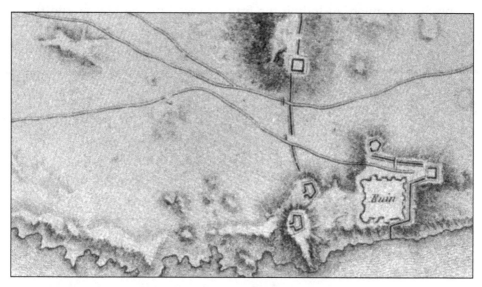

Roman Ruins as fortified by Coote: detail from Captain Thomas Walsh's plan

All the while Hutchinson and his army were adventuring up the Nile, Major General Coote was maintaining a thankless, but not altogether uncomfortable, vigil just to the east of Alexandria.

There was no question of undertaking any operations against the City. From a distance the fortifications appeared far too formidable:

> ... It was really astonishing [said Walsh on inspecting them afterwards] to behold the numerous works which had been made.

130

A wall flanked with bastions had been built round the new town, and the lines to the eastward were much stronger, than we could ever have imagined. Nothing could exceed the care and attention, which had evidently been employed in strengthening them; and our whole army agreed, that no field works superiour to these were ever seen. The old walls, and ruined towers, had been repaired, and turned to the best advantage; in fine, nothing was omitted by Menou, which could in any manner add to the strength of the place. Forts Caffarelli and Cretin, which, at a distance, always appeared to us so formidable, were, on a nearer inspection, far from being so. They were both built exactly alike, and consisted of a large and elevated cavalier [an inner raised platform, able to fire over the main parapet] encompassed at its foot by a deep entrenchment. In these cavaliers were nine pieces of heavy ordnance, with four or five smaller guns in the entrenchments. Being built upon two heights, they completely commanded the town and other works; but were themselves easy of approach: while having no casemates, and but small cisterns, they could not make a long defence. Beside these disadvantages, the weight of the guns, &c., being too much for the cavaliers, which were built on eminences composed entirely of rubbish and of loose sand, they needed frequent repairs, the works constantly crumbling down, and filling the lower entrenchment. They were both within the Enceinte des Arabes, and about eight hundred yards distant from each other.

The next principal fortification was the Pharos, a poor substitute for the noble structure which formerly bore that name. The approach to it was over a narrow causeway, shut in on both sides from the sea by a thin wall. It consisted of a low square tower, enclosed by a double rampart and ditch; the whole of Turkish construction, but kept in very good repair by the French.

Its best defence was its very formidable and beautiful artillery, brought over from France, all brass, and cast in the reigns of Lewis the XIVth and XVth. It was also well supplied with very fine mortars. Several furnaces for heating shot were also disposed along the faces looking toward the sea. Some of the stone shot formerly used by the Turks still remained in the fort.

On the top of the tower stands the present lighthouse. All the prisoners taken from us since our landing in the country were confined in this fort, and could not boast of having been well treated. How cruel must their situation have been, when, on the 21st of March, they could see every movement, and hear every shot, without being able to learn the result …

The redoute de Cleopatra, and that of Pompey, were two very good works; but all the other fortifications were totally insignificant, being either field works, or old towers crumbling to pieces under the weight of their guns, and calculated only to stop Arabs, or undisciplined troops. Against a regular and spirited attack, Alexandria could not have held out more than ten or twelve days.[1]

Even if the weakness of the fortifications had been appreciated, there were far too few men to mount such an attack. When Hutchinson marched off to the Nile, he left behind no fewer than five of his infantry brigades, including most of the Reserve:[2]

Brigade of Guards:	Coldstream and 3rd Guards
1st Brigade:	1/54th, 2/54th and Marine Battalion
3rd Brigade:	13th, 2/27th and 44th Regiments
5th Brigade:	Stuart's; De Roll's and Dillon's Regiments
Reserve:	23rd Fusiliers, 28th, 42nd and 50th Regiments

The 26th Light Dragoons were also assigned to Coote, although at this point in time just over half its 438 men were fortunate enough to be mounted.

In addition, there were 292 Royal Artillerymen (with just thirty horses between them, ten of which were returned as sick or lame) and eighty-eight Maltese of the Staff Corps under two ensigns and two sergeants.

In all, therefore, on paper Coote appeared to have been assigned a total of slightly less than 10,000 infantry, but already only 7,000 of them were actually fit for duty and that number would drop substantially over the next three months. Indeed his ADC, Walsh, claimed that at the outset, his entire division had consisted of about 5,000 men, 'of whom upwards of fifteen hundred were afflicted with sore eyes and fluxes, which soon reduced it to little more than three thousand fit for duty'.

What was more, notwithstanding their crucial role in the 21 March battle, some officers continued to fret over the fact that half of the remaining men were the foreigners belonging to Stuart's brigade – and were therefore quite unfairly stigmatised as unreliable. Then, to make matters worse, plague broke out behind them at Aboukir, forcing Coote to send a detachment back to Mandara for a while to establish a security cordon and quarantine his camp.

As if all that was not enough, although a reinforcement arrived on 10 May when about twenty store-ships and victuallers arrived in Aboukir

Bay carrying the now recovered 1/27th Regiment from Malta, with an additional 500 recruits and convalescents from other corps, making in all 1,066 reinforcements, nearly all of them were immediately marched off to Rosetta.[3] Then on 1 June, Coote was also ordered to forward the 28th and 42nd Regiments to the Nile front, all of which 'left his entrenched position very destitute of troops, and without a second line'.

Consequently, he was not even blockading the city, far less besieging it, for French gold still ensured the passage of supply columns brought in by local contractors (mainly Bedouin) via its western side. Rather, Coote's primary focus was on protecting the landing site and depots at Aboukir Bay. Acutely aware that he was outnumbered by the French and vulnerable to a sudden sortie, he heavily fortified the line earlier established along the sand hills and escarpment stretching south from the old Roman fortress.

In the meantime, both sides engaged in an early species of trench warfare in which the chief activity was not fighting but rather improving, extending and repairing the constantly eroding sandy ditches and earthworks, and as Captain Walsh rather pompously declared, 'every precaution was taken to make up in vigilance what we wanted in numbers'.

As the weeks went by, the only real excitement occurred on 23 June, when it was noticed that the once dry Alexandria Canal was nearly filled with water. This was, of course, due to the annual rising of the Nile, but the French were quick to take advantage by cutting the canal to let it flow into the plain. Coote responded by throwing up a dam to prevent the water spreading too far, but the French still ended up with about a quarter of their frontage flooded, but otherwise, except for an occasional reconnaissance pushed towards the south, activity was generally kept at a very low level as both sides tried to avoid provoking the other.[4]

Then, for a time a French fleet was reported to be offshore. This was no chimera, but a long-heralded squadron under Admiral Ganteaume, consisting of four sail of the line, one frigate, one corvette, and five small transports. As early as 27 March, Admiral Sir James Bickerton, soon joined by Keith himself, had been waiting for the French admiral off Alexandria, but in fact Ganteaume did not leave Toulon until nearly a month later on 25 April. However, when he did sail, his men of war had a reputed 3,000 to 4,000 troops on board, all destined to reinforce Menou. Supposedly, their original intention, incredibly enough, was to avoid interception by landing near Derna, in far-off Cyrenaica and then they were expected to march for 500 miles along the sea coast to

Alexandria! Instead, a number of men were rather more sensibly set ashore in Locabsis Bay, near El Alamein, on 8 June – by mistake, says Walsh.[5] This landing place was located a rather more realistic 74 miles, or just three marches, west of Alexandria. Had all of them come ashore there, this would have been an altogether more dangerous development than the fantastical notion of marching all the way from Derna, but not surprisingly the locals were hostile and the distant appearance of some sails (which in reality was no more than a convoy of transports) provided Ganteaume with sufficient excuse to re-embark the men, cut his cables and run for home. Menou was on his own, but he remained defiant and indeed two weeks earlier had strengthened his personal position by arresting and expelling General Reynier and some of his other more vocal critics.[6] No matter the collapse of the French regime elsewhere in Egypt, he was still determined to hold on to the trump card of Alexandria until peace was signed in Europe.

The stalemate, however, was about to be broken at last.

For all its faults, the British government had the great good sense to recognise and reinforce a victory on the rare occasion when it was presented with one, and having received the news of the 'brilliant and decisive success' in the 21 March battle, it voted Abercromby a handsome memorial in St Paul's Cathedral and a baronetcy for his widow, while Hutchinson, by virtue of surviving, became a Knight of the Bath. Rather more practically, in consultation with the King, the government also took immediate steps to confirm Hutchinson's status. Abercromby had named him his second-in-command, but Abercromby was dead and the senior officer in the Mediterranean was now Lieutenant General Fox. However, Fox was on Minorca, while Hutchinson was on the spot and actively conducting operations, and so he was promoted to the local rank of lieutenant general in the 'Mediterranean and the dominions of the Grand Seignor' with effect from 29 March.[7] That done, the government also set about scraping up every man reckoned fit for service and shipping them out to Egypt.

The first of these reinforcements arrived on board the frigate HMS *Leda*, which anchored in Aboukir Bay on 5 July, carrying a draft of 150 men for the 3rd Footguards and, what was probably even more welcome, £50,000 in specie 'for the use of the army'. Aside from the usual uses, this sum allowed for the payment of the considerable arrears of pay owing to the troops. Then, three days later, 150 Coldstreamers also turned up on HMS *Active* and on 9 July two new battalions; the 25th and 26th Regiments, appeared, once again accompanied by large sums of money and the promise of yet more reinforcements still to come. A delighted

Coote ordered them all to land at once and marched up to join him in front of Alexandria, before they could be snatched away from him. Then, on 14 July, the 24th Regiment also arrived, followed four days later by a convoy from Minorca carrying both battalions of the 20th Regiment and the curiously titled Ancient Irish Fencibles,[8] along with the riflemen of the *Löwenstein Jäger*, a German mercenary unit in British pay, which had until recently been serving in Bavaria. Nor was this all, for on 24 July the 22nd Light Dragoons also arrived from Cork, albeit they were dismounted, since the Transport Board had been unable to find suitable shipping for their horses, and then finally, a convoy from Malta arrived in the bay on 3 August, carrying 1,600 men of two more foreign mercenary units, the *Chasseurs Britanniques* and the *Regiment de Watteville*, and 120 Royal Artillerymen from Gibraltar.

Even as these various reinforcements were arriving, so were Hutchinson's men, who were now steadily making their way back down the Nile together with the surrendered Cairo garrison. Their return was a carefully phased operation, managed by Major General Moore, who was by this time sufficiently recovered, and on 25 July, the day after the 22nd Dragoons came ashore, the greater part of the Allied forces arrived at Ramanieh and then halted there while Brigadier Oakes supervised the embarkation of the French army from Rosetta on board a series of convoys. The terms of the Cairo capitulation had left Belliard and his men fully armed, both with their personal weapons and even their field artillery, and while there was never the slightest suggestion that the French might repudiate the agreement and resume hostilities, common prudence demanded that an equally substantial force remained closely at hand until the embarkation was completed on 5 August. Indeed, while everyone waited, 2/1st Royals and the 58th Regiment were posted to prevent the Turks getting into the town, where as Walsh wryly commented, 'their presence might have created some unpleasant circumstances'.

Hutchinson himself only arrived at Rosetta on 29 July. Ever since the initial landing at Aboukir and then throughout the Nile campaign he had been feeling unwell, and as a result became more distanced from his subordinates than before, culminating in something of a collapse after the surrender of Cairo. The nature of Hutchinson's illness has always been unclear, although numerous eyewitnesses testified anent his looking ill, but the likelihood is that it was primarily psychosomatic rather than physical in origin and therefore hardly likely to elicit any sympathy from his critics. At any rate, Sir John spent the next two weeks resting in a house at Giza, and now, on returning north, he promptly went aboard Keith's flagship, HMS *Foudroyant*, and to the dismay of some and the resentment of others, he remained isolated there to continue his convalescence and to concert plans with the admiral for the forthcoming operations against Alexandria.

Earlier, the options open to him had been limited and unattractive. Thus far the British Army had been confined to the eastern approaches, and while it had won two pitched battles in the open, no one in their right mind could relish the prospect of attacking the heavily fortified Nicopolis Lines head on. Now, however, to the great bemusement of the returning members of the Nile expedition, what had been a flat, boggy plain when they marched away, was transformed into a vast inland sea that now offered itself as the key to Alexandria.

By using the Innundation, the focus of operations could be shifted to the western side of the city instead, but first, in his usual slow and methodical fashion, Hutchinson was determined to make all the necessary preparations.

He began with a thorough reorganisation of the army, promulgated on 9 August, which incorporated the newly arrived reinforcements and thereby both enlarged the existing brigades and added a sixth one, – see the appendix to the end of this chapter – which provided a nominal total of 9,698 infantry fit for duty, excluding the 13th Regiment out at Rosetta.

On the same day, Doyle's brigade marched back into the camp in front of Nicopolis and over the next week, as the rest of the Nile army followed it, a parallel effort was made to pre-position guns, ammunition and other supplies. Conversely, two of the cavalry regiments, the artillery horses and the pack animals, including a large and extremely noisy collection of donkeys, were largely sent back to the Rosetta area, where they could be fed without interfering with the build-up of men and munitions at the front.

Operations were thus beginning to move apace and a significant development was the advent of Turkish gunboats on to the Innundation. These were described by Walsh as very large, each with two masts, square rigged and mounting a heavy 24-pounder gun at the bow, and a 12-pounder on each quarter. They were also flat bottomed, drawing very little water and therefore ideally suited to operations on the lake, which although vast was only some 3 m deep.[9] Having been dragged across from Lake Maadje, a flotilla of twenty-four of these gunboats sailed up Lake Mareotis on the morning of 13 August, and positioned themselves off Alexandria, menacing the handful of French gunboats that had hitherto controlled the navigation of the lake.

As long ago as 10 July, Major General Coote had gone aboard a brig and reconnoitred the seaward side of the isthmus to the west of Alexandria. At the time he assessed that it might be practical to land a force of up to 5,000 men there in order to then move against the city's western defences, which were shrewdly assumed to be much less formidable than the Nicopolis lines. Now Hutchinson was giving him the chance to attempt it.

In the general orders of 12 August, Coote was allocated three brigades for the task; Cavan's brigade of Guards, Ludlow's 1st Brigade and Finch's 2nd Brigade, making about 4,000 rank and file in total, with in addition 'a certain proportion of artillery, engineers, &c.' and a detachment of 100 men of the 26th Light Dragoons.

The intention was to launch the operation three days later and even Sir John finally came ashore to see it off. Unfortunately, when the boats arrived it was found at the last moment that due to a misunderstanding they had not been victualled and so the start had to be delayed by twenty-four hours until about 7.00 pm on the evening of 16 August. There were then about 400 boats in all. Some were provided by the fleet, and three of Finch's battalions were embarked on the Turkish gunboats, but more than half of the boats were a miscellany of Greek and Egyptian vessels rounded up by the *Kapūdān Pasha* in Rosetta. Even loading everyone on to the motley collection may have been a notable accomplishment in itself, but by 9.30 pm they were all under way.

Unfortunately, the wind then changed during the night and dawn found half of the boats sagging away to leeward. By the time they were all collected together and shepherded in the right direction again, it was about 10.00 am and the French, or at least some of them, were waiting. Coote estimated them as only 300 to 400 strong – perhaps a single battalion – with two pieces of horse artillery, so he directed Finch to take his brigade straight in, while he himself simply landed the rest of his division, without any opposition, about 2 miles further west.

While Coote's landing was taking place, Hutchinson launched a parallel attack from the east. This was one of those opportunistic affairs, primarily intended as a diversion to pin down French troops who might otherwise be rushed to oppose Coote, but at the same time, was hopefully capable of being turned into a full-scale attack in its own right. Moore explained:

In order to favour this movement two lodgements were directed to be made on the flank of the enemy's position. The one on the left was made under the orders of General Cradock; that on the right under mine.[10] The troops for this attack – Stewart's Regiment and the Lowenstein Rangers – assembled under Brigadier-General Stewart after dark in front of our works, and moved forward half-an-hour before daybreak. They drove in the enemy's outposts, and pushed forward a part as far as a commanding hillock within 900 yards of the enemy's works. From this we had a perfect view of their position; but the fire was too great to retain it, and the hillock too distant for support. Upon the French coming out in force we retired to a position which had been previously selected, where 400 men were at work making an entrenchment. Our taking possession of the hillock mentioned was done with no view but to reconnoitre. We had no hopes of retaining it.

On the left, Doyle was rather more successful in clearing the Green Hill position. Although he had insisted on rising from his sickbed to take command, it was actually the fiery Colonel Spencer who volunteered to go forward with the 30th and 50th Regiments, and the 92nd in support, quickly clearing two small redoubts and occupying the hill. However, seeing Moore fall back from the other hill (known as the Sugarloaf), the French essayed a counterattack, launching a column of about 500 men of *75e Ligne* against the Green Hill.[11] Spencer's men were by then very sensibly taking cover from artillery fire on the reverse slope, but on realising the French infantry were coming forward, Lieutenant Colonel William Lockhart of the 30th hastily conferred with Spencer and suggested 'the propriety of marching out to meet and attack this party instead of waiting for them in the trenches'. This was music to Spencer's ears and he immediately agreed. As soon as the French reached the brow of the hill, with drums beating, colours flying, and covered by showers of grapeshot and round-shot, Lockhart, although outnumbered two to one and in his men no very good order, stood up, fired a ragged volley and immediately charged with the bayonet. The French, recorded Moore disapprovingly, 'behaved very ill, and fled the moment they were charged, though it was by inferior numbers'.[12] Behind them they left upwards of 100 men killed, wounded or taken prisoner. By contrast, the whole day cost Doyle and Spencer about thirty killed and wounded, mainly to cannon fire. The dismal performance by *75e* was very much a foretaste of what was coming. French morale was crumbling fast.

Next day, Moore's entrenchment was enlarged to be able to accommodate the whole of Stuart's regiment, which was in turn relieved that evening by Colonel Paget with the 23rd and 28th Regiments, the

40th (flank companies), and the Corsican Rangers. During the night a working party of 250 men was employed in erecting a two-gun battery to the front and right of the entrenchment and on the next night it was the turn of De Roll's and Watteville's regiments under Colonel Jost Dürler.[13] And so on it went. Moore and Cradock had pushed forward the front line by 700 to 800 m, but although more trenches and batteries were being dug to consolidate the advance, and Moore was grumbling in orders anent the poor performance of the troops on the picquet line, who seemingly fell back at the slightest excuse, all of them were very much aware that they were just going through the motions. The Nicopolis position, as he admitted, was 'very formidable. Nature had made it strong, and they have added to it much by art', and no one was much inclined to get themselves killed for the sake of a demonstration.

Instead, the expectation was growing that the operations now opening on the western front offered a much more promising approach. There Coote and his men found the terrain to be altogether different from that on the eastern side of the city. The isthmus at this point was only 2 miles across and dominated by a broad spine of flinty limestone, pitted by ancient quarries.

At 5.00 pm in the evening of 18 August, Coote moved forward about 2 miles without any opposition beyond a few stray shots exchanged between his advanced guard and the retiring enemy, before halting and taking up a defensive position with the Guards extending across the quarries in two lines with their right to the Innundation and Major Generals Ludlow and Finch's brigades formed *en potence* fronting the sea.

This pause in the advance was to secure the fort of Marabout, otherwise known as the *Tour de Arabes*, situated on a small rocky islet just off the Mediterranean shore of the isthmus.[14] It was a sea mark for the entrance to the lagoon variously known as Marabout Bay or the Old or Western Harbour of Alexandria, where Napoleon Bonaparte had landed nearly three years before. Now the fort needed to be neutralised to allow British and Turkish gunboats to get into the harbour and cover Coote's advance on the city. That evening a battery of two 12-pounders and two howitzers was planted against it and at daybreak on 19 August, Coote ordered the guns to commence firing. To the delight of all concerned, within an hour or so two French gunboats anchored just inside the harbour entrance were sunk and a third fled back to Alexandria 'in a very crippled state'. A *djerme* boldly coming out that evening suffered the same fate, but the 12-pounders proved unequal to battering the fort itself and so Captain Duncan of the Royal Artillery, deciding that he needed bigger guns, paused the bombardment until he could bring up a couple of 24-pounders instead. In the meantime the 1/54th Regiment was left to maintain the pressure, and its commanding officer, Lieutenant Colonel Christopher Darby (a veteran of the American war), pushed forward his battalion's light company to the end of the promontory leading to the island, where they found a vantage point that allowed them to sweep the ramparts and pick off every gunner who dared to stick his head above the parapet.[15]

In the end it took four battalions to drag the guns over 'steep quarries and precipices' across the spine ridge between the lake and the sea, but by daybreak on 21 August both of them were in position. Their heavier calibre soon told and at 11.30 am the signal tower came down with a tremendous crash, burying one of the French guns in the rubble. Still game, the French rehoisted their colours and managed an occasional shot in reply, but most of them by now had to take cover outside the fort on the other side of the islet, so it was obvious that they could not last much longer. Coote, growing impatient, decided to storm the place that night, but first, at 5.30 pm Colonel Darby and Captain Walsh went forward to summon the garrison to surrender. After some genteel haggling, *Chef de Battallon* (Major) Etienne of the *88e Ligne* capitulated and two companies of the 54th Regiment took possession of the ruins at 11.00 pm.[16]

At 6.00 am next morning Coote resumed his advance. A flotilla of two British and five Turkish sloops had already been taken into the harbour the previous evening by Captain Alexander Cochrane RN, despite the removal of the navigation marks and buoys. Now they moved forward covering his left wing while the gunboats on the lake covered his right.

'Our little army' [as Walsh styled it] moved forward in three columns; the Guards under Major General Lord Cavan forming two columns on the right, near the lake, and Major General Ludlow's brigade on the left, close to the sea, while Major General Finch's brigade was designated the reserve. In front of them was a heavy skirmish line, comprised of the battalion light companies, and 174 riflemen of the *Löwenstein Jäger* under Captain Perponcher, who had been fetched round from the eastern front during the night, and just behind them all were six field-pieces under Major George Cookson.[17]

Opposing them were about 1,200 men under *General de Brigade* Georges-Henri Eppler, primarily comprising four battalions strung out in a line athwart the ridge[18] at a point where the isthmus narrowed to just a mile across. Their front was covered by a deep cutting, originally excavated as a canal linking the Old Harbour with Lake Mareotis, and they were supported by two heavy guns *en batterie* on the right, and on their left by two batteries containing three more guns. Besides these, various small pieces of artillery were planted in the intervals between the battalions, and two regiments of cavalry; the *14e* and *18e Dragoons* stood close behind the centre; otherwise there was no reserve.

It ought to have been a strong position and at first the French greeted the British advance with a heavy fire of artillery and musketry, but as the Redcoats moved steadily forward into what would be the last battle of the campaign, Walsh, for one, was moved to eulogy:

> Never, perhaps, was there a more grand or superb spectacle, than that which the affair of this morning afforded. The army moving in separate and regular columns over the narrow isthmus; the fire of our great guns and musketry; the ships of war and the gunboats keeping up a constant cannonade upon our right and left, and advancing gradually with the troops; presented all together, assisted by the fineness of the morning, a sight rarely to be seen, and in beauty seldom equalled.

There was also an astonishing irony in the way that, in a complete reversal of the popular picture of how these battles were fought, while the French defenders were drawn up in a single long thin battle line stretching along the crest, their British attackers were advancing upon them in battalion columns covered by a heavy skirmish line.

As the British moved forward 'with the greatest coolness and regularity', enjoying close fire support from the gunboats conforming to their advance on either flank, the French not only abandoned their position behind the deep cutting, and with it all seven of their heavy guns, but then allowed themselves to be driven all the way back across rocky ground that ought to have been capable of being contested at every step, and into the Alexandria defences. For the French, the day was an utter disaster. Coote's men advanced no less than 4 miles, overrunning tents and abandoned equipment, killing, wounding and capturing about 200 of the enemy, at a cost of just three men killed and forty-two wounded, including Lieutenant Richard Hockings of the 25th Regiment, who lost a leg.[19] The state of French demoralisation was exemplified when the single squadron of the 26th Light Dragoons present under Major James Moore charged and routed a body of French cavalry. Pursuing the French too far, they suddenly found themselves in the presence of an infantry battalion, but it too was so rattled that a volley unleashed at just 30 m distance from the dragoons flew harmlessly overhead!

By 10.00 am it was all over and the headlong advance came to a halt within cannon-shot of the outlying *Fort de Bains*. Any further operations were going to have to wait until some heavy guns could be brought up, and for once in his life Hutchinson had to think quickly. During the last couple of days there had been signs that the French might be thinning out the Nicopolis Lines. If so, it was most likely being done to stabilise their western front, and so he ordered the new 6th Brigade to reinforce Coote. This was complicated. Its original commander, Brigadier General John Blake, appears to have been sick and had to be replaced at the last moment by the capable Brent Spencer. Assembling sufficient boats for the lift also took time, which meant the brigade could not be embarked until after dark.

An immediate diversion was needed and so, at 4.00 am in the morning of 23 August, having literally crawled up the slopes under cover of darkness, Moore and Cradock drove the French outposts in front of the Nicopolis Lines, and pushed parties of infantry up the slopes behind them. A party of Turks even took possession of the Sugarloaf Hill, and in return were answered by a gratifyingly heavy, but near harmless fire from the French.

Afterwards there was a decided feeling that if the false attack had been pressed, the French would have given way, and under cover of the racket, Colonel Spencer landed to the westward, with the 6th Brigade, and later in the day Coote was also reinforced by 250 *Mamlūk* cavalry, under Captain Chollet of the Hompesch Hussars, who arrived by land from Damanhūr, and then later, a body of 700 Turks, detached from the *Kapūdān Pasha*'s contingent, was brought round and took up their ground in the rear of Spencer's brigade. Even Hutchinson turned up in the afternoon, to have a look for himself, accompanied by Cradock and by Captain Brice of the Engineers. For months the British had been staring up at the Heights of Nicopolis with not a glimpse of their ultimate objective. Now, from the high ground on the western front, Hutchinson and his colleagues gazed down upon the ancient city and its crumbling, surely indefensible walls:

> Everyone was astonished at the unexpected appearance of Alexandria; instead of being, as heretofore, removed by superior heights from view of the city, nothing intervened to hide the old crumbling walls. Such an approach seemed nearly absolute possession. The scene, which before had always been so frightfully bleak, became animatingly gay. The shipping in the harbour, the full view of everything passing in the town, and the bustle on the quay, afforded considerable interest.'"

Clearly, this side rather than the eastern front offered the best approach, but first the necessary guns would have to be carried round to deal with the French forts, and rather more urgently a water supply needed to be organised. When Coote and his men first landed they found plenty of water at no great depth on the sandy north side of the isthmus, but 4 miles nearer to the city the rock yielded none. Fortunately, the *Mamlūks* stepped in and organised a shuttle, carrying water bags on camels. Conveniently too, roads running into the city on either side of the isthmus allowed four 24-pounders and four mortar pieces to be brought forward and on the morning of 25 August they opened on the *Fort des Bains*. The French response was feeble, but so too, alas was the effect. The guns were simply too far away to make an impression on the fort. In conventional terms, that normally required a lengthy process of digging forward and opening a new trench or parallel for a battery closer to the fort. In this case, however, there was a low ridge, in just the right place, 600m away from the fort.

The French had a strong outpost there, but in the current mood of optimism, Colonel George Smyth was instructed to take it, with 1/20th Regiment and a thirty-strong detachment of the 26th Light Dragoons under Lieutenant Thomas Kelly. Just 'in case of accident', 2/54th were also deployed along a line of sand hills, but in the event the operation went without a hitch. About 9:00 pm, Smyth went forward with his men in column formation, their firelocks unloaded but bayonets fixed. However, instead of going straight forward, he first turned the left of the French picquet line and then scoured along the ridge, killing or capturing the lot. Once again, the casualties were wholly disproportionate and aside from an optimistic estimate of the French dead and wounded, Walsh records that eight officers, five sergeants and forty-seven men were brought in as prisoners, against three of Smyth's men and Lieutenant Kelly slightly wounded.

The French quickly organised a counterattack and opened a furious fire on the captured position, but both had petered out by midnight without accomplishing anything. Then, at 4.30 pm, one of General Menou's ADCs turned up on the western picquet line with a letter for Coote, requesting a seventy-two-hour ceasefire. Another was sent to Hutchinson.

Next morning, white flags were flying all along the lines. Menou, was in an awkward, almost dangerous position. Personally, he was committed to holding out, clinging on to Alexandria in the hope that the imminent peace in Europe would save him, yet only too aware that his army was on the point of collapse. Just as on the Nile, the events of the last few days had shown that his army was no longer willing to fight. He attempted to prevaricate, requesting an extension of time and even proposing that he be free to resume hostilities if reinforcements reached him before 17 September. Hutchinson responded bluntly that if Menou did not surrender, he would storm the place. The long-delayed Indian army under Major General Baird had just arrived at Rosetta and he had enough men to do it. Menou bowed to the inevitable and accepted what were by now the usual terms, repatriation of his men and their dependants to France with their arms, their personal possessions and a token ten guns. All in all it turned out that there were 10,524 soldiers and sailors, including Egyptian, Greek and Syrian auxiliaries and another 685 non-combatant personnel, hospital staff, commissaries and the like and even a few civilians requiring passage, but just as they had been uncounted when Napoleon Bonaparte embarked on his Oriental adventure, no one counted the women who sailed home from Egypt.

Captain Walsh recorded:

At twelve o'clock on the 2d of September, agreeably to the capitulation, we took possession of the French lines. Major-general Cradock occupied the entrenched camp of the French on the east of the town, with the grenadiers of that division of the army. To the westward Major-general Ludlow, with two hundred men of the brigade of guards, and the grenadiers of his division, took possession of forts le Turc and du Vivier, and the fortified heights of Pompey's pillar. The French had previously evacuated all these posts, and we marched in with our bands playing and drums beating. The British and Turkish flags were immediately hoisted together, and the whole was conducted with the greatest precision and regularity.

The day was extremely fine, and the whole of the scene, heightened by the reflections, which must have arisen in every breast on the termination of a glorious campaign, was certainly one of the most pleasing and gratifying, that a soldier can feel.

This day crowned our efforts, and gave us the entire possession of Egypt. The effusion of human blood now ceased; the torrent subsided; and the long hovering dove at length found a place for the sole of her foot. An enemy, who during the war had considered himself as invincible, was taught by this campaign, that British troops, meeting him on fair ground, will ever maintain a fair superiority.

And they were indeed to do just that, many times over the next fifteen years.

Appendix

New Arrangement for brigading the Army under Lieutenant General Sir John Hely Hutchinson, K.B.; Camp near Alexandria, 9 August 1801.[21]

The Brigade of Guards (1,142)
This was largely unchanged with a battalion apiece from the Coldstream and 3rd Footguards, but it should be noted that, despite an infusion of 300 fresh men a month earlier, it was still weaker by a third than it had been when it landed at Aboukir. It also had a new commanding officer in the Earl of Cavan.[22]

1st Brigade (1,863)
This was a new formation, commanded by Major General George Ludlow, having no connection to the original 1st Brigade.
25th Regiment
1/27th Regiment
2/27th Regiment
44th Regiment

2nd Brigade (1,555)
Again, a new creation, commanded by Major General Edward Finch.
2/1st (Royal) Regiment
26th Regiment
1/54th Regiment
2/54th Regiment

3rd or Foreign Brigade (2,035)
Originally designated the 5th Brigade, Brigadier General Stuart's very large brigade now boasted a fourth battalion in the shape of de.
Stuart's Minorca Regiment
De Roll's Regiment
Dillon's Regiment
Watteville's Regiment

4th Brigade (1,449)
This had originally been Cradock's 2nd Brigade, but the very sickly 13th Regiment was replaced by the 79th Highlanders, and it was now commanded by Brigadier General John Hope as Cradock would have a division in the forthcoming operations.

8th (King's) Regiment
18th (Royal Irish) Regiment
79th Regiment
90th Regiment

5th Brigade (1,331)
Brigadier General Doyle's brigade was effectively a new creation, although all its battalions had been in Egypt from the beginning.
30th Regiment
50th Regiment
89th Regiment
92nd Regiment

6th Brigade (1,946)
This was formed entirely of recently arrived reinforcement units and commanded by Brigadier General John Blake of the 24th Regiment.[23]
1/20th Regiment
2/20th Regiment
24th Regiment
Ancient Irish Fencibles

Reserve (2,934)
This formation was expanded to comprise two full brigades under Moore and Oakes,[24] those units marked with an asterisk having been added to it since the beginning of the campaign.
2nd (Queen's) Regiment*
28th Regiment
42nd Regiment
58th Regiment
40th Regiment (flank companies)
23rd Fusiliers
Löwenstein's Jäger[25]
*Chasseurs Britanniques**
Corsican Rangers

Cavalry
11th Light Dragoons (one troop)
12th Light Dragoons
22nd Light Dragoons
26th Light Dragoons
Hompesch' Hussars

Chapter 11

Abercromby's Legacy

The surrender of Alexandria more or less coincided with the Peace. As it happens, its preliminaries were signed in London on 1 October 1801, which turned out to be the day before the news actually broke there. Nevertheless, although Sir Arthur Conan Doyle would use the coincidence as the basis for one of his historical short stories, the late arrival of the despatch announcing the surrender actually made no difference to the settlement for everyone was well aware that the capture of Bonaparte's last foothold in Egypt was both inevitable and imminent.[1]

Nevertheless, it was not news the First Consul of France wanted to hear. Just a few months before, he bestrode Europe in something of a commanding position. But on 23 March his most surprising ally, Paul I of Russia, was assassinated and the new Tsar, Alexander, proved less susceptible to Bonaparte's flattery and bullying. Not only were Britain and Russia able to reconcile the differences that had spawned the League of Armed Neutrality, and so reopen the Baltic, but Alexander displayed no interest in succeeding his unstable father as Grand Master of the Order of Knights Hospitaller of St John of Jerusalem. That in turn meant that Britain could afford to disregard the stipulation in the peace treaty that Malta be evacuated and returned to the Order or its representatives. Minorca had to go back to Spain, but by continuing its occupation of Malta, Britain (and the Royal Navy) gained a far more valuable prize as a legacy of Napoleon Bonaparte's ill-fated attempt to establish an Eastern empire.

Egypt, perhaps predictably, descended at first into anarchy. The last British troops were not withdrawn until March 1803 and in the meantime their principal task was to protect their *Mamlūk* allies from their vengeful Ottoman overlords. No one had any confidence in the

Turks, and the *Mamlūks* were seen as a vital bulwark against Napoleon's ambition. They were also doomed; factional infighting followed Britain's departure and they eventually lost out in a three-cornered fight between Turks, *Mamlūks* and Albanian mercenaries, which left the latter in control of Egypt.

The acquisition of Malta aside, for Britain the Egyptian legacy went far beyond territorial gain and strategic advantage, for the campaign proved to be a transitional moment in the history of the British Army, as a shambolically inefficient army began to flower into what would very soon be described (by the Duke of Wellington no less) as 'Probably the most *complete machine* for its numbers now existing in Europe'.

Although he is chiefly remembered, if at all, only for his victory at Alexandria/Canope on 21 March 1801, Sir Ralph Abercromby's responsibility for that transformation is to be found in the weeks before the landing in Aboukir Bay. The ultimate point of drill, as any instructor will tell you, is to move a body of men to where they need to be – without losing too many of them on the way. First on Minorca, then on Malta and finally at Marmaris, Abercromby unrelentingly practised his men in the manoeuvres devised by his good friend Colonel David Dundas. Yet notwithstanding his own faith in the drill book and the praise heaped upon it by some of the officers who were in Egypt, there was nothing revolutionary about its tactical precepts. On the contrary, the teachings in the 1792 *Rules and Regulations* were downright reactionary and outdated in concept, particularly in their neglect of light infantry work, and they would attract increasing criticism over the coming decade. On the other hand, the book – or rather instruction manual – was well written, clearly explained, and had a modular approach allowing for far more flexibility than its critics allowed. Just as importantly, perhaps, practice on such a scale allowed both officers and men to work out the wrinkles and agree a common approach, so that by the time they went ashore at Aboukir they were more than capable not just to perform the various manoeuvres laid down, but above all they were confident enough in their own proficiency to surmount anything they encountered, whether it was in the book or not. They were indeed truly *aguerri* and all of the regiments involved received an unprecedented and unique Royal gift in the form of a handsome badge, bearing a sphinx and the simple word EGYPT.

Appendix 1

Opposing Forces March 1801

NB: This appendix surveys the British and French forces at the outset of the campaign. It does not include the Anglo-Indian army intended to enter Egypt by way of the Red Sea, and other reinforcements, and nor for lack of reliable information, does it include the Turkish and *Mamlūk* forces.

The British Expeditionary Force
General Abercromby's army was organised into seven infantry brigades, one of which was the two-battalion-strong Guards Brigade, while the seventh was a reinforced one designated as the Reserve.

All British infantry battalions comprised ten companies, two of which were referred to as Flank Companies and were designated as grenadiers and light infantry respectively. The first were formed from the older and steadier men (hence sometimes being unkindly referred to as the 'grannies'), while the latter were generally younger and more active ones. Collectively they were the battalion's elite and were still from time to time employed on detached service, sometimes in dedicated Flank Battalions.[1]

The figures given in parentheses beside each regiment are the number of rank and file returned as present and fit for duty on the evening of 7 March 1801, prior to their going into the boats for the landing in Aboukir Bay next morning. Officers, NCOs, and drummers are not included. Names of commanding officers at Aboukir are largely taken from the list printed in Colonel David Stewart's narrative.[2]

Guards Brigade
First in terms of seniority was a brigade of Footguards, commanded by Major General Hon. George James Ludlow.[3] The brigade comprised

only two battalions, albeit both were very strong and were obviously superbly disciplined ones:

1/Coldstream (766) – Colonel Arthur Brice
1/3rd Footguards (812) – Colonel Samuel Dalrymple

1st Brigade

Major General Eyre Coote, the senior brigadier, was an experienced officer, who would later go on to serve as second in command of the army under General Hutchinson.[4] Coote had the usual four battalions in his brigade, all of which had previously served at the Helder in 1799 and afterwards formed part of General Pulteney's force at Ferrol, before sailing south to join Abercromby:

2/1st (Royal) Regiment (626) – Lieutenant Colonel Peter Garden
1/54th Regiment (490) – Colonel Christopher Darby
2/54th Regiment (484) – Lieutenant Colonel John Layard
92nd Highlanders (529) – Lieutenant Colonel Charles Erskine

2nd Brigade

This was commanded by Major General Sir John Cradock, who had previously served extensively in the West Indies before being appointed quartermaster general in Ireland. In 1800 he was ordered to the Mediterranean, where he was given command of one of the excellent brigades formed by Abercromby on Minorca:[5]

8th Kings Regiment (439) – Colonel Gordon Drummond
13th Regiment (561) – Lieutenant Colonel the Hon. Charles Colville
18th Royal Irish Regiment (411) – Lieutenant Colonel Henry Tucker
    Montresor
90th Perthshire Volunteers (727) – Colonel Rowland Hill

3rd Brigade

The third brigade was assigned to Major General Richard Lambart, Earl of Cavan.[6] Like Coote's 1st Brigade, his command had originally been part of Pulteney's force at Ferrol, and at that time it comprised four battalions, two of them belonging to the 27th Regiment, the Inniskillings. Unfortunately, the latter regiment was largely made up at this time of volunteers from the Irish militia and a reputed combination of poor discipline, negligent officers and all of them being tossed about on transports for five months, meant that by the time they arrived off

Gibraltar both battalions were very sickly indeed. Seven companies of 2/27th were immediately sent away to Lisbon to recuperate while the supposedly fit men of both battalions sailed eastwards with the rest of the expeditionary force. Nevertheless, en route, their condition continued to deteriorate and Abercromby was compelled to set them all ashore on Malta.

As a result, when the brigade landed at Aboukir on 8 March it would only field two battalions:

50th Regiment (477) – Lieutenant Colonel Benjamin Rowe
79th Cameronian Volunteers (604) – Colonel Allan Cameron of Erracht

Fortunately, 2/27th caught up almost immediately afterwards and re-joined the brigade two days after the landing, just in time for the Mandara battles, but 1/27th would not turn up until 7 May and in the meantime its place in the brigade was partially filled by a hastily formed provisional battalion of marines under Lieutenant Colonel Walter Smith.

4th Brigade

Another Irishman, Brigadier General John Doyle,[7] commanded the 4th Brigade. In 1798 he was employed as Secretary for War in the Irish administration based in Dublin Castle, but he then joined the staff at Gibraltar and, so fortuitously placed, he gained command of a brigade being formed on Minorca. This was an unashamed exercise of influence – his son had served as Abercromby's ADC in Flanders – but nevertheless, while Doyle enjoyed no great distinction, he turned out to be a competent and very popular officer.

His brigade followed the same pattern as the others, with four battalions being assigned to it, but it had a difficult gestation. At Cadiz it had consisted of the 2nd Queen's Regiment, the 1/40th and 2/40th, and the 63rd Regiments, but only the first was a general service battalion. Therefore, when the orders came to move east, the brigade was broken up; the 63rd Regiment was set ashore at Gibraltar in exchange for the 44th Regiment, which although considerably weaker, was available for general service, and similarly, the two battalions of the 40th Regiment were carried only as far as Malta, where they exchanged with two of the general service battalions there who had earlier taken part in the siege of Valletta; the 30th and the 89th Regiments.

A personal appeal by Abercromby then resulted in the four flank companies of the 40th Regiment volunteering to go to Egypt, but they went out there as part of the Reserve rather than remaining with Doyle's Brigade.

On landing at Aboukir, the brigade therefore comprised:

2nd Queen's Regiment (530) – Colonel the Earl of Dalhousie
30th Regiment (412) – Major William Lockhart
44th Regiment (263) – Lieutenant Colonel David Ogilvie
89th Regiment (378) – Lieutenant Colonel William Stewart

5th (Foreign) Brigade

Unusually, Brigadier General John Stuart was an American by birth.[8] Another Guardsman, his brigade comprised three battalions of foreign mercenaries, who proved to be a particularly *aguerri* crew:

Roll's Regiment (528) – Lieutenant Colonel Jöst Durler
Dillon's Regiment (530) – Lieutenant Colonel Baron Henrick Georg Perponcher[9]
Minorca Regiment (929) – Lieutenant Colonel Peter John James Dutens

The Reserve

The Reserve was actually a reinforced brigade, built around the usual four battalions to whom were attached an eclectic collection of smaller units with no other obvious home. Despite its title, far from being a second-line formation, the combat elements of the Reserve were in fact employed as a spearhead.

In principal charge of the Reserve was Major General John Moore, who would prove to be one of the finest British generals of his age, before being fatally wounded at the battle of Corunna in 1809. Even at this early stage he was a rising star in the Army and had previously served creditably under Abercromby in the Caribbean, then even more creditably in Ireland in 1798, and again at the Helder in 1799.[10]

No doubt because the Reserve was so large and so heterogenous in its composition, Moore was given the luxury of a second-in-command, Brigadier General Hildebrand Oakes. A heavy, dull-faced man, Oakes' previous experience was limited to staff work and while he would fight bravely in the Aboukir landing and at Alexandria, it was probably this staff expertise that recommended him to his appointment to second Moore.[11]

23rd Royal Welch Fusiliers (457) – Lieutenant Colonel John Hall[12]
28th Regiment (587) – Colonel the Hon. Edward Paget

42nd Royal Highland Regiment (754) – Lieutenant Colonel William
   Dickson
58th Regiment (469) – Lieutenant Colonel William Houston

In addition, at Malta the four flank companies (two of grenadiers and
two of light infantry) belonging to the 40th Regiment (250) were formed
into a small battalion under the intrepid Colonel Brent Spencer[13] and
there was also another small light infantry unit known as the Corsican
Rangers (209), commanded by Major Hudson Lowe.

Adding to its diversity, the Reserve also included two small cavalry
units; one was a single reinforced troop of the 11th Dragoons, mustering
five officers, two sergeants, one trumpeter and fifty-three men. This had
been solicited by Abercromby before setting out for the Mediterranean
presumably in order to provide him with a source of orderlies. The
other unit, which had also joined more or less accidentally, was a
detachment of a small foreign corps, Hompesch's Light Dragoons or
Hussars, numbering 138 troopers under Major Robert Wilson, who had
originally been attached to the abortive Isle de Houat expedition.[14]

Reference is also made in the returns to an eighty-strong Staff
Corps, although it properly belonged to the Quartermaster General's
Department. Its British officers were trained as engineers, while the
rank and file probably belonged to a rather ephemeral unit otherwise
known as the Maltese Pioneers.[15]

Cavalry
The two small mounted units attached to the Reserve were obviously
totally inadequate as a cavalry force, and the original intention appears
to have been to rely upon the Turks to supply the deficiency, but
when the expeditionary force in Portugal was withdrawn, Pulteney
was ordered to send the two cavalry regiments there to reinforce the
Egyptian expedition. They joined on 12 January, by which time the
army was already at Marmaris.

The two regiments were the 12th Light Dragoons and the 26th Light
Dragoons, commanded by Lieutenant Colonel Mervyn Archdall and
Lieutenant Colonel Robert Gordon respectively. The 12th mustered
474 troopers, besides officers and NCOs on 7 March 1801, while the
26th had 369. Unfortunately, they had arrived without horses and as
those initially offered by the Turks were useless, local purchasing had
to be resorted to that eventually saw most of them mounted on sturdy
little Anatolian ponies. Unfortunately, as we have seen, most of the
horse transports temporarily went astray during the voyage to Egypt,

which meant that both regiments could still field only a single mounted squadron apiece on their first landing. The rest therefore served as infantry in the early part of the campaign.

Royal Artillery

As to the artillery, this was directed by Brigadier General Robert Lawson.[16] Born in about 1741, Lawson was an intelligent and innovative officer, who among other things had been responsible for the organisation and training of the original Royal Horse Artillery troop and would exercise some considerable ingenuity and energy in overcoming the manifold difficulties that lay ahead.

He and Lieutenant Colonel Henry Thompson took a total of twenty-four light 6-pounders, four light 12-pounders, twelve medium 12-pounders and six 5½in howitzers to Egypt, together with a suitable siege train, manned by the 13th, 14th, 26th, 28th, 55th, 69th, 70th 71st companies of the Royal Artillery, totalling twenty-five officers, ten sergeants and nine drummers, together with 557 gunners and seventy-two members of the Horse Department.

The siege train as originally embarked comprised four iron 12-pounders, twenty 24-pounders, two 10in and ten 8in howitzers, eighteen 5½in, ten 8in and twelve 10in mortars. In the event, a desperate shortage of horses to draw even the field guns saw Lawson borrowing Naval carronades as a lighter substitute for some of the larger pieces.

The French Army

French line infantry and light infantry regiments were properly designated *Demi-brigades de Bataille* or *Demi-brigades de Légére* respectively. For convenience, we will anticipate later practice by identifying them simply as (No.) *Ligne* and (No.) *Légére*. Officially both types of unit comprised three battalions apiece, each with an establishment of eight companies of fusiliers and one of grenadiers (or carabiniers in light infantry units), although the latter were often detached and grouped into scrappily small provisional battalions. The odd term 'demi-brigade' itself derives from the fact that in the French army of the Ancien Regime infantry brigades had normally fielded *four* battalions, rather than the present three battalions established in 1793.[17]

As outlined in the previous chapter, the French army in Egypt was initially organised into five divisions of uneven size, each of which was responsible for a different sector of the country as described in a set of

154

tables presented as an appendix to Reynier's narrative.[18] The numbers attached to each unit were dated to 1 March 1801 but while there might have been some variation a week later, they will be substantially correct for the opening of the campaign.

Friant's Division

As it turned out of course, the critical sector was going to be on the west side of the Delta, where *General de Division* Louis Friant was in command at Alexandria. Defending this particular sector was shaped by the need to cover a number of key points. The all-important port of Alexandria itself had a permanent static garrison of 2,350 troops assigned to it, including small detachments holding the outlying coastal castles at Aboukir and Marabout, and in addition another 450 artillerymen and miners were scattered between the nearby towns of Rosetta (and the neighbouring Fort Julien), Bourlos and Rahmanieh.

That particular dispersal was unavoidable, but Reynier's detailed list shows Friant's own mobile division, comprising three demi-brigades of infantry, backed up by two regiments of dragoons, and totalling something over 2,000 men, was not only just as scattered but it was also rather jumbled into the bargain:

> *25e Ligne* had 580 men stationed at Rahmanieh; but there were also 100 men detached to the Rosetta garrison and another 230 men detached to the central reserve in Cairo.
> *61e Ligne* had 750 men at Alexandria and 150 more at Rosetta.
> *75e Ligne* had a very respectable 950 men at Alexandria but once again a detachment of 80 men was posted at Rosetta.

In addition, 200 men of *51e Ligne* (and a reported 600 artillerymen) had just arrived from France, running through the blockade aboard the frigate *Régénérée* only a few days before.

As for Friant's cavalry, all 150 mounted and seventy-five dismounted troopers of *18e Dragoons* were stationed at Alexandria, but *3e Dragoons* were split up with 150 mounted and thirty dismounted men at Rosetta, and another seventy-five men up in Cairo.

Rampon's Division

Similarly, and despite its supposed importance, the neighbouring Damietta sector on the east side of the Nile Delta was assigned to *General de Division* Antoine-Guillaume Rampon with a rather weak division notionally comprising just two demi-brigades of infantry and a single cavalry regiment:

20e Dragoons	213 mounted and 60 dismounted
2e Légére	540 in the Damietta area
32e Ligne	542 in the Damietta area

In addition, there were 530 artillerymen and miners stationed in Damietta itself and another 462 men drawn from both demi-brigades back at Cairo.

Reynier's Division

By contrast, *General de Division* Jean-Louis Reynier,[19] who was reluctantly assigned to cover the anticipated appearance of the Grand Vizier and his Turkish host on the Sinai front, had a full division under his command comprising four demi-brigades and a regiment of dragoons amounting to a total of 245 mounted cavalry and 3,300 infantry:

14e Dragoons	245 & 67 dismounted
9e Ligne	894
13e Ligne	841
85e Ligne	890
22e Légére	744

However, at the outset apart from about 200 artillerymen and miners scattered between Salahieh, Suez and Belbeis, and a couple of battalions of *22e Légére* posted well forward to serve as a tripwire, nearly all of them, including the sixty-seven dismounted cavalrymen belonging to the *14e Dragoons*, were actually positioned in Cairo.

Donzelot's Division

To the south, *General de Brigade* François-Xavier Donzelot was posted in Upper Egypt with just a single demi-brigade, the *21e Légére*, comprising 1,650 men, and another 110 artillerymen and miners. He was tasked along with Murād Bey (who had accepted the post of governor under the French regime!) with watching for any threat from the south, although in this case that was initially more likely to come from local Bedouin and other dissidents rather than from the British Army and the East India Company.

Reserve

The dedicated core of this reserve or *mass de manoeuvre* was a weak cavalry brigade under *General de Brigade* César-Antoine Roize, and no fewer than four demi-brigades of infantry under *General de Division* Francois Lanusse, numbering a total of 600 mounted cavalry and 3,326 infantry, viz:

7e (bis) Hussards[20]	240 and 30 dismounted
22e Chasseur a Cheval	230 and 40 dismounted
15e Dragoons	129 and 52 dismounted
4e Ligne	790
18e Ligne	790
69e Ligne	959
88e Ligne	883

These were marching units and there were also in addition another 2,600 artillery and security troops serving in Cairo itself, and although it was obviously not contemplated that they would be available for field operations, they freed the reserve from any immediate responsibility for the city.

Appendix 2

The British Army in Egypt

This appendix is intended to summarise the known information about each regiment serving in Egypt, including details of service, uniform and equipment.

All infantrymen (other than Highlanders) wore short red jackets, white knee-breeches, black calf-length black gaiters and cylindrical black caps. Since 1798 the jacket had been single breasted with a stand-up collar and plain round cuffs in the regimental facing colour and a double row of lace down the front. The shoulder straps were also in the facing colour and terminated in a tuft of white worsted, although the flank companies were distinguished by crescent-shaped wings. The lining and jacket turnbacks were white.

Highlanders were, of course, distinguished by the wearing of kilts, chequered hose and feathered bonnets. There is no evidence of any variations acknowledging the climate.[1]

Equipment comprised a firelock musket and bayonet – mainly at this date the 42in barrelled Short Land Pattern – and two whitened buff leather cross-belts, one carrying a black leather cartridge box on the right hip and the other supporting the bayonet in a scabbard on the left. A canvas knapsack was normally carried on the back, but in Egypt this was as far as possible left with the transport and a blanket, with a spare shirt rolled inside slung diagonally instead. In addition, a linen haversack for rations and a wooden canteen for water were issued as 'camp equipage'.

The clothing situation was, however, complicated by distance and circumstances. In theory new clothing was issued in the summer of each year, but for various reasons Abercromby's regiments did not receive their 1800 issue on time. A quantity of clothing supposedly arrived while the army was at Marmaris but comments on the state of the soldiers' boots and clothing as the campaign went on raises doubts as to just how much was actually delivered.

It should also be noted that certain variations in clothing styles were traditional in hot stations. Loutherbourg's well-known paintings of the campaign certainly depict round hats being universally worn by officers, but there is evidence they were also worn by many rank and file, and those units earlier serving in the Mediterranean were probably wearing loose linen pantaloons or trousers, as recommended by Abercromby on Minorca.

Besides the round hats, and the wearing of calf-length boots, officers were normally distinguished by their swords, epaulettes and a crimson silk net sash around the waist and by the wearing of double-breasted scarlet tailcoats of a much brighter shade than that used for the rank and file. A short-lived single-breasted jacket had been introduced in 1797, but although it should have been discontinued by the end of 1798, there is evidence that it continued to be worn in hot stations.

All infantry regiments each carried two colours; the King's colour, which was a Union flag with the regiment's badge or number in the centre, surrounded by a 'Union wreath' of roses and thistles, the second was the regimental one displaying the facing colour with the Union flag confined to the canton. It should be noted that while the union of Britain and Ireland took effect from 1 January 1801, adding St Patrick's cross to the Union flag, there is no evidence that the old colours carried by the British regiments in Egypt were replaced until after the campaign.

Light Dragoon regiments did not carry guidons on active service – a reflection of their role.

Cavalry uniforms were quite different from those worn by the infantry, consisting of a dark blue dolman or hussar jacket with white cords across the front, white or buff buckskin breeches, and calf-length riding boots, the whole being topped with a bearskin-crested Tarleton helmet.

Equipment comprised a narrow buff leather belt around the waist, from which was suspended a 1796 pattern sabre in a plain steel scabbard. A buff leather sling-belt over the left shoulder carried a black leather cartridge box on the back and a clip for the carbine, which at this date will have been the 28in barrel Elliott pattern.

NB: British cavalry in Egypt spent a substantial period dismounted. When serving as infantry, shoes will have been substituted for riding boots, with ankle gaiters, and their sabres and carbines temporarily exchanged for borrowed Sea Service muskets that generally had a 36–37in barrel, but were otherwise very similar to infantry ones.

The Regiments: Infantry

Footguards

The Footguards contributed two service battalions to the Egypt expedition; one each from the 2nd or Coldstream Guards and the 3rd (or Scots) Guards. Both were at the Helder in 1799 and on the Ferrol expedition in the following year before joining Abercromby. They were unique among the Egypt regiments in each receiving drafts of reinforcements during the campaign.

Facings were dark blue and officers had broad gold lace and appointments. The two regiments were distinguished one from another by their buttons, which were placed in twos for the Coldstream and in threes for the 3rd Footguards.

2/1st (or Royal) Regiment of Foot

The Royals, or Royal Scots as they officially became in 1812, were the oldest corps in the British Army and had always mustered two battalions, albeit they had entirely separate service histories. 1/1st began the war in garrison on Jamaica and over the next four years was gradually destroyed on St Domingue. The 2/1st, on the other hand, started off on Gibraltar and served at Toulon and then on Corsica before briefly returning home to serve at the Helder and then back to the Mediterranean via Ferrol.

In Egypt it served first in Coote's 1st Brigade and then, as of 9 August 1801, in Finch's 2nd Brigade.

As a Royal regiment, it had dark blue facings, while officers had gold lace and by way of a regimental peculiarity carried broadswords with the regulation 1796 pattern hilt.

2nd (or the Queen's Royal) Regiment of Foot

The Queen's history since the outbreak of war was tangled. Almost at the outset they were put aboard the Channel Fleet to serve as marines and were not set ashore again until November 1794. At that point most of the regiment, designated as 2/2nd Queen's, was sent to the West Indies, although a nucleus of two companies designated 1/2nd Queen's remained behind as a depot. Eventually the two were reunited as one battalion in October 1797 and served in Ireland in the following year, then at the Helder in 1799, then the abortive Belle Isle expedition and finally the Mediterranean.

In Egypt it served in Doyle's 4th Brigade before transferring to the Reserve in the 9 August reorganisation.

160

Again, as a Royal regiment, it had dark blue facings, but the officers had silver lace and appointments.

8th (or the King's) Regiment of Foot
The 8th had served in Flanders at the beginning of the war and then under Abercromby in the West Indies before being assigned to serve as part of the Minorca garrison, where Sir Ralph encountered it again and insisted on taking it to Egypt.

There it served first with the 2nd Brigade under Cradock and then from 9 August in Hope's 4th Brigade.

It had dark blue facings and gold lace for officers.

10th (or the North Lincolnshire) Regiment of Foot
Serving in the Bengal Presidency, the 10th under Lieutenant Colonel Richard Quarrell, embarked in Saugor Roads for Egypt, landing at Kosseir on 15 June, afterwards marching across the desert and being carried in boats down the Nile to Alexandria. On the conclusion of the campaign it returned home via Malta.

Facings were light yellow with silver lace and appointments for officers. However, coming from India white pantaloons will have been worn rather than breeches and gaiters, and almost certainly round hats rather than caps.

13th (or the 1st Somersetshire) Regiment of Foot
The 13th began the war by immediately being sent from garrison on Jamaica to St Domingue without first being brought up to strength. There they fought well in a number of small-unit actions that offered little or no opportunity to follow David Dundas' teaching, but did call for much use of loose files and American scramble. Inevitably, disease and exhaustion took their toll and only sixty rank and file remained by the time the battalion embarked for home in August 1797. Sent to Ireland to recover, the regiment was still too weak for service when the rebellion broke out there in the following year, but afterwards it was brought up to strength with volunteers from the Irish Militia, and once reckoned fit for service again was ordered first to join Pulteney's expedition to Ferrol and then to go to Egypt under Lieutenant Colonel the Hon. Charles Colville.

The regiment went ashore with Cradock's 2nd Brigade but became so sickly in the camp outside Alexandria that it had to be assigned to garrison duty at Rosetta.

The regiment had yellow facings with silver lace for the officers.

18th (or the Royal Irish) Regiment of Foot

At the outset of the war the regiment was on Gibraltar and from there went first to Toulon and then to Corsica, before returning to Gibraltar via a spell on Elba. A search of the *Army List* reveals that, unlike many of Abercromby's regiments, they had experienced no great turnover in personnel, and if anything, the officers were rather older and more settled than the general run. As a result, they must have been a very close-knit regiment, very probably tightly drilled and disciplined.

It served first with the 2nd Brigade under Cradock and then from 9 August in Hope's 4th Brigade.

As a Royal regiment, it had dark blue facings and gold lace for officers.

20th (or the East Devonshire) Regiment of Foot

This was not part of the original expeditionary force and its two battalions were actually limited service units, but they both arrived from the Minorca garrison on 18 July and were assigned to the newly-formed 6th Brigade on 9 August.

Facings were pale yellow and for officers, lace and appointments were silver.

23rd Regiment of Foot (or the Royal Welch Fusiliers)

The 23rd Fusiliers had gone to the West Indies in 1794 and as usual, only a skeleton returned. It was then rebuilt, largely with militia recruits, but suffered heavily both at the Helder and in a subsequent shipwreck. Notwithstanding, the survivors went to Belle Isle, Ferrol and then to the Mediterranean temporarily commanded by Major James Mackenzie, although Lieutenant Colonel John Hall led the regiment in Egypt, where it served with the Reserve.

As a Royal regiment, it had dark blue facings with gold lace for officers. As a fusilier regiment, all soldiers had grenadier-style wings on their shoulders and in full dress had bearskin caps. It is unlikely that they had them in Egypt but it should be noted that they do appear in Loutherbourg's paintings.

24th (or the Warwickshire) Regiment of Foot

This was not part of the original expeditionary force but arrived from England on 14 July and was assigned to the newly formed 6th Brigade on 9 August.

Facings were willow green and for officers lace and appointments were silver.

25th (or the Sussex) Regiment of Foot
Another reinforcement regiment, arriving in front of Alexandria on 9 July and assigned to Ludlow's 1st Brigade a month later. Despite its title, it was a Scottish regiment.

Facings were deep yellow with gold lace and appointments for officers.

26th (or Cameronian) Regiment of Foot
Not to be confused with the 79th (Cameronian Volunteers), this was another reinforcement regiment, arriving with the 25th in front of Alexandria on 9 July and assigned to Finch's 2nd Brigade a month later.

Facings were pale yellow with silver lace and appointments for officers.

27th (or Inniskilling) Regiment of Foot
The Inniskillings had been recruited up to two battalions by taking volunteers from the Irish Militia and were involved in the Ferrol fiasco. As discussed in the text, they were very sickly and at first both battalions were hospitalised on Malta and at Lisbon respectively. However, 2/27th (less three companies set ashore on Malta) did catch up with the army in time to fight at Mandara with Cavan's 3rd Brigade, but the regiment was not fully reunited until 10 May. In the 9 August reorganisation both battalions went to Ludlow's 1st Brigade.

Facings were deep buff. Ordinarily this also meant that buff-coloured breeches were worn and accoutrements were also buff rather than white.

28th (or the North Gloucestershire) Regiment of Foot
The 28th under Colonel the Hon. Edward Paget began the war by going to Flanders and then, while six companies went to the West Indies, the other four went to Gibraltar. Reunited in 1797, it took part in the capture of Minorca and remained as part of the island's garrison until joining Abercromby.

In Egypt it formed part of the Reserve, but was temporarily detached on 9 June to go up the Nile, before returning to the Reserve afterwards.

Facings were yellow with silver lace for officers.

30th (or the Cambridgeshire) Regiment of Foot
The 30th Regiment, commanded by Major William Lockhart, was embarked as marines with the Mediterranean Fleet at the start of the war and took part in the defence of Toulon and the occupation of Corsica. Inevitably, it became somewhat fractured in the process but was pulled

together again in Ireland before returning to the Mediterranean, first on Minorca and Sicily, and then to Malta to take part in the blockade of Valletta.

In Egypt the regiment served throughout under Doyle, in the 4th Brigade, which then became the 5th Brigade under the 9 August reorganisation.

Facings were pale yellow with silver lace for officers.

42nd (or the Royal Highland) Regiment of Foot

The 42nd Highlanders led by Lieutenant Colonel William Dickson had a good war, beginning in Flanders, and then was split with five companies going to the West Indies and five to Gibraltar. As usual, there were heavy losses in the Caribbean, but when recalled these were offset by taking a substantial draft from the 79th – much to Cameron of Erracht's disgust. Afterwards it went to Minorca before being selected for Egypt.

In Egypt it formed part of the Reserve, but was temporarily detached on 9 June to go up the Nile, before returning to the Reserve afterwards.

The 42nd had dark blue facings and gold lace for officers. David Stewart is positive that Highland dress was worn in Egypt, ie a feathered bonnet with a red hackle, and a kilt that at this period will have still borne a red over-stripe on the standard army or 'Black Watch' tartan, but sporrans were not worn on active service. Officers wore short double-breasted jackets and carried broadswords with brass basket hilts.

44th (or the East Essex) Regiment of Foot

The 44th also had an active war, serving in Flanders and in the West Indies before going to the Gibraltar garrison in 1798, from where they were hurriedly plucked by Abercromby as one of the few available general service units.

In Egypt it was originally part of Doyle's 4th Brigade but the 9 August reorganisation saw it transferred to Ludlow's 1st Brigade.

Facings were yellow with silver lace for officers.

50th (or the West Kent) Regiment of Foot

The 50th, commanded by Lieutenant Colonel Benjamin Rowe, was another Mediterranean regiment, which had begun the war at Gibraltar, where it had been in garrison for nearly ten years, and then taken part in the capture of Corsica in 1794. Since then it had been briefly on Elba before spending the last two years in Portugal.

In Egypt it served in Cavan's 3rd Brigade and then from 9 August in Doyle's 5th Brigade.

Facings were black with gold lace for officers. On the regimental colour the black field was relieved by a red cross overall.

54th (or the West Norfolk) Regiment of Foot
The 54th went to the West Indies and then to Ireland to recover, where sufficient volunteers were entered from Irish militia units to reorganise the regiment into two battalions, one commanded by Colonel Christopher Darby and the other by Lieutenant Colonel John Layard.[2] Immediately prior to going to the Mediterranean, it was at Ferrol.

In Egypt both battalions served in Coote's 1st Brigade and then from 9 August in Finch's 2nd Brigade.

Facings were yellowish green with silver lace for officers.

58th (or the Rutlandshire) Regiment of Foot
Lieutenant Colonel William Houston's 58th Regiment was another of the battalions that went to the West Indies and then, having been rebuilt, went to the Mediterranean to help take Minorca.

It served throughout the Egyptian campaign in the Reserve.

Facings were black with gold lace for officers. On the regimental colour the black field was relieved by a red cross overall.

61st (or South Gloucestershire) Regiment of Foot
The 61st was serving in South Africa when the campaign began, and was ordered to the Red Sea, where it formed a part of Major General Baird's Anglo-Indian army.

Facings were a yellowish buff. Ordinarily this also meant that buff-coloured breeches were worn and accoutrements were also buff rather than white. However, a remarkable pair of watercolours by Private William Porter shows the whole regiment wearing round hats – except for the grenadiers and drummers in bearskin caps! – and loose white trousers, or white breeches in the case of the officers. Belts also appear to be white rather than buff.[3]

79th Regiment of Foot (or Cameronian Volunteers)
The 79th or Cameronian Volunteers are not to be confused with the 26th (Cameronian) Regiment. The second new regiment to be raised at the beginning of the war, it found itself hurriedly shipped to Flanders with just one officer to a company and five rounds of ammunition a man. Having survived that particular baptism of fire, it then spent two years

165

on Martinique, but was rebuilt in time to go to the Helder in 1799 and Ferrol before joining the Egyptian expedition.

Despite its later reputation, the regiment did not enjoy good relations with the other Highland regiments in Egypt. There was a feud between the Camerons and the Gordons stretching back to their first raising, which had been revived when the two regiments were brigaded together at the Helder and was serious enough for care to be taken to separate them in Egypt. Similarly, when the 79th were ordered home after serving in the West Indies under Abercromby, the general had ordered the rank and fire to be drafted into the 42nd – a move bitterly resented by Erracht, who was already on bad terms with him.

In Egypt therefore, the regiment first served with Cavan's 3rd Brigade and then from 9 August with Hope's 4th Brigade.

The 79th had dark green facings and gold lace for officers. David Stewart is positive that Highland dress was worn in Egypt, ie a feathered bonnet with a white over red hackle, and a kilt of the regiment's unique 'Cameron of Erracht' tartan, but sporrans were not worn on active service. Officers wore short double-breasted jackets and carried broadswords with brass basket hilts.

80th Regiment of Foot (or Staffordshire Volunteers)
Raised in 1793, the 80th had taken part in the seizure of the Cape of Good Hope in 1796, after which it was transferred to Ceylon (Sri Lanka) before joining the Anglo-Indian expeditionary force to Egypt. Two companies under Lieutenant Colonel Josiah Champagne turned back and the regiment was commanded in Egypt by Lieutenant Colonel William Ramsay. After the campaign the regiment returned to India.

Facings were yellow with gold lace and appointments for officers. However, coming from India white pantaloons will have been worn rather than breeches and gaiters, and almost certainly round hats rather than caps.

86th Regiment of Foot
Raised in 1793, it initially served as marines before going to the Cape of Good Hope in 1796 and then to India in 1799, first in Madras and then Bombay. A wing of the regiment, comprising three companies under Lieutenant Colonel James Lloyd, was embarked from there by Admiral Blankett to secure Suez and subsequently marched across the desert to join Hutchinson's army outside Cairo. Another wing, again of three companies, under Captain George Middlemore, formed part of Baird's Anglo-Indian expeditionary force.

Facings were yellow with silver lace and appointments for officers. However, as related in the text, Lloyd's wing burned their uniforms after an outbreak of plague at Jeddah, and may have adopted Arab dress – Wilson states that 'their appearance excited great interest'.[4]

88th Regiment of Foot (or Connaught Rangers)
Raised in 1793 and served in Flanders and the West Indies before going to Bombay in 1799 and then to Egypt as part of Baird's expeditionary force.

Facings were yellow with gold lace and appointments for officers. However, coming from India white pantaloons will have been worn rather than breeches and gaiters, and almost certainly round hats rather than caps.

89th Regiment of Foot
The 89th Regiment under Lieutenant Colonel William Stewart was raised in Dublin at the start of the war and immediately pitched into the Flanders debacle. Afterwards it returned to Ireland and gained a rather unsavoury reputation after the victory at Vinegar Hill in 1798. Since then it had been in the Mediterranean and latterly on Malta, taking part in the blockade of Valletta.

In Egypt the regiment served throughout under Doyle, first in the 4th Brigade, which then became the 5th Brigade under the 9 August reorganisation.

Facings were black with gold lace for officers. On the regimental colour the black field was relieved by a red cross overall.

90th Regiment of Foot (or the Perthshire Volunteers)
Raised in 1794, it was not only the highest numbered regiment to legitimately survive the great cull of 1796, but it was also a little different from the ordinary run. In the first place, it was the only regiment raised benorth the Forth at this time that was *not* designated a Highland one. Instead it was trained as light infantry and served first on the abortive Quiberon expedition in 1795 and then on Minorca before going to Egypt.

In Egypt it initially served with Cradock's 2nd Brigade and with effect from 9 August with Hope's 4th Division.

Facings were deep buff. Ordinarily this also meant that buff-coloured breeches were worn and accoutrements were also buff rather than white. As a light corps, wings appear to have been worn on the shoulders.

A 27 October 1801 order confirms that officers wore short jackets rather than tailcoats and had red waistcoats.[5] Appointments, including the fringing on wings, were silver but buttonholes were unlaced.

Headgear was usual. Officers had Tarleton-style helmets as worn by light dragoons, but the rank and file may have had round hats with a worsted crest resembling bearskin.

92nd Regiment of Foot

Raised in 1794 as the One Hundredth Regiment of Foot, the Gordon Highlanders narrowly escaped drafting two years later thanks to political influence and the convenient excuse that it was serving at Gibraltar at the time![6] Subsequently the regiment served in Ireland in 1798, at the Helder and then Ferrol.

In Egypt the Gordons first served in Coote's 1st Brigade and then from 9 August with Doyle's 5th Brigade.

The 92nd had light yellow facings and silver lace for officers. David Stewart is positive that Highland dress was worn in Egypt, ie a feathered bonnet with a white over red hackle, and a kilt of the standard army tartan with a yellow over-stripe, but sporrans were not worn on active service.

Officers wore short double-breasted jackets and carried broadswords with brass basket hilts.

Ancient Irish Fencibles

Raised on 4 June 1799 and liable for limited service anywhere in Europe, it was assigned to Minorca garrison, taking part in Abercromby's training exercise in late 1800. On Hutchinson's appealing for reinforcements it was sent by Fox to Egypt. Legally, this could only be done if the men volunteered, but Stewart of the 42nd declared that they were not given the opportunity to do so.[7] Arriving at Aboukir on 18 July, they were assigned to the newly formed 6th Brigade on 9 August.

There appears to be no surviving information as to uniforms, although yellow facings were common among Irish regiments during this period. Hats are referred to by Stewart and linen pantaloons were presumably also worn.

Marines

The Marine battalion, commanded by Lieutenant Colonel Walter Smith, was landed to fill the deficit in Cavan's brigade arising from the need to leave behind both battalions of the 27th Regiment, but the provisional battalion's lack of expertise in manoeuvring proved to be a liability at Mandara and it was eventually sent back to undertake garrison duties at Aboukir.

Ordinary infantry uniform, accoutrements and equipment, with white facings and gold lace and appointments for officers. Due to the inevitable delays involved, a mixture of uniform styles may have been worn in Egypt with some ship's companies wearing single-breasted short jackets while others may still have had the older long-tailed coat with lapels. Round hats were worn by all ranks. Home-based divisions included grenadier and light companies but there is no evidence they were formed in Egypt.

Foreign Regiments

Chasseurs Britanniques

Not part of the original expeditionary force. This regiment was formed in May 1801 from the remnants of units belonging to a body of *emigres* led by the Prince de Conde. Although at one time in Russian pay, it latterly served alongside the Austrian Army before being disbanded after the Peace of Luneville in February 1801. Some, however, were taken into British pay as the *Chasseurs Britanniques*. Hastily shipped from Trieste in June and then after a stopover on Malta, arrived in Egypt on 3 August and assigned a few days later to the Reserve.

Details of the uniform at this time are unclear. They certainly had green jackets but sources differ as to whether these had half-lapels and whether the facings were black or yellow. Caps and grey pantaloons are also said to have been worn.[8]

Corsican Rangers

Formed on Minorca in 1799 from the numerous refugees and French emigres who had accompanied the British forces on the evacuation of Corsica in October 1796.

In Egypt the regiment served throughout as part of the Reserve.

The uniform of this small but useful corps is unclear. According to a contemporary uniform chart, they had red jackets with yellow facings, which was the uniform of their predecessor corps, the Corsican Regiment. A sketch, said to date from the Egyptian campaign depicts a quite different uniform of a green jacket with black facings, grey pantaloons and a cylindrical cap, although the sketch may actually depict a member of the Swiss regiment De Watteville, which certainly did wear that uniform.

Edward Dillon's Regiment

This had no direct connection with the old Irish regiment in the French service, but was raised in northern Italy in 1795 from an eclectic mix of French, Italians, Germans and deserters from everyone else's army.

Served in Italy, Elba and Portugal before going to Egypt, where it served in Stuart's Foreign Brigade.

Ordinary British uniform: Red coats with yellow facings and silver lace for officers. May have worn caps but round hats seem more likely.

Hompesch Hussars

One of a number of mercenary units recruited in Germany by the Hompesch family with a confusing history. The original regiment was raised in the Dusseldorf area by Karl von Hompesch in 1794 and after service on the Continent went to the West Indies, where it was effectively wiped out by fever on St Domingue. The unit that served in Egypt was raised by Karl's younger brother, Ferdinand, in 1796 as a light infantry unit, but included a mounted element. When the infantry went to the West Indies the mounted chasseurs remained in Britain and were augmented to four troops now referred to as Hompesch's Mounted Riflemen. The unit then served in Ireland in 1798 and in July 1800 a detachment commanded by Major Robert Wilson sailed with Pulteney first to Ferrol and then to the Mediterranean. There Wilson consistently referred to them as Hussars, perhaps because the fourth troop added in the 1798 augmentation may have been formed around the remnants of Frederick von Hompesch's Hussars. Following the desertion of three troopers, the unit was dismounted and assigned to garrison duties at Aboukir. A little poignantly, the 13 September return records that the two trumpeters present when the detachment landed in Egypt had been replaced by a single drummer.

A watercolour by William Loftie shows an officer wearing a green jacket turned up with red, including false lapels, red breeches and a red cap with gold lace. Horse furniture was green with red trim. It is, however, clearly identified as Hompesch's Mounted Riflemen. If Wilson's men were indeed Hussars, they will have worn green dolmans with red facings and white cords, and green pelisses with white cords and black fur trim.

Löwenstein's Jäger

One of a number of units raised by another military contractor named Karl, Prince von Löwenstein-Wertheim. The first, known as Löwenstein's Chasseurs or Jägers, was originally in the Dutch service but passed into British pay in April 1795 and went to the West Indies, as did Löwenstein's Fusiliers, raised in 1796. Both regiments were eventually absorbed into the 5/60th Regiment. Another, quite separate regiment, was raised chiefly in Bavaria in 1800 and after the Peace of Luneburg was evacuated, with Watteville's and the *Chasseurs Britanniques*, through Trieste to Malta and then on to Egypt, where it served with the reserve.[9]

The uniform is unclear. A contemporary illustration shows the original regiment, which was taken into British service in 1795 wearing bluish grey jackets with dark green facings displayed on collar, cuffs, turnbacks and half-lapels. Secondary sources give this same uniform to the later regiment, but there is no evidence for this. Instead it is possible that it wore the same uniform (and for the same reason) as Watteville's and the *Chasseurs Britanniques*. Unlike those units, however, it was armed with rifles rather than common firelocks.

Roll's Regiment
Nominally a Swiss regiment, originally recruited in 1794 by Baron Louis de Roll, a former officer of the Swiss Guard in France. As was often the case, a substantial number of men were actually found in Germany and Alsace. Most of its service was in the Mediterranean, then in Portugal before joining the forces assembling on Minorca. Served in Egypt in Stuart's Foreign Brigade.

British-style uniform: Red coats with sky blue facings and silver lace for officers. Sketched wearing round hats and pantaloons in Egypt.

Stuart's Minorca Regiment
This had an unusual origin. Having captured Minorca in 1798, Sir Charles Stuart proceeded to raise a regiment from among the numerous Swiss troops found in the surrendered Spanish garrison. They were in fact nothing of the sort, being mostly Germans captured from the Austrians by the French in Italy and trafficked to the Spaniards, reputedly at two dollars a head.[10] Commanded in Egypt by Lieutenant Colonel Dutons, they evidently found the British service a good deal more congenial, gained a good reputation and were eventually taken into the line as the Queen's own German Regiment in 1802 and renamed the 97th (Queen's own Germans) in January 1805.[11]

Ordinary British uniform: Red coats with yellow facings and silver lace for officers. May have worn caps but round hats seem more likely.

Watteville's Regiment
Newly formed on 1 May from the remnants of various Swiss regiments in British pay that had been serving with the Austrian army. Hastily shipped

from Trieste in June and then after a stopover on Malta, arrived in Egypt on 3 August and assigned a few days later to Stuart's Foreign Brigade.

At this stage the regiment was still wearing the same uniforms it had in Germany; green single-breasted jackets of Austrian cut, with black facings, sky-blue Hungarian pantaloons and Austrian caps.[12]

Indian Regiments

The East India Company's Native infantry units had short red jackets with narrow lapels, but turbans and *jangheas* (drawers) varied in style according to the Presidency of origin.

1st Bombay Native Infantry

Red jacket worn open to expose white shirt, with orange facings displayed on collar, cuffs, lapels and turnbacks. White knee-length *jangheas* (drawers), tall dark blue sugar-loaf shaped turban with brass front plate similar to Prussian fusiliers, bearing regimental number and edged with facing colour fringe.

7th Bombay Native Infantry

As above but pea-green facings.

Bengal Volunteers

Red jacket as above; all Bengal Native Infantry regiments at this time had yellow facings. Despite its diverse origins, this unit will therefore have presented a relatively uniform appearance.

However, *jangheas* were very short indeed and bore unrecorded regimental distinctions in blue. Turbans were dark blue but very low and broad, sometimes referred to as 'sundial' turbans and not unlike a Basque beret in outline and size.

Cavalry
8th Light Dragoons

Served in Flanders at the start of the war and then to the Cape in 1796. From there a troop was sent north by sea to Egypt to join with Baird's Anglo-Indian army, but like the rest of that force, it arrived in Rosetta too late for service, other than the rounding up shoals of deserters from the French army making their way south to join with the *Mamlūks*.

The regiment's uniform was a tropical one, unique in Egypt, introduced in January 1796. The dark blue dolman was replaced by a version in French grey (actually a light blue shade) with red facings, and the Tarleton helmet by a tin version, with a red horsehair crest in

172

place of the heavy bearskin one. The regiment's Irish Harp badge was placed on the front.[13]

11th Light Dragoons
Served in Flanders at the beginning of the war and then at the Helder in 1799, before Abercromby made a direct appeal to the Duke of York for a detachment to accompany him to the Mediterranean. As a result, a reinforced troop commanded by Captain-Lieutenant Archibald Money went with him to Minorca and eventually five officers, two sergeants, one trumpeter and fifty-three men would go ashore at Aboukir as part of the reserve – all of them mounted.[14]

Distinguished by buff facings and breeches.

12th Light Dragoons
The regiment had been serving in Portugal, but on the decision being taken to withdraw Pulteney's contingent, both the 12th and 26th were added to Abercromby's expeditionary force as a brigade under Brigadier General the Honourable Edward Finch. In fact, a shortage of horses meant that initially, although Lieutenant Colonel Mervyn Archdall mustered 474 troopers on 7 March 1801, only a single squadron of 124 men could be mounted in each and the rest at first served as infantry until horses were procured little by little.

Distinguished by yellow facings.

22nd Light Dragoons
Raised in 1794 and disbanded in 1802, so not to be confused with the later 22nd Light Dragoons who served in the Peninsula. Sent out directly from Ireland as a reinforcement, arriving without horses on 24 July and seeing no action.

A watercolour sketch by William Loftie depicts an officer wearing a blue dolman with black facings and silver cords, blue breeches, and a leopard-skin turban on his Tarleton helmet.

26th Light Dragoons
Raised in 1794, the regiment served in the West Indies and in Portugal before being sent to Egypt. Lieutenant Colonel Robert Gordon landed with 369 troopers at Aboukir but only 124 were mounted at that time. It should be noted that as a result of the inevitable reductions in the military establishment at the war's end, the 26th Light Dragoons became the 23rd Light Dragoons in 1803 and were disbanded in 1817.

Distinguished by dark blue facings.

Other Units and Departments

General officers wore double-breasted scarlet tailcoats with dark blue facings (collars were red with a dark blue patch on either side) and gold lace and appointments. Usually, plain coats without gold lace were worn on service. Senior staff officers, ie quartermaster generals and adjutant generals, wore the same but with silver lace.

Junior staff, including officers of the Staff Corps, had single-breasted coats, which were usually plain and unlaced on service. Aides-de-Camp also had single-breasted coats and were distinguished by a single gilt epaulette on the left shoulder.[15]

All staff officers in Egypt wore round hats.

The Royal Artillery wore the same uniform as the infantry, except that coats and jackets were dark blue, faced with red. Officers had gold lace and appointments and the rank and file had yellow lace. Accoutrements were white buff leather including cartridge boxes.

Round hats were worn by all officers, and probably by the rank and file of a number of companies serving in Mediterranean garrisons.

Royal Engineers officers wore blue coats with black facings. There were no rank and file at this time and officers' servants will therefore have been drawn from the Royal Artillery.

NB: the clothing worn by the officers and men of the Military Mission with the Grand Vizier's army may have been various as they were at least three years away from home, and Captain Leake for one wore 'Tartar' dress on occasion.

Appendix 3

The East India Company in Egypt

The campaign against the French in Egypt was waged from beginning to end by the Turks and their allies and by the British Army that General Abercromby had landed on the Mediterranean coast in March 1801, but there was also another British army, or more accurately an Anglo-Indian army, in Egypt. Regretfully, although this army exercised a certain influence on the campaign, despite its best efforts it did so only remotely and while its composition and its operations need to be recorded, it is best dealt with separately.

Major General David Baird was a competent and particularly determined commander, and if he was also renowned as an abrasive and sometimes foul-mouthed one, then his career provided ample justification. A Scot, born in East Lothian in 1757, he went out to India with what became the 71st Highlanders and in 1780 was wounded and captured at the battle of Pollilur. He then spent the next three years in captivity with a bullet lodged next to his spine – which was hardly calculated to improve anyone's temper. Promoted a major general in the brevet of 18 June 1798, he led the assault on Seringapatnam that killed the Tippoo Sultan and removed the threat to the East India Company that General Bonaparte had intended to exploit. Afterwards, however, Baird was denied the customary plum of being appointed governor of the city, and instead the post went to Colonel the Hon. Arthur Wellesley. Of itself, that was disappointment enough, but then when an expeditionary force was ordered to be sent to the Dutch East Indies at the end of 1800, Wellesley, who had the great good fortune to be a younger brother of the Governor General of British India, was nominated to have the command of what promised to be a lucrative conquest.[1] This blatant nepotism was going too far and under pressure from every senior officer in sight, the Governor

175

General eventually gave way and instead appointed Baird to the command on 24 January 1801.

What followed was something akin to the *Odyssey* played out on a grand scale. The first of the troops assigned to the expedition, HM 10th Regiment together with 1,200 volunteers from the Bengal Native Infantry and artillery,[2] embarked in Saugur Roads (the mouth of the Ganges) on 1 December 1800, and sailed five days later, but by the time they reached Ceylon (Sri Lanka) and the rendezvous at Trincomalee on 13 December, fresh orders had arrived from London, changing the destination to Egypt.

At this point, young Colonel Wellesley was still in charge of the expedition and on consulting with the Royal Navy and with the Company's sea officers, he was swiftly appraised that timing was now going to be critical. If the expeditionary force did not leave Aden for the 1,000-mile passage through the Red Sea to Suez by the middle of May, then the arrival of the annual monsoon winds would see them stuck there for months on end. Wellesley did not hesitate, he was due in any case to pick up both additional supplies and reinforcements from Bombay, and so he sailed north on 9 February. Not until twelve days later, while he was actually at sea, did he receive the news of his supersession – and resolved to keep going. Wellesley did at least send Baird a tactful letter of explanation, which the general received on arriving at Trincomalee, but Baird's temper must have been sorely tested as he set off in pursuit of his absent command. He finally caught up with it at Bombay on 3 April, and from there the transports, under the orders of Rear Admiral Sir Home Popham, proceeded in small divisions across the Persian Gulf to Aden and then up the Red Sea to Jeddah. This piecemeal despatch was necessary because the intricate and dangerous navigation of the coral reefs of the narrow Red Sea prevented the fleet sailing in a large body and so it was not until the end of the month that the last of the transports cleared Bombay – without Wellesley. The Irish aristocrat had gone down with an uncommonly bad case of the dreaded Malabar Itch and if Baird was disappointed, he betrayed no obvious sign of it. In any case, he soon had a far more serious problem to contend with than the loss of an unwanted second-in-command.[3]

The first of the divisions of transports reached Jeddah on the Arabian side of the Red Sea on 28 April, but by then they were too late, for the seasonal monsoon had set in. Battling constant headwinds and an occasional shipwreck, they next pushed up to Kosseir (Quseer) on the African side, where the first troops were landed on 21 May. It had taken three weeks to cover just 50 miles and at this point Baird acknowledged that making Suez at any time soon was an unrealistic prospect.

Nor, of course, could he remain at Kosseir indefinitely, but Admiral John Blankett turned up on 15 June with a despatch from Hutchinson, requesting him to join with the Grand Vizier in operations against Cairo. The news was by then well out of date, but Baird, ignorant that General Belliard was just a week away from surrendering the city, decided to march directly across the desert to strike the Nile at Kenneh (Quena) and then move north down the river.

From Kosseir the Indian army began its 120-mile march across the desert on 21 June. Although some of the transports were still missing, by this time Baird had assembled a total of 5,227 officers and men at Kosseir, together with another 439 lascars or native labourers. During the day the thermometer rose to 110 and even 115 degrees, but fortunately the Indian army was not only acclimatised but well-used to conducting operations in such arduous conditions and prepared for it accordingly. Some of the difficulties were overcome by marching at night in small detachments and at two of the wells Baird established depots of provisions, from which the troops were supplied with sheep and biscuits. Water was a bigger problem as some of the wells were separated by more than a day's march. There the gap was covered by relays of camels, laden with leather water bags, which accompanied each detachment to the next well and then returned again the next day to their post.

All in all, no more than fifteen men were lost during the march and afterwards Baird justifiably considered that conveying his army across the desert was one of his greatest achievements, but to his great disappointment, when he reached the Nile, he learned that Cairo had already fallen. At that point he immediately despatched an ADC down there to meet with Hutchinson and question the necessity for his continued presence in Egypt. The conquest of Batavia still beckoned and he was fully prepared to turn around, recross the desert and re-embark his men while the monsoon was still favourable to take him out of the Red Sea and across the Indian Ocean.

It was a reasonable enough proposal but to Baird's disappointment, Hutchinson insisted that he should still move down the Nile. In terms of manpower, the campaign was still being run on a shoestring, and although reinforcements were promised to be on their way, Baird's army was wanted to garrison Cairo (or at least Giza) after Hutchinson's men returned north and then to take over Rosetta and the other garrisons in the lower Delta in order to cover the rear of the forthcoming operations against Alexandria. Once the city had fallen, the Indian army was again intended to form its garrison while Hutchinson and the Mediterranean army sailed off to do the government's bidding elsewhere – wherever that might turn out to be.

While the final act was being played out, Baird and his men therefore waited at Cairo and by the time they were called forward, the Nile had risen by 10m and was in full flow so that when they again embarked on the boats, the strong current brought them all the way down to Rosetta in just three days.[4] It was 31 August and Brigadier General Hope was in Alexandria, putting his signature to the armistice. To his frustration, despite all his efforts Baird and his men had come late to the ball and were to play no active part in it.

The Indian army was organised into two infantry brigades, with artillery, engineers – and seventy-five largely dismounted troopers of the 8th Light Dragoons sent up from South Africa![5]

Indian Army, 24 August 1801

Right Brigade (Colonel William Carr Beresford)
10th Regiment	(854)
88th Regiment	(390)
Bengal Volunteers	(563)

Left Brigade (Lieutenant Colonel John Montresor)
61st Regiment	(857)
80th Regiment	(314)
1st Bombay N.I.	(717)

Technically, the 61st were not an 'Indian' regiment, but like the detachment of the 8th Light Dragoons, had been sent up from South Africa and took part in the march from Kosseir to Kenneh.

On the other hand, not included in this 24 August return (Walsh App 24) were Lieutenant Colonel Lloyd's wing of the 86th Regiment and five companies of 7th Bombay N.I. at Damietta, and various other detachments, including the rest of the 86th and the 7th Bombay N.I. under Colonel Ramsay at Giza.

Appendix 4

The French Army in Egypt

Infantry

French infantry units were designated as *Demi-Brigades de Bataille* (or *Ligne*) or *Demi-Brigades Légére* (light infantry) comprising three battalions, each in turn mustering nine companies, one of which was designated either as *Grenadiers* or *Carabiniers* according to arm.

While it is suggested that some of the weaker demi-brigades had consolidated their regulation three battalions into two by 1801, the actual situation was more complicated in that it was common to find units fielding two battalions for operations, while the third battalion was employed on garrison duties, and the grenadier companies were also detached to serve as skirmishers, either by themselves or joining with the companies drawn from other units in order to form consolidated battalions.

At the time of its first landing in Egypt, the French army was officially dressed in the 'National' uniform as worn in Europe; a long dark blue coat with white lapels, red collar, cuffs and turnbacks, with a white waistcoat and breeches (blue for *Légére*) and a large bicorne hat. *Grenadiers* and *Carabiniers* were officially distinguished by worsted fringed epaulettes and bearskin caps, although bicorne hats with falling plumes were a common substitute. Resupply was problematic at the best of times, and first a blue linen single-breasted jacket was locally sourced, but by 1801 the so-called 'Kleber' uniform was in use featuring a short, single-breasted Austrian-style jacket in a variety of colours and a blackened sheepskin 'petit-casquette' or cap. White linen or cotton trousers were worn, with white ankle gaiters.

Sources vary to some extent anent the colour combinations worn by each demi-brigade, largely because of the vagaries of the available dye-stuffs and a decided tendency to fade or discolour. Nevertheless, as can be seen below, although the four light infantry units wore light green or light blue jackets by way of distinction, all ten *Demi-brigades de Ligne* wore either red jackets or at least of a sufficiently red hue to potentially cause confusion when fighting British troops. For that reason, they were ordered to wear their undyed canvas frocks or greatcoats in action, and indeed for the sake of consistency, the whole army may well have done so. Captain Stewart of the 42nd, for example, describes the 21e *Légére* wearing white frocks in the fight for the Roman ruins at Alexandria/Cano, and implies that this was a characteristic of French infantry.

The listing below is based on a variety of largely secondary sources and is indicative only:[1]

9e Ligne
Scarlet jacket with green facings, red crest on cap.

13e Ligne
Crimson jacket with puce (brownish purple) facings, later blue collar and crest on cap.

18e Ligne
Scarlet jacket with yellow facings, possibly brown collar, with a black crest on the cap.

25e Ligne
Crimson jacket with sky blue facings and white lining, and a white over red crest.

32e Ligne
Brown or crimson jacket, deep blue facings, pos. orange cuffs and turnbacks, white over blue crest.

51e Ligne
This was a last-minute reinforcement, arriving in Egypt just days before the landing in Aboukir Bay and therefore still wearing the 'National' uniform, including long coat and bicorne hat.

61e Ligne
Brown jacket with yellow facings and white over blue crest.

69e Ligne
Dark brown jacket, scarlet facings, pos. white cuffs and turnbacks, white over yellow crest.

75e Ligne
Scarlet jacket, sky blue facings and red over blue crest on cap.

85e Ligne
Brown jacket, scarlet collar, yellow cuffs and turnbacks, red over yellow crest.

88e Ligne
Crimson jacket, or possibly a mixture of crimson and violet or purple jackets, blue collar, green cuffs and turnbacks and blue over yellow crest.

2e Légére
Light green jacket with dark blue facings, and green crest on cap.

4e Légére
Light green jacket with crimson or brown facings, and a white over green crest.

21e Légére
Sky-blue jacket originally with yellow facings – seemingly changed to rose pink facings. Yellow over green crest on cap.

22e Légére
Sky blue jacket with crimson facings and crimson over green crest on cap.

Cavalry

The cavalry comprised five regiments of *Dragoons* and one each of *Hussards* and Chasseurs a Cheval. To a degree the style of their uniforms was little affected by the Kleber regulations. Dragoons continued to wear long-tailed coats 'as in Europe', although these are likely to have been cut single-breasted rather than with lapels. Cloth trousers replaced the breeches and jacket boots. Elting suggests that these were closely fitting *pantalons a cheval* with leather strapping, but it seems more likely that they may have been the local baggy *sarouel* style, which later became popular with French troops in Spain.

In theory, dragoons retained the classical-styled brass helmet, with a trailing black horsehair crest, but there are suggestions that the leather infantry cap may have been more popular by 1801.[2]

As to the individual regiments; *3e Dragoons* had scarlet facings, *14e, 15e* and *18e Dragoons* had rose pink facings and *20e Dragoons* yellow.

7bis Hussards were clothed in traditional style with a dark blue dolman, headgear consisted of a cylindrical cap in dark blue with a square cut visor and a cloth wing lined with red.

22e Chasseurs a Cheval also wore hussar dress with a green dolman and breeches, with orange collar and cuffs, and an apple-green pelisse. Cords and braiding were white and the cap was green with an orange wing. Elting states that green *pantalons a cheval* were adopted with an orange stripe on the outside leg.

Both units carried short barrelled carbines, slung by their right hips.

Other Units

Artillery companies retained their traditional dark blue uniforms with red facings, but while foot companies adopted the short jacket and leather cap, the horse artillery retained their tailcoats and hussar-style caps in dark blue with red wings. Similarly, miners had blue jackets with black facings and artillery drivers continued to wear steel grey – a bluish shade.

The most famous of the colonial units was unquestionably the **Regiment de Dromedaires**. It was formed in 1799 from infantry volunteers and employed first in a contra-guerilla role and then as its expertise grew, in foraging, reconnaissance and courier duties. Its only regular combat role came as part of Bron's diversionary attack in the Canope battle of 21 March 1801. The uniform evolved over time, but by 1801 a light blue dolman with white cords was worn with red breeches for formal occasions, and a short-sleeved scarlet caftan is also illustrated. On active service, however, white *sarouel* trousers were worn and a Turkish-style cahouk, resembling a bell-topped shako, substituted for the bicorne hat.

The **Legion Nautique** formed from Naval personnel stranded ashore after the destruction of the French fleet in Aboukir Bay went through various iterations, but essentially the ships' marines were drafted into army units, and the gunners employed accordingly. Some were attached to the engineers and others employed on gunboats. Those remaining formed security companies in Alexandria and elsewhere. None were fielded as combat units. In 1799 it was noted that yellow uniforms were provided for sailors (it could not be given to the army), but red jackets faced with blue are also recorded and perhaps worn by the security companies. A glazed round hat was worn instead of the leather cap issued to army personnel.

Local Units

A considerable amount of local recruiting took place, partly in an effort to maintain numbers in the Metropolitan units, but there were also some discreet units of irregular cavalry and even two sizeable infantry battalions. Reynier described the latter thus:[3]

> Kleber … prevailed on them to raise a battalion of 500 men, whom he trained to arms, and clothed in the French uniform. He proposed to augment these auxiliary troops as circumstances might permit.
>
> This formation of a body of Copts was useful as introducing a military taste but it was a still more important object to induce the inhabitants of Egypt (Christians and Mussulmen) to enroll themselves in the demi-brigades, where they would more readily imbibe the principles, and learn the discipline, of the French soldiery, Kleber gave the greatest encouragement to these enrolments. In Upper Egypt they became frequent. The 21st demi-brigade in a short time recruited 300 men, who quickly learnt their exercise. The inhabitants of Lower Egypt seemed less disposed to enter the service, but their repugnance might have been removed.
>
> The Greeks, of a more warlike character, offered themselves with a great deal more zeal. Two companies of Greeks had been raised by Bonaparte. One of these was at the siege of Cairo, and fought with great bravery. General Kleber raised a Greek legion, in which were enlisted numbers of Greeks who had newly arrived in the ports of Egypt. It soon amounted to nearly 1,500 men.

The Legion Copte
This was employed only on garrison and policing duties in Cairo and did not take part in active operations. A green uniform is illustrated with yellow facings, topped by a bicorne hat.

Grenadiers Grecs
Some of the Greeks were employed as gunners and on the gunboats and *djermes*, but the infantry formed a battalion designated the *Grenadiers Grecs* that fought at Canope. Details of the uniform are sketchy but they appear to have had brown jackets and a red crest on their caps.

Appendix 5

Returns

State of the Army under the Command of Lieut. General Sir Ralph Abercromby, k. b., in confequence of the feparation which took place on the 20th of October, 1800, in Gibraltar Bay.

BRIGADES.	REGIMENTS.
Brigade of Guards: Hon. Major General Ludlow.	Battalion Coldftream Guards. Battalion 3rd Guards.
1 ft Brigade of the Line: Major General Coote.	2nd Battalion Royal. 1 ft Battalion 54th Regiment. 2nd Battalion 54th Ditto.
2nd Brigade: Major General Cradock.	8th Regiment. 13th Ditto. 18th Ditto. 90th Ditto.
3rd Brigade: Major General Earl of Cavan.	1ft Battalion 27th Regiment. 2nd Battalion 27th Ditto. 50th Regiment. 79th Ditto.
4th Brigade: Brigadier General Doyle.	2nd, or Queen's. 1ft Battalion 27th Ditto. 50th Regiment. 79th Ditto.
5th Brigade: Brigadier General Stuart.	Stuart's or Minorca Regiment. De Rolle's Ditto. Dillon's Ditto.
Referve: Major General Moore, Brigadier General Oakes.	23d Regiment. 28th Ditto. 42nd Ditto. 58th Ditto. Derachment Hompefch Rifleman. Corfican Rangers.
Brigadier General Lawfon.	Artillery.

(A)

Appendix, No. 36.----------State of the ARMY Under the Command of General Sir RALPH ABERCROMBY.

7th March 1801.

REGIMENTS and CORPS.		Field Officers.	Captains.	Subalterns.	Staff.	Sergeants.	Drummers.	Rank and File fit for Duty.	Sick prefent.	Sick abfent.	Total Rank & File.
Major General Ludlow	Coldftream Guards	-	3	20	5	44	13	766	93	31	890
	3d Reg' D° -	-	2	14	5	50	13	812	85	26	923
Major Gen¹ Coote	Royals - - - -	3	4	17	2	31	20	626	38	31	695
	54th 1ft Battalion -	3	6	25	4	38	18	490	6	100	596
	54th 2d Battalion -	2	4	21	5	37	14	484	5	83	572
	92d - - - - -	3	6	16	6	50	22	529	134	9	672
Major Gen¹ Cradock	90th - - - - -	3	3	13	3	50	21	727	31	18	776
	8th - - - - -	3	6	16	4	43	19	439	8	36	483
	13th - - - - -	4	6	34	4	41	21	561	89	86	736
	18th - - - - -	2	5	16	5	32	14	411	38	39	488
Major Gen¹ Lord Cavan	50th - - - - -	2	7	19	5	31	13	477	20	28	525
	79th - - - - -	4	6	15	5	47	19	604	11	107	722
Brigadier Gen¹ Doyle	Queen's - - - -	3	10	22	4	46	19	530	22	23	575
	30th - - - - -	2	6	17	5	41	21	412	9	5	426
	44th - - - - -	3	4	14	4	40	17	263	16	38	317
	89th - - - - -	3	10	16	-	33	12	378	20	3	401
Brigadier Gen¹ Stuart	Stuart's - - - -	3	7	24	6	52	21	929	16	34	979
	De Roll's - - - -	2	7	14	5	52	21	528	6	26	560
	Dillon's - - - -	2	6	13	6	50	22	530	18		574
Major General Moore Brigadier Gen¹ Oakes.	23d - - - - -	3	6	18	5	41	13	457	20	67	544
	28th - - - - -	2	8	20	5	41	18	587	12	29	628
	42d - - - - -	4	5	21	5	37	15	754	28	18	800
	58th - - - - -	3	9	18	4	33	13	469	14	21	504
	Corfican Rangers -	-	2	6	2	9	3	209	9	9	227
	Flank Comp' 40th Regᵗ	1	4	8	2	16	8	250	-	1	251
	Staff Corps - - -	-	-	3	-	2	-	82	2	6	90
TOTAL - - - -		60	142	440	106	987	410	13304	750	900	14950

185

State of the ARMY, &c.——*continued.*

CAVALRY.

REGIMENTS and DETACHMENTS.	Officers.				Non-Commiffioned.			Rank & File.		Total.	Horfes.		
	Field Officers.	Captains.	Subalterns.	Staff.	Quarter-Mafters.	Sergeants.	Trumpeters.	Fit for Duty.	Sick.		Officers.	Troop.	Sick.
11th Light Dragoons - - - - -	-	1	4	-	-	3	1	53	-	53	6	57	
12th D° D° - - - - - - -	1	3	10	4	4	28	7	474	12	486	26	124	
26th D° D° - - - - - -	3	1	7	5	7	31	10	369	14	483	30	124	
Hompefchs - - - - - - - -	1	2	4	1	2	8	2	138	3	141	16	142	7
Total - - -	5	7	25	10	13	70	20	1034	29	1163	78	447	7

ARTILLERY.

	Officers.						Rank and File.				Horfe Department. Rank and File.							Horfes.		
	Field Officers.	Captains.	Subalterns.	Staff.	Sergeants.	Drummers.	Fit for Duty.	Sick prefent.	Sick abfent.	Total Rank and File.	Quartr Maftr Commy	Sergeant Conductors.	Corporal D°	Farriers.	Fit for Duty.	Sick.	Total.	Fit for Duty.	Sick.	Total.
Total - - -	1	8	20	7	10	9	557	24	5	586	2	2	5	2	70	2	72	173	—	173

Appendix, No. 9. ——State of the Troops under the immediate Command of Major-General Coote.

CAMP, 4 Miles from Alexandria, the 25th of April, 1801.

Regiments		Comm^ed Officers.						Sergeants.		Rank and File.					Grand Total.
		Lt. Colonels.	Majors.	Captains.	Lieutenants.	Ensigns.	Staff.	Sergeants.	Drummers.	Present fit for Duty.	Sick present.	Sick at Aboukir and on board.	Sick in the Mediterranean.	On Command.	
Brigade of Guards.	Coldstream - -	-	-	2	12	4	4	34	11	646	97	78	20	2	843
	3rd Guards - -	-	-	2	8	2	4	35	10	585	105	123	13	7	833
1ft Brigade.	54th, 1ft Batt^n	2	-	5	11	4	2	32	18	395	64	35	73	5	572
	54th, 2d Batt^n	1	2	3	12	7	5	38	12	357	82	42	51	9	541
	Marines- - -	1	1	8	21	-	3	28	17	367	88	15	-	6	476
3d Brigade.	13th - - -	1	2	5	10	12	2	39	13	404	157	75	34	28	698
	27th - - -	-	1	2	14	8	5	34	10	497	63	23	121	-	704
	44th - - -	-	1	3	10	2	4	37	16	224	30	14	17	1	286
5th Brigade.	Stuart's - -	-	2	4	14	5	5	53	22	728	83	82	31	-	924
	De Roll's - -	1	1	5	4	5	4	43	21	421	26	58	15	7	527
	Dillon's - -	1	1	5	7	5	4	45	18	422	33	64	21	-	540
Reserve.	23d - - -	1	1	5	11	2	4	35	12	372	47	61	48	2	530
	28th - - -	2	-	6	17	4	5	43	18	451	36	64	25	-	576
	42d - - -	1	2	3	11	2	3	37	18	517	67	243	15	-	842
	50th - - -	2	1	6	16	3	5	28	11	405	48	41	14	4	512
Staff Corps- - - -		-	-	-	-	2	-	2	-	73	3	12	-	-	88
92d at Aboukir - - -		-	2	6	10	5	6	21	20	305	183	94	17	15	614
Total - - -		12	17	70	188	72	65	584	247	7169	1212	1124	515	86	10106

187

CAVALRY.

REGIMENTS.	Lt. Col.	Majors.	Captains.	Lieuts.	Cornets.	Staff.	Quar. Masters.	Sergeants.	Trumpeters.	Fit for Duty.	Sick at Aboukir.	Aboard & in Camp.	On Command.	Total.	Officers.	Horses Fit for Duty.	Sick or Lame.	On Command.	Total.
26th Light Dragoons { Mounted	1	1	-	4	-	4	4	13	3	183	-	-	48	231	-	190	9	51	250
Dismounted	-	-	1	2	2	-	3	13	6	170	2	35	-	207					
TOTAL	1	1	1	6	2	4	7	26	9	353	2	35	48	438	46	190	9	51	250

ROYAL ARTILLERY.

Captains.	Lieutenants.	Staff.	Sergeants.	Drummers.	Fit for Duty.	Sick.	Total.	Gunner Drivers Fit for Duty.	Sick.	On Command.	Total.	Horses Fit for duty.	Sick or Lame.	Total.	Royal Engineers Corps	Captains.	Lieutenants.	Total.
3	10	2	3	5	247	29	276	12	4	-	16	20	10	30	Royal Engineers	1	4	

188

Appendix, No. 11.

Correct Statement of the Divifion of the Army under the Command of Major General Hutchinson.

Derout on the Nile, the 6th of May, 1801.

Major General Cradock's Brigade - -
- 8th Regiment - - - -
- 18th Ditto - - - - -
- 79th Ditto - - - - -
- 90th Ditto - - - - -
} 1650

Brigadier General Doyle's Brigade - -
- 2nd Battalion Royal - -
- 30th Regiment - - -
- 50th Ditto - - - - -
- 92nd Ditto - - - - -
} 1650

Referve, under Colonel Spencer - - -
- 2nd, or Queen's - - -
- 58th Regiment - - -
- 40th Flank Companies
- Corfican Rangers- - -
} 1150

Column in the Delta, under Col. Stewart - 89th Regiment - - -   350

Total Infantry - - - - - -   4800

Cavalry:
12th Light Dragoons - - - - - - - - - - - - 350
26th Ditto - - - - - - - - - - - - - - - - 80
Detachment of the 11th Light Dragoons, with the Referve - 50
Detachment of the 12th Ditto, with Colonel Stewart's Column 30

Total Cavalry - - - - - - - 510

Making Total Britifh, not including Artillery - - - - 5310

Albanians, with Colonel Stewart's Column - - - - - - - - - 1000
Turkifh Regulars, under the Capoutan Pacha - - - - - - - - 1100
Irregulars, under Ditto - - - - - - - - - - - - - - - 1500
Turkifh Cavalry, under Ditto - - - - - - - - - - - - - - 600

Total Combined Forces - - - - - - - - - - - - - - - 9510

Appendix, No. 20.—New Arrangement for BRIGADING the Army under Lieut. General Sir JOHN HELY HUTCHINSON, K. B.; Camp near Alexandria, the 9th of Auguft, 1801.

Major General COOTE, Second in Command.

BRIGADES.	REGIMENTS and CORPS.	Effective Rank and File.	TOTAL STRENGTH.
Brigade of Guards: Major Gen. Earl of Cavan.	Coldftream Guards	552	Brigade Major Carey. 1142.
	3rd Regt. Ditto	590	
1ft Brigade: The Hon. Major Gen. Ludlow.	25th Regiment -	526	Brigade Major Ramfay. 1863.
	27th, 1ft Battalion -	538	
	27th, 2nd Ditto -	465	
	44th Regiment -	334	
2nd Brigade: The Hon. Major Gen. Finch.	2nd Bat. Royal	352	Brigade Major Popham. 1555.
	26th Regiment -	438	
	54th, 1ft Battalion	381	
	54th, 2nd Ditto -	384	
3rd, or Foreign Brigade: Brigadier General Stewart.	Stuart's Regiment	690	Brigade Major Miffett. 2038.
	De Roll's Ditto - -	383	
	Dillon's Ditto - -	393	
	Watteville's Ditto -	572	
4th Brigade: The Hon. Brigad. Gen. Hope.	8th Regiment -	285	Brigade Major M'Kenzie. 1449.
	18th Ditto - -	293	
	79th Ditto - -	434	
	90th Ditto - -	437	
5th Brigade: Brigadier General Doyle.	30th Regiment -	269	Brigade Major Sutton. 1331.
	50th Ditto - -	337	
	89th Ditto - -	311	
	92nd Ditto - -	414	
6th Brigade: Brigadier General Blake.	20th, 1ft Battalion -	604	Brigade Major Chatterton. 1946.
	20th, 2nd Ditto -	484	
	24th Regiment -	438	
	Ancient Irifh -	420	
Referve: Major General Moore, Brigadier General Oakes.	2nd, or Queen's -	327	Brigade Major Groves. Ditto - - - Bowles.
	28th Regiment -	338	
	42nd Ditto - -	490	
	58th Ditto - -	238	
	40th Flank Comp. -	146	
	23rd Regiment -	343	
	Rifle Corps - -	397	2934.
	Chaffeurs Britanniques	595	Grand Total - 14258.
	Corfican Rangers	60	

Appendix, No. 22.—RETURN of the Troops to the Weftward of Alexandria, commanded by Major General Coote.—Camp Weft of Alexandria, the 23rd of Auguft, 1801.

BRIGADES, and by whom commanded.	REGIMENTS and CORPS.	Effective Rank & File	DEPARTMENTS.
Brigade of Guards: Major Gen. Earl of Cavan.	Coldftream Guards	501	Quarter Mafter Generals:
	3rd Regt. Ditto -	619	Deputy, Lieut. Col. Duncan.
		1120	Affiftant, Captain Brownrigg. Ditto, Lieut. Coffin.
1ft Brigade: Major General Ludlow's.	25th Regiment -	448	
	27th, 1ft Battalion	508	Adjutant General:
	27th, 2nd Ditto -	418	Affiftant, Capt. Farquharfon.
	44th Regiment -	307	
		1681	Engineers:
2nd Brigade: Major General Finch's.	24th Regiment -	389	Captain Ford, commanding.
	26th Ditto - - -	362	Lieutenant Graham.
	54th, 1ft Battalion	424	Lieutenant Kennett.
	54th, 2nd Ditto -	374	Affiftant, Lieut. Harrifon.
		1549	Ditto - - - Leonard.
6th Brigade: Brigadier Gen. Blake's, Commanded by Col. Spencer.	20th, 1ft Battalion	547	Medical Staff:
	20th, 2nd Ditto -	477	Ralph Green, Infpector of Hofpitals.
	Ancient Irifh - -	289	Alexander Grant, Surgeon.
		1313	L. Parker - - Ditto.
Lieut. Colonel Schoedde.	Rifle Corps - -	260	G. Marmeon,⎫ Hofpital
	Total Infantry -	5923	— Hipp, -⎬ Mates. — Reynolds,⎭
Major Moore.	26th Light Drag.	103	Commiffariat:
Major Cookfon.	Royal Artillery -	146	Affiftant Commis. Bennatt.

N. B. The Brigade commanded by Colonel Spencer, the Rifle Corps, and the Detachment of Cavalry, were not prefent at the landing on the 17th of Auguft.—The Cavalry, and 174 Men of the Rifle Corps under the Command of Captain Perpoucher, acted with the Weftern Divifion on the 22nd of Auguft.—Colonel Spencer, with his Brigade and the remainder of the Rifle Corps, joined on the 23rd of Auguft.

Ordnance intended to have been employed to the Weftward of Alexandria, the Night following the Commencement of the Armistice:

Ten	24	Pounders.	Two	10	Inch Mortars.
Two	12	Ditto, medium.	Two	8	Inch Ditto.
Two	12	Ditto, light.	Four	5½	Inch Ditto.
Six	6	Ditto, Ditto.	Two	8	Inch Howitzers.
			Two	5½	Inch Ditto.

Appendix, No. 24.—RETURN of the INDIAN ARMY, under the Command of Major General BAIRD. Camp, near Rofetta, the 24th of Auguft, 1801.

BRIGADES.—CORPS.	REGIMENTS and CORPS.	Effective Rank & File	STAFF and DEPARTMENTS.
Artillery - - - - - - - - -	- - - - - -	311	Col. Auchmuty, Adj. General.
Native Ditto - - - - - - -	- - - - - -	583	Major M'Quarrie, Dep. Do.
Bengal Horfe Ditto - - - -	- - - - - -	120	Colonel Murray, Quarter Mafter General.
*Troop 8th Light Dragoons	- - - - - -	80	Capt. Cox, 68th Reg. } Affift. Lieut. White, 13th Dⁿˢ } Do.
Right Brigade:	10th Regiment -	815	Captain Tucker, 22nd Regt. Brigade Major.
Colonel Beresford, 88th.	88th Ditto - - -	272	
	Bengal Volunteers	603	W. R. Shapter, Infpector of Hofpitals.
		1690	
			A. L. Emerfon, Apothecary.
Left Brigade:	*61 ft Regiment -	933	John Foreman, Surgeon.
Lieut. Colonel Montréfor.	80th Ditto - -	272	W. J. Price, } A. White, } Hofp. Mates. J. Rice }
	Bombay Nat. Inf.	714	
		1919	Richard Mofs, Purveyor of Hofpitals.
Pioneer Corps - - - - - -	- - - - - - -	92	W. Hayman, Deuputy Ditto.
Royal Engineers - - - - -	- - - - - - -	33	

DETACHED CORPS.	Strength.	By whom commanded.	To what Place.
86th Regiment - - - - - - - - - - - - -	167	Lt. Col. Lloyd, 86th	Damietta.
5 Companies 7th Bombay Native Infantry	339		
Detachments 10th, 61ft, 80th, 88th Regts.	150	Colonel Ramfay	Gizeh, & Ifland of Rodda.
5 Companies 7th Bombay Native Infantry	338		
Total- - - - - - - - -	5805		

N. B. Five Companies of the 80th, and Two of the 88th, have never yet reached Coffeir; they are fuppofed to have returned to India, as alfo a Battalion of Native Infantry.—The Corps marked thus [*] are from the Cape of Good Hope, but now put on the India Eftablifhment. The Garrifon of Damietta was recalled in the Beginning of September, as that Place is to be garrifoned by the Turks. Out of the above Total, the following was the Number of Sick, on the 26th of September.—Sick, prefent, 999—In the Hofpital 126.

Appendix, No. 25.—Difembarkation Return of the Troops under the Command of Major General Baird, at Coffeir and Suez.

Column groups: **OFFICERS** — *Commissioned* (Colonels, Lieut. Colonels, Majors, Captains, Lieutenants, Enfigns); *Staff* (Pay-Matters, Adjutants, Quarter-Matters, Surgeons, Afflt. Surgeons); *Native* (Subadaurs, Jemmidaurs). **Non-Comm. Officers, Rank and File** (Conductors, Sergeants, Drummers, Rank and File). **Lafcars** (Syrangs, 1ft Tindals, 2d Tindals, Lafcars).

CORPS.	Colonels	Lieut. Colonels	Majors	Captains	Lieutenants	Enfigns	Pay-Matters	Adjutants	Quarter-Matters	Surgeons	Afflt. Surgeons	Subadaurs	Jemmidaurs	Conductors	Sergeants	Drummers	Rank and File	Syrangs	1ft Tindals	2d Tindals	Lafcars
Royal Artillery	-	-	-	2	-	-	-	-	-	-	-	-	-	1	1	1	41	-	-	-	-
Bengal Horfe Artillery	-	-	-	1	-	-	-	-	-	-	1	-	1	1	6	-	69	-	1	3	51
Bengal Foot Do.	-	-	-	2	1	-	-	-	-	-	1	-	1	1	7	-	74	1	3	3	87
Madras Do.	-	-	1	1	2	-	-	-	-	-	1	-	1	-	5	2	84	3	6	5	143
Bombay Do.	-	-	-	2	4	-	-	-	-	-	-	-	-	2	7	1	133	2	6	5	158
Royal Engineers	-	-	-	-	-	-	-	-	-	-	-	-	-	-	-	-	-	-	-	-	-
Bengal Do.	-	-	-	1	1	2	-	-	-	-	-	-	-	-	-	-	-	-	-	-	-
Madras Do.	-	-	-	-	1	-	-	-	-	-	-	-	-	-	-	-	-	-	-	-	-
Bombay Do.	-	-	-	-	1	-	-	-	-	-	-	-	-	-	-	-	-	-	-	-	-
Madras Pioneers	-	-	-	1	-	-	-	-	1	-	-	-	1	-	4	-	88	-	-	-	-
His Mahefty's 8th Light Dragoons	-	1	-	1	2	1	-	1	1	-	2	-	-	-	4	1	75	-	-	-	-
—— 10th Foot	-	2	2	6	16	5	1	1	1	1	1	-	-	-	46	18	854	-	-	-	-
—— 61ft Do.	-	2	2	9	18	7	1	1	1	1	2	-	-	-	52	22	857	-	-	-	-
—— 80th Do.	-	1	1	3	9	1	-	1	-	1	1	-	-	-	23	6	314	-	-	-	-
—— 86th Do.	-	1	-	4	8	1	-	-	1	-	-	-	-	-	20	11	308	-	-	-	-
—— 88th Do.	-	1	1	5	7	1	-	1	-	1	1	-	-	-	27	19	390	-	-	-	-
Bengal Volunteers, Native Infantry	-	-	-	2	10	1	-	-	-	-	-	6	6	-	31	11	563	-	-	-	-
1ft Bombay Regt. Do.	-	1	1	1	11	-	-	1	-	-	1	10	10	-	51	18	717	-	-	-	-
7th Do.	-	1	1	1	13	-	-	-	-	-	1	10	9	-	48	15	660	-	-	-	-
Total	-	10	9	42	104	19	2	6	5	4	12	26	28	5	332	125	5227	6	16	16	439

Disembarkation Return &c.—*continued.*

CAMP, near El Hamed. PRESENT STATE. 5th October, 1801.

CORPS.	Colonels	Lieut. Colonels	Majors	Captains	Lieutenants	Enfigns	Pay-Masters	Adjutants	Quarter-Masters	Surgeons	Affift. Surgeons	Subadaurs	Jemmidaurs	Conductors	Sergeants	Drummers	Fit for Duty	Sick prefent	Sick in Hofpital	On Command	Total	Syrangs	1ft Tindals	2d Tindals	Fit for Duty	Sick prefent	Sick in Hofpital	Total	Joined	Dead	Difcharged	Deferted	Invalided
																	Rank and File				Lafcars.							Alterations fince Difembarkation				
Royal Artillery	-	-	-	2	-	-	-	-	-	-	1	-	-	1	1	1	39	2	-	-	41	-	1	3	45	6	-	51	-	-	-	-	-
Bengal Horfe Artillery	-	-	-	1	1	-	-	-	-	-	1	-	-	1	5	1	63	6	-	-	69	1	3	3	82	4	-	86	-	-	-	-	-
Bengal Foot Do.	-	-	-	-	-	-	-	-	-	-	1	-	-	1	7	-	56	5	-	14	75	3	6	6	112	16	5	133	-	1	-	-	6
Madras Do.	-	-	-	1	2	-	-	-	-	-	1	-	-	1	5	2	77	5	-	-	82	2	6	6	117	10	3	130	-	5	-	1	5
Bombay Do.	-	-	-	2	4	-	-	-	-	-	1	-	-	1	7	1	95	22	1	3	121	-	-	-	-	-	-	-	3	31	-	1	-
Royal Engineers	-	-	-	1	-	-	-	-	-	-	-	-	-	-	-	-	-	-	-	-	-	-	-	-	-	-	-	-	-	-	-	-	-
Bengal Do.	-	-	-	-	1	2	-	-	-	-	-	-	1	-	-	-	-	-	-	-	-	-	-	-	-	-	-	-	-	-	-	-	-
Madras Do.	-	-	-	-	1	-	-	-	-	-	-	-	1	-	-	-	-	-	-	-	-	-	-	-	-	-	-	-	-	-	-	-	-
Bombay Do.	-	-	-	-	1	-	-	-	-	-	-	-	1	-	-	-	-	-	-	-	-	-	-	-	-	-	-	-	-	-	-	-	-
Madras Pioneers	-	-	-	1	1	-	-	1	-	-	1	-	1	-	4	-	73	12	-	-	85	-	-	-	-	-	-	-	-	-	-	-	-
His Majefty's 8th Light Dragoons	-	-	-	1	3	1	-	1	1	1	2	-	-	-	4	18	63	1	6	5	75	-	-	-	-	-	-	-	-	-	-	1	-
10th Foot	-	2	2	6	15	4	1	1	1	1	1	-	-	-	46	22	515	231	29	51	826	-	-	-	-	-	-	-	1	27	-	1	2
61ft Do.	-	2	2	10	17	6	1	1	1	1	2	-	-	-	52	6	492	222	24	103	841	-	-	-	-	-	-	-	1	15	5	2	-
80th Do.	-	2	-	3	9	1	-	1	1	-	1	-	-	-	23	11	211	94	6	-	311	-	-	-	-	-	-	-	-	3	-	-	-
86th Do.	-	1	-	4	8	1	-	1	1	-	1	-	-	-	20	17	247	41	4	-	292	-	-	-	-	-	-	-	-	16	-	-	-
88th Do.	-	2	1	5	7	1	-	1	1	-	1	-	-	-	25	11	240	116	11	-	367	-	-	-	-	-	-	-	-	25	-	2	-
Bengal Volunteers, Native Infantry	-	-	-	2	2	1	-	1	1	-	1	6	6	-	31	15	460	86	3	-	549	-	-	-	-	-	-	-	-	7	-	-	7
1ft Bombay Regt. Do.	-	-	1	1	10	1	-	1	1	-	-	10	10	-	51	15	582	64	-	30	676	-	-	-	-	-	-	-	-	20	-	10	11
7th Do. Do.	-	-	-	1	11	1	-	1	-	-	-	9	9	-	50	15	276	51	17	255	599	-	-	-	-	-	-	-	-	47	-	12	-
Total	-	9	6	41	101	17	2	6	5	3	14	25	28	5	331	120	3489	936	96	461	5009	6	16	18	356	36	8	400	4	197	5	29	31

194

Disembarkation Return, &c.—*continued.*

DISTRIBUTION.

STATIONS.	Officers.											Native.		Non-Commissioned Officers. Rank and File.				Lascars.			
	Commissioned.						Staff.														
	Colonels.	Lieut. Colonels.	Majors.	Captains.	Lieutenants.	Ensigns.	Pay-Masters.	Adjutants.	Quarter-Masters.	Surgeons.	Assistant Surgeons.	Subadaurs.	Jemmidaurs.	Conductors.	Sergeants.	Drummers.	Rank and File.	Syrangs.	1st Tindals.	2d Tindals.	Lascars.
At Head Quarters, near El Hamed -	-	9	5	39	90	15	2	6	5	3	13	21	25	5	297	107	4452	6	12	18	368
At Gizeh - - - - - - - -	-	-	1	2	9	2	-	-	-	-	1	4	3	-	30	9	442	-	2	-	24
On the Way to Suez - - -	-	-	-	-	2	-	-	-	-	-	-	-	-	-	4	4	115	-	2	-	8
Total - - -	-	9	6	41	101	17	2	6	5	3	14	25	28	5	331	120	5009	6	16	18	400

195

Difembarkation Return, &c.—*concluded.*

GENERAL STAFF.

Major General Baird	54th Foot	Commanding in Chief.
Colonel Auchmuty	10th Do.	Adjutant General.
Colonel Murray	84th Do.	Quarter-Mafter General.
Major Macquarie	77th Do.	Deputy Adjutant General.
Captain Falconer	71ft Do.	Deputy Quarter-Mafter General.
Captain Molle	Scotch Brigade	Private Secretary and A. D. C.
Captain Tucker	22d Foot	Major of Brigade to General Baird.
Lieutenant Budgen	84th Do.	Additional A. D. C. and Mufter Mafter.
Major Harris	Bombay Infantry	Auditor of Bombay Accounts.
Captain Michie	Bengal Volunteers	Auditor of Bengal and Madras Ditto.
Captain Scott	Madras Artillery	Commiffary of Stores.
Lieutenant Warden	Bombay Do.	Deputy Commiffary of Ditto.
Captain Burr	Bombay Infantry	Commiffary of Cattle.
Lieutenant Fagan	Bengal Do.	Boat Mafter.
T. White, Efq.		Pay Mafter to the Troops.
T. Shubrick, Efq.		Commiffary of Provifion to Ditto.
Mr. Secluno		Deputy Commiffary of Provifion to Ditto.

BRIGADE STAFF.

RIGHT BRIGADE.

Colonel Beresford - - 88th Foot, Commanding.
Captain Trotter - - - Ditto, Brigade Major.
Captain Cox (Affiftant Q. M. G.) 68th, Acting Quarter-Mafter.

LEFT BRIGADE.

Lieutenant Colonel Montrefor, 80th Foot, Commanding.
Lieutenant White (Affift. Q. M. G) 13th Dragoons, Acting Brigade Major.
Ditto, Ditto, Ditto, Acting Quarter-Mafter.

GARRISON STAFF.

Colonel Ramfay	80th Foot	Commandant of Gizeh.
Lieutenant Harvey	61ft Do.	Brigade Major.
Lieutenant M'Donald	10th Do.	Town Adjutant.
Lieutenant Denoe	61ft Foot	Garrifon Quarter-Mafter.
Lieutenant Colonel Barlow		Commandant of Rofetta.

Appendix, No. 30.—French and Auxiliary Troops in Egypt, with the Numbers of the feveral Corps.—Each Demi-brigade being compofed of 3 Battalions.

Artillerie à pied et à Cheval.
Régiment de Dromadaires.
7eme Régiment de Huffards.
22eme de Chaffeurs à Cheval.

3eme	
14eme	
15eme } Régiments de Dragons.	
18eme	
20eme	

9eme
13eme
18eme
25eme
32eme
51eme } Demi-brigades de Ligne, ou Infan-terie de Battaille.
61eme
69eme
75eme
85eme
88eme

2eme
4eme
21eme } Demi-brigades d'Infanterie légère, ou Tirailleurs.
22eme

Régiment de Grenadier Grecs.
Corps de Cophts, Syrien, et Mamelouks.
Guides à pied et à Cheval du Général en Chef
Corps du Génie, Sapeurs, et Soldats de Marine.

Thefe demibrigades were very unequal in their ftrength, fome having recruited blacks from Africa; it is, however, very moderate, to eftimate them upon an average at 1200 each demibrigade, and the regiments of cavalry at 300, exclufive of artillery, guides, and auxiliaries.

General Officers of the French Army in Egypt:

Abdoullahy Jacques François Menou, Commander in Chief.

Generals of Divifion:

Reynier.
Rampon.
Lanuffe { (wounded on the 13th, and killed on the 21ft of March).

Damas.
Friant.
Béliard.
Lagrange.

Generals of Divifion:

Roize { (commanding the cavalry, killed on the 21ft of March).
Bron.
Donzelot.
Morand.
Bouffart.
Martinet (killed at the landing)
Eppler (wounded on the 21ft of March).
Almeyras.

Deftin (wounded on the 21ft of March
Beaudot (killed on the 21ft of March).
Delegorgne.
Silly (wounded on the 21ft of March).
Valentin.
Songis (commanding the Artillery).
Sanfon (commanding Engineers).
Zayonfeck.

Appendix, No. 29.

Fair Eftimate of the number of French in Egypt, at the Time of the Arrival of the Britifh Army in Aboukir Bay, accounting for the Manner in which they have been difpofed of.

	Number.
Marched out of Cairo in confequence of the Convention, and embarked for France, in Aboukir Bay- -	14000
Surrendered in Alexandria, and embarked thence - - - - - - - - - - - -	11500
Made Prifoners of War in Aboukir Caftle, the 18th of March- - - - - - -	200
Ditto, in Fort Julien, near Rofetta, the 19th of April- - - - - - - - - - -	300
Convoy in Germes from Cairo to Rahmanieh, the 10th of May - - - - -	150
Taken in the Fort of Rahmanieh - - - - - - - Ditto- - - - - - - - - -	200
Large Convoy under Cavalier, by Brigadier Gen. Doyle, the 17th of May	600
Garrifon of Lefbeh, near Damietta, and Fort Bourlos- - - - - - - - - -	700
Garrifon of Marrabout, Prifoners of War, the 21ft of Auguft - - - - - - -	200
25th of Auguft, taken Prifoners- -	100
Killed and Taken in the different Actions- - - - - - - - - - - - - - - - -	3000
	30950
Allowing for Women, Children, and Noncombatants - - - - - - - - - -	10000
Total Fighting Men - - - - - - - - - - - - - -	20950
Effective Force under the Command of General Sir Ralph Abercromby, on the 7th of March -	14967
Superiority of the French - - - - - - - - - - -	5983

Bibliography

Anon., *The Military Panorama or Officers Companion*, London, 1814.

Anon., *Partial account of the action in North Holland on the 2nd October 1799; by an officer engaged in Sir R. Abercromby's division.*

Barthorp, *Michael Napoleon's Egyptian Campaigns 1798–1801*, Osprey, 1978.

Bunbury, Lieutenant General Sir Henry, *Narratives of Some Passages in the Great War with France, from 1799–1810*, London, 1954.

Cannon, Richard, *Historical Record of the First or Royal Regiment of Foot*, London, 1847.

Cannon, Richard, *Historical Records of the Ninety-Second Regiment*, London, 1851.

Chartrand, Rene, *Émigré & Foreign Troops in British Service (1) 1793–1802*, Osprey, 1999.

Crowdy, *Terry French Soldier in Egypt 1798–1801*, Osprey, 2003.

Delavoye, Alexander *Records of the 90th Regiment, (Perthshire Light Infantry); with roll of officers from 1795 to 1880*, London, 1880.

Flaherty, Chris, *Napoleon's 1798 Pyramid Campaign & The Egyptian Army*, Partisan, Eastwood, 2019.

Fortescue, J.W., *A History of the British Army* 4, London, 1915.

Gardyne, Charles Greenhill, *Life of a Regiment; The History of the Gordon Highlanders*, Edinburgh, 1901.

Gates, David, *The British Light Infantry Arm 1790–1815*, London, 1987.

Gould, Robert W., *Mercenaries of the Napoleonic Wars*, Brighton, 1995.

Grant, Charles S., *Napoleon's Campaign in Egypt Vol.1 The French Army*, Partisan, Leigh on Sea, 2006.

Grant, Charles S., *Napoleon's Campaign in Egypt Vol.2 The British Army & Allies*, Partisan, Leigh on Sea, 2006.

Graves, Donald, *Dragon Rampant; The Royal Welch Fusiliers at War 1793–1815*, Barnsley, 2010.

Harman, William, *A History of Malta during the period of the French and British occupations 1798–1815*, London and New York, Longmans Green and Company, 1909.

Haythornthwaite, Philip, *Uniforms of the French Revolutionary Wars 1789–1802*, London, 1981.

Houlding, Dr John, *Fit for Service; The Training of the British Army 1715–1795*, Oxford, 1981.

Larrey, Dominique Jean *Memoirs of Military Surgery and Campaigns of the French Army*, Baltimore, 1814.

Mackesy, Piers, *British Victory in Egypt*, Routledge, London, 1995.

Moore, *Diary of Sir John Moore*, Ed. Sir J.F. Maurice, London, 1904.

Return of the names of the officers in the army who receive pensions for the loss of limbs, or for wounds; WO 30 April 1818.

Reynier, Jean Louis Ebenezer, *State of Egypt after the Battle of Heliopolis, Preceded by General Observations* ... G. and J. Robinson, London, 1802.

Stewart, David, *Sketches of the Highlanders of Scotland*, 2nd Edn, Edinburgh, 1822.

Walsh, Thomas, *Journal of the Late Campaign in Egypt*, London, 1803.

Weller, Jac, *Wellington in India*, London, 1972.

Wilkinson, Sir John Gardiner, *Modern Egypt and Thebes: Being a Description of Egypt* ..., J. Murray, London, 1843.

Wilson, Robert, *Narrative of the Expedition to Egypt*, 4th Edn, London, 1803.

Notes

Chapter 1: The Mediterranean War

1. Corresp. Napoleon 3:235 quoted in William Harman *A History of Malta During the Period of the French and British Occupations 1798–1815*, London and New York, Longmans Green and Company, 1909, 10.
2. Corresp. Napoleon 3:293 per Harman, 11. The Venetian ships had recently been seized along with the old naval base at Corfu, but they turned out to be in very poor condition and could not be fitted up and manned in time.
3. Hompesch was the first German to become Grand Master of the Order, when he was elected in 1797. Two of his nephews, Franz Karl and Ferdinand von Hompesch, were professional soldiers, or rather military contractors in the British service, who between them raised and commanded a number of mercenary units. A detachment belonging to one of those units, the Hompesch Hussars, would serve in Egypt under Major Robert Wilson.
4. William Harman, *A History of Malta during the period of the French and British occupations 1798–1815*. (London and New York, Longmans Green and Company, 1909), 45.
5. The statement in at least one secondary source that Bonaparte's *Legion Maltaise* (commanded by an Irish adventurer named Bernard MacSheehy) numbered 1,500 men seems a touch optimistic, given that only 500 regulars had surrendered and the French showed no interest in taking on the 'hideous' Cacciatori.
6. Ibid.
   The regiments in question were:
6e Ligne	518
7e Légére	900

19e Ligne	700
41e Ligne (detachment)	285
80e Ligne	650

7. Each infantry battalion comprised eight companies of fusiliers and an elite company of grenadiers – designated as carabiniers in light infantry or *Légére* units.

8. *Guns in the Desert: General Jean-Pierre Doguereau's Journal of Napoleon's Egyptian Expedition* (Westport, Con, 2002): 14.

9. Sir Sydney Smith had rather dubiously obtained his knighthood while temporarily in the Swedish service, and although he very properly obtained King George III's formal dispensation to use the foreign title, most of his colleagues were not so accommodating and mocked him unmercifully. He did eventually become a KCB but not until after Waterloo in 1815.

10. Stuart's official dispatch identifies them as the *Valencia* Regiment (three battalions), the Swiss Regiment *Ruttiman* (two battalions) and the Swiss Regiment *Yann* (one battalion). In addition, there was a detachment of the *Numancia* Dragoons, and the obligatory artillery detachment.

11. Harman: 109–110.

12. Not yet the *Royal* Marines; that distinction would not be granted until 29 April 1802.

13. Vivion somehow managed for most of his career to be misidentified in the *Army List* (and most secondary sources) as *James* Vivion – an error that was not corrected until his eventual return from Malta in 1814. Commissioned a lieutenant in the Royal Artillery 14 August 1794, he enjoyed the local rank of captain on Malta prior to being regimentally promoted captain-lieutenant and captain 3 December 1800. A substantive captain in the Royal Artillery on 6 December 1803, he was made a brevet major 1 January 1812 and major in the Royal Artillery 3 July 1815, and finally lieutenant colonel 20 June 1823. He died at Gravesend 11 October 1832. Aside from these steps in rank be served as quartermaster general on Malta under Graham, and afterwards was assistant quartermaster general with responsibility for the Maltese forces and Inspector of the Coast and of the Maltese Cannoneers and Militia. (*United Services Magazine*)

14. A thorny political dimension had arisen, revolving around the status of King Ferdinand IV vis-à-vis the Tsar of all the Russias! Following the capitulation of Malta to the French in 1798, the disgraced Hompesch had been deposed and rather irregularly replaced as Grand Master of the Knights by the Russian Tsar, Paul I,

and as a result Russian troops had been hopefully expected on Malta ever since. However, although there were already Russian ships and Russian troops in the Mediterranean, they seemed curiously reluctant to intervene, largely as it turned out because they were far too busily occupied in capturing the island of Corfu from the French (ironically enough with Turkish co-operation) ultimately in order to use the old Venetian outpost as a base for interfering in the western Balkans.

15. BM Addl Mss 34940 Vivion to Ball 1 July 1799.
16. Lindenthal appears to have originally been in the Austrian service, but transferred to the British one amidst the widespread recruitment of German mercenary units in the 1790s and went on to serve in Flanders and the West Indies, before being appointed DQMG in Portugal in November 1796. From there he went to Minorca and helped raise Stuart's Minorca Regiment. As its lieutenant colonel, he went to Egypt and was temporarily lent to discipline the *Kapūdān Pasha's* men. He died a lieutenant general at Chelsea in 1837.
17. TNA:WO 17/2117 Strength of 30th and 89th Regiments on their disembarkation at St Paul's Bay on 10 December 1799.

Regiment	Officers	Serjeants	Rank and File	Women	Children
30th	31	34	418	20	15
89th	29	32	426	42	
Total	58	66	840	62	15

The rear parties of both regiments under Major William Lockhart must have been brought forward very quickly as a 1 January 1800 return for the 30th Regiment (WO12/4565) revealed 460 rank and file and twenty-one sick.
18. Graham to Sir William Hamilton 19 May 1800 IN Harman: 295–298. The Maltese independent companies were commanded by British junior officers seconded from the 30th and 89th Regiments under the overall direction of Captain James Weir of the marines, holding the local rank of major. The officers seconded from the 30th Regiment were Lieutenant Philip Edward Bulkeley, Lieutenant William Fitzthomas and Ensign Peter Dumas, assisted by Sergeant Major Peter Wallace and Corporal Charles Wharton. Captain Richard Hare was also recorded as serving with the Maltese companies in July, but the names of the 89th Regiment's officers are not stated. (WO12/4565) The British officers retained their regimentals but

the Maltese rank and file had bluish grey round jackets with red collar and cuffs and buckskin coloured gaiter trousers. This was topped off with a round hat and in a distinctive touch they all had red sashes with the knot tied at the rear in Maltese style. A white nankeen jacket was worn in hot weather. Vivion's Malta Coast artillery, which he raised and trained, wore white cotton jackets and trousers and were distinguished by wearing blue sashes rather than red ones.

19. Having been filled with volunteers from the Militia, the two battalions were both very strong. On 1 January 1801 1/35th Regiment mustered 744 rank and file fit for duty, seventy-seven rank and file sick, while 2/35th had 777 rank and file fit for duty, 102 rank and file sick. On arrival they were quartered at Naxxar, near St Paul's Bay.

20. Two companies of the regiment were still serving as marines on HMS *Generaux* at the time, but most of the regiment arrived on Malta on 21 July and was quartered at Gudja. It appears to have been rather sickly and a return of 1 January 1801 revealed 481 rank and file fit for duty and no fewer than eighty sick.

21. There is a curious story in the regimental history of the 30th that the four flank companies of the 30th and 89th Foot and a detachment of the 35th, all under the command of Lieutenant Colonel Lord Blayney of the 89th, suddenly stormed Fort Ricasoli four or five days before the general surrender. None of the other histories mention the incident, and although the circumstantial details of the supposed assaulting force are intriguing, the terms of the capitulation agreed on 5 September specifically required the surrender of Fort Ricasoli by the French. The likeliest explanation is that once the French surrendered, Blayney was directed to formally take possession of the fort with the force named, but afterwards the story was improved and accorded a spurious legitimacy by Blayney's entry in the *Royal Military Calendar*.

Chapter 2: General Abercromby and his Army

1. Bunbury, Lieutenant General Sir Henry, *Narratives of Some Passages in the Great War with France, from 1799–1810* London 1954: vii–xviii. The caveat ought to be recorded that Bunbury's first commission was as an ensign in the Coldstream in January 1795, therefore he encountered the Army at its worst during the chaotic midst of the great recruiting boom of the 1790s, rather than at the very outset of the war.

2. Bunbury's assertion that the army was 'very weak in numbers' in the beginning was literally correct in that when the war began, infantry battalions were on a peacetime establishment of just 370 rank and file. Obviously enough they could not be completed up to their wartime establishment of 850 men at a moment's notice, especially as they were competing for recruits with dozens of other units. Independent Companies were therefore authorised for the sole purpose of enlisting men in a hurry, and they were no sooner completed than they were shut down and their personnel decanted into needy regiments of the line. Purely in terms of numbers enlisted, they were effective enough but they were also notorious for the poor quality of the recruits thus gathered in, often by unscrupulous crimps.
3. Bunbury: 29.
4. Two years after that precocious first commission he transferred as an ensign to his uncle's 75th Highlanders, rising to the rank of captain by 1792 despite not going out with the regiment to India. Further promotion followed at a rapid pace; he became major of John Hely Hutchinson's short-lived 94th Regiment in 1794 and then lieutenant colonel successively of the 112th Regiment, commanded by Hutchinson's elder brother, the Earl of Donoughmore, and then the 53rd Regiment, under Wellbore Ellis Doyle – one of the Doyles of Bramblestown. There is no evidence of any talent on the part of young Abercromby to justify these appointments, either at the time or in his subsequent career, and it is difficult not to conclude that he is a clear example of how the promotion system could be abused – and together with the equally blatant and unjustified favouritism displayed towards Hutchinson, does not cast Sir Ralph in quite such a flattering light.
5. Officers in the Footguards enjoyed a system of dual rank. Lieutenants in the Footguards took precedence as captains in the Army, while captains in the Footguards enjoyed the rank of lieutenant colonel in the Army.
6. Like Murray, Campbell of Monzie not only came from 3rd Footguards, but was quite literally a next-door neighbour to the Murrays of Ochtertyre! There is no mystery therefore as to why young Murray was taken on as his ADC.
7. *Hart; ODNB.*
8. See Houlding, Dr John, *Fit for Service; The Training of the British Army 1715–1795* (Oxford, 1981) for a very thorough and eminently sensible study of this important and frequently misunderstood issue.

9. It should, of course, be emphasised at this point that Harry Dundas the politician and David Dundas the soldier are not to be confused and were not closely related.

10. Platooning required that a battalion be drawn up into a long, three-man deep firing line and then arbitrarily told off into a number of platoons, which were intended to fire volleys in a tightly controlled sequence, producing a constant and supposedly effective rolling fire. Under the simpler Alternate system, companies were paired off and then fired alternately. Latterly however the preference was to fire by wings or even by whole battalions preparatory to closing with the bayonet. To do this effectively, battalions were increasingly drawing up in only two ranks; a practice deplored by Dundas, who firmly advocated the 'solidity' of three ranks.

11. (Anon.) *Partial account of the action in North Holland on the 2nd October 1799; by an officer engaged in Sir R. Abercromby's division.* Quoted in Gardyne, Greenhill, *Life of a Regiment.* 1:67–68.

12. Again referencing later experience, although there was an sensible policy that experienced officers drawn from the Half Pay should form at least part of the cadre of newly raised units (gaining a step in the process) and retired NCOs were encouraged to re-enlist, it was inevitable that in the first years of the war their experience pre-dated the adoption of the 1792 *Regulations* and understandable therefore that they should teach what they knew, which may have contributed to some of the confusion alluded to by Bunbury.

13. Moore, *Diary of Sir John Moore,* Ed. Sir J.F. Maurice (London, 1904) 1:377–9.

14. They did not remain in Portugal for very long. On 17 November Harry Dundas informed Pulteney not only that no further reinforcements could be spared to him, but that on the contrary nearly all of his existing troops were urgently needed for internal security duties in England and Ireland. He was therefore directed to send one of his six battalions to Minorca, to embark the remaining five for England immediately, and finally to despatch some 500 men of the 12th and 26th Light Dragoons to join Abercromby. Thus, all British troops were withdrawn from Portugal, and the three foreign regiments of *Mortemarte, Castries* and *Le Chastre* alone remained; the British government having now made up its mind, quite erroneously, that the country was no longer in any danger from the menaces of France and Spain. Pulteney himself was given the option either to join Abercromby or to return home, but once

again the earlier difficulty arose that Pulteney was the officer next in seniority to Abercromby in the Mediterranean, and so displaying great good sense he took himself home, although he was destined not to be employed again.

15. While there is no denying that Tsar Paul was mentally unstable, his shift in attitude was triggered in large part first by the Helder fiasco and then by Britain's refusal to surrender Malta.

16. The troops in question were originally intended for an expedition to the Dutch East Indies and the Governor General of British India, Richard Wellesley, Earl of Mornington, originally intended to give command of the force to his brother, Arthur Wellesley, but this blatant act of nepotism aroused a storm of protest that forced him to back down and appoint Major General David Baird instead. See Weller, Jac, *Wellington in India* (London, 1972): 106–113.

17. The combat losses at the Helder had not been unduly heavy but 247 officers and men were lost by shipwreck on the way home.

18. *Aguerri* was originally a French term that roughly translates as hardened or fit for service. but it was used by more than one officer involved in the campaign, suggesting that it was then in common currency in the British Army. Surprisingly enough, the term appears to have survived into the author's day in slightly mangled form as '*warry*' – and probably still does.

Chapter 3: The Iliad and the Odyssey

1. Moore 2:56–7.
2. TNA WO1/345. Abercromby to Dundas 15 January 1801.
3. Walsh, Thomas, *Journal of the Late Campaign in Egypt* (London, 1803): 50; Wilson, Robert, *Narrative of the Expedition to Egypt* (4th Edn., London, 1803) 1: 7.
4. Walsh: 53. He also mentioned, in passing, that most of the horses were greys, as these were much favoured by the Turks.
5. Moore 2:56–7.
6. Moore, *Diary*, op. cit. Walsh commented that fortuitously there was a plain by the landing place, which was broad enough for two brigades to exercise at the same time.
7. Walsh: 66.
8. Walsh: 67. In fact, this was one of the more notable intelligence failures and once they arrived at Aboukir, drinking water was found quite readily, both by digging wells and by rediscovering ancient aqueducts.

9. Alexander Cochrane, born in 1768, was the sixth surviving son of Thomas Cochrane, 8th Earl of Dundonald, and like his siblings, was a somewhat equivocal character, later best known for successfully burning the White House and unsuccessfully bombarding Fort McHenry during the American War of 1812.

10. Like many of the high-ranking Ottoman officers, the Grand Vizier, Yusuf Pasha, was a Georgian rather than a Turk and the appellation *Kör* (blind) referred to his having lost an eye to an accident with a javelin. Devout and fatalistic, he was regarded by many European observers as woefully incompetent, but from the Ottoman viewpoint he was effective enough to hold his army together after its defeat at Heliopolis, however shambolic it may have appeared, and eventually he surprised everyone by defeating the French in open battle at El Khanka, near Cairo, on 16 May 1801, albeit with the aid of the officers and men of the British military mission, who not only manned his artillery but effectively ran the battle for him.

11. Walsh: 55. Robert Wilson (Wilson 1:9) amplifies this by claiming that: 'The Grand Vizier wished to muster the troops; but as each chief drew for as many rations as he chose to demand, which this inspection would have checked, a few shots were fired at his highness's tent in the morning it was to take place, which hint was well understood and the muster was immediately countermanded.'

12. Georg Koehler was a Royal Artillery officer of German extraction who had served for many years at Gibraltar.

13. Charles Holloway actually held the substantive rank of captain in the Royal Engineers, but was granted both the brevet rank of major with effect from 1 January 1801 and the local rank of lieutenant colonel within the 'Dominions of the Grand Seignior' from the same date. (*Army List*)

14. Moore, *Diary of Sir John Moore* Ed. Sir J.F. Maurice (London, 1904) 1:390–6.

15. An unexpected hazard to navigation in the shallow waters of the bay turned out to be the sunken wreck of *L'Orient* and other debris scattered around the seabed by Nelson's victory.

16. Walsh App 29 and 30 *124–5. A more detailed breakdown and estimate by Mackesy (56) raises the disposable French total to 23,493, largely by reducing the number of 'non-combatants' by half – on the reasonable grounds that a substantial number of them, including artillerymen and auxiliaries, such as the *Legion Nautique* and the *Grenadiers Grec*, were perfectly capable of fighting.

17. These figures (for 1 March 1801) form an appendix to Reynier, Jean Louis Ebenezer *State of Egypt after the Battle of Heliopolis, Preceded by General Observations* ... G. and J. Robinson (London, 1802).

18. It is unclear how much credence may be placed on the involvement of slave traders, but Reynier also emphasises the degree to which the ranks of *21e Légére* were filled with Coptic and other local volunteers.

19. A notable example, once again, was the *21e Légére*, which fielded two battalions at the battle of Alexandria/Canope, while *1/21e* was still serving in Upper Egypt with Donzelot.

20. Unlike their British counterparts, French dragoons were still officially regarded as mounted infantry and while they undoubtedly preferred being cavalrymen, they were also fully trained and equipped as infantry and were still employed in that role from time to time.

21. Richard Fletcher, who had earlier been in Syria with Koehler's mission, later went on to serve as Wellington's chief of engineers in the Peninsula before being killed in action at the storming of St Sebastian in 1813.

Chapter 4: Aboukir Bay

1. The flat-bottomed boats or barges were purpose-built landing craft, originally designed in the 1750s, and are not to be confused with the ordinary ship's boats carrying Coote's brigade, which although very useful for towing barges, had a rather smaller capacity for carrying troops, and less room for sufficient rowers to match the speed of the barges.

2. Walsh: 74 et. seq.

3. Moore, *The Diary of Sir John Moore* (Edward Arnold, London, 1904) 2:3.

4. Wilson 1:20, recorded that the right flank of the boats was protected by the *Crueile* cutter and the *Dangereuse* and *Janissary* gun vessels; while the left was similarly covered by the *Entreprenant* cutter, *Malta* schooner and *Negresse* gun vessel; on each flank were also two launches taking the place of the missing Turkish gunboats. Otherwise, close fire support for the landing was primarily provided by the *Tartarus* and the *Fury* bomb vessels while the *Peterell, Camelion* and *Minorca* were moored with their little broadsides to the shore.

5. Grapeshot was primarily a close-range anti-personnel round, each containing several copper or iron balls packed in a canvas

bag. It differed from the canister rounds employed by the army in that it was generally used in large calibre weapons and the balls themselves were correspondingly larger in order to be able to smash through ships' bulwarks, as well as flesh and bone. Langrage was very similar in concept, but the balls were replaced by chopped up pieces of scrap metal. This makeshift substitute was obviously more frightful in its execution, but it tended to be used reluctantly by gunners since it inevitably scored and damaged the bore of the gun.

6. Reynier: 241, 243 enumerates Friant's force in detail:

61e Ligne (two battalions including grenadiers)	700
75e Ligne (two battalions)	600
51e Ligne (half battalion plus detachment 25e Ligne)	250
18e Dragoons	100
20e Dragoons (detachment)	80

7. Stewart, David, *Sketches of the Highlanders of Scotland* (2nd Edn., Edinburgh,1822) 1:452. It should be noted that while Stewart went out to the Mediterranean as the captain-lieutenant of the 42nd Highlanders, on paper at least he had become a substantive captain in the 90th Perthshire Volunteers on 15 September 1800, and then did not officially exchange back into the Black Watch until 23 July 1802, long after the campaign was over. However, the 7 March 1801 state shows the 42nd with five captains, while the 90th had only three captains present, and it is clear from his narrative that despite his promotion into a different regiment, Stewart continued to do duty with the Black Watch throughout the campaign.

8. *Return of the Killed, Wounded, and Missing, of the Army under the Command of Sir Ralph Abercromby, K.B., in the Landing on the Coast of Egypt; Aboukir, 8th of March 1801.* Walsh App 2: *4–5. Stewart 1:453, identifies the wounded officers of the 42nd as Lieutenant Colonel James Stewart, Captain Charles Macquarrie, Lieutenants Alexander Campbell, John Dick, Frederick Campbell, Stewart Campbell, and Charles Campbell and Ensign (Adam) Wilson.

9. All in all, those temporarily left behind on the ships for lack of boats to carry them amounted to a company of the Black Watch, the entirety of the 92nd Highlanders and the rest of 2/54th Regiment, although all of them would eventually be brought ashore later in the day or that evening.

10. *Return of the Killed, Wounded, and Missing, of the Army under the Command of Sir Ralph Abercromby, K.B., in the Landing on the Coast of Egypt; Aboukir, 8th of March 1801.* Walsh App 2: *4–5. These figures will have included those men lost in the sunk landing craft. The wounded

officers were Captain Hon, Edward Plunkett, Captain Richard Beadon, Captain John Frederick, Captain James Myers and Surgeon George Rose. – of whom Captain Frederick and Surgeon Rose joined Ensign Warren (the son of Admiral Sir John Borlace Warren) on the Guards memorial in the Royal Military Chapel in Wellington Barracks. Myers would later die commanding the Fusilier Brigade at Albuera in 1811.

11. Wilson 1:23.
12. The Royals' losses included four officers wounded; Captain Alexander McDonald and Lieutenants James Graham, Thomas Fraser and Thomas Lister. The Scots Guards' losses included a drummer and seven rank and file missing, so at least some of their casualties must have been killed or wounded in the boats. By contrast, both battalions of the 54th escaped more or less unscathed with a total of four killed and nineteen wounded.
13. Mackesy, Piers, *British Victory in Egypt* (Routledge, London, 1995) citing Admiralty records gives a total of seven officers and ninety seamen killed or wounded, but this seems rather high in relation to the army's casualties and most likely refers to the total losses for the campaign as a whole rather than on the day of the landing alone.
14. *Return of the Killed, Wounded, and Missing, of the British Army, during the Campaign in Egypt*. Walsh App 37: *141. Confusingly, Lieutenant Guiterra of the Corsican Rangers, his sergeant and thirteen of his men taken prisoners on 11 March were added as 'missing' to the official return for the Aboukir landing.
15. There is some confusion as to the name of this lake. The French named it as Lake Maadje, and some of the British did likewise, while others insisted on calling it Lake Aboukir. However in a note to the second edition of his *History* (2:6), Wilson complicates matters even further by insisting that it was properly called Lake Sed (after the breached wall or causeway mentioned by Walsh), and that Lake Maadje was actually another name for Lake Edko and so called for the passage or ferry on the road to Rosetta! For the sake of clarity and consistency I have chosen to stick with Lake Maadje.
16. Walsh: 81–3.
17. Moore similarly remarked in the run-up to the landing that 'Contrary also to every previous information of the climate upon this coast, there has been constant and very hard rain.' (*Diary* 2:2).
18. The lieutenant was John Woodgate of the 26th Light Dragoons. The nature of his wound is unknown but he next turns up as a captain in the 1st Royal Garrison Battalion, a traditional refuge for disabled veterans.

19. The 90th Regiment was a particularly good choice for the assignment, for although the regiment was not officially designated as light infantry, it had, quite exceptionally, been trained as such from its first formation and it is hard to avoid the impression that Moore's acquaintanceship with the regiment (and with its trainer, Major Kenneth Mackenzie) at Mandara led directly to Shorncliffe and the creation of what would become the famous Light Division of Peninsular fame.

Chapter 5: Mandara

1. Appreciating that he was badly outnumbered, Lanusse had marched out with every man he could muster, leaving only the *Legion Nautique* to hold Alexandria.
2. Dundas' *Rules and Regulations* were enthusiastically praised by a number of officers observing this performance, but while Dundas' manoeuvres were indeed well conceived, organised and explained; the real credit should be given to Abercromby's intensive training programmes on Minorca, Malta and at Marmaris prior the commencement of the campaign, which gave everyone (except the marines) the opportunity to become proficient in their use.
3. Reynier: 253. Although Reynier himself was not actually present, he was a personal friend of Lanusse and no doubt got the story from him just a few days later: 'The [British] centre marched slowly on the other side of a height, by which it was hid from the French so that the left wing appeared isolated. General Lanusse, hoping to overpower it by a brisk attack, before it could be supported ...'
4. Mackenzie actually held the brevet rank of lieutenant colonel.
5. Delavoye, Alexander *Records of the 90th Regiment, (Perthshire Light Infantry); with roll of officers from 1795 to 1880* (London, 1880): 39. In total the 90th had twenty-two rank and file killed over the course of the battle, besides eight officers, eleven sergeants and 203 rank and file wounded. Remarkably, the wounded officers included both of the two regimental lieutenant colonels and the assistant surgeon. Rowland Hill was shot in the head, but saved by his Tarleton helmet (which is still preserved and displaying the damage) and, of course, he lived to be the most reliable of Wellington's generals and eventually succeeded him as Commander-in-Chief of the Army. The engagement was also a remarkable one in that the 90th counterpointed the earlier demonstration of Dundas' Prussian-style precepts by delivering a masterclass in the light infantry tactics that

212

NOTES

Mackenzie would later go on to teach at Shorncliffe under Moore. Captain McNair's account of the action, which he related to the regiment's colonel, Sir Thomas Graham in a letter of 17 March, bears quoting at length:

'With the most heartfelt satisfaction I congratulate you on the unparalleled gallantry of your regiment in the action of the 13th inst. The Commander-in-Chief was pleased to say we had gained immortal honour; we proved to our own army and also the enemy how futile the attempts of the most determined cavalry is on infantry that meet them with resolution. Col. Mackenzie, who commanded three companies for the support of the light company which was in front, behaved with singular coolness and most determined heroism. I had Mr. Wright [Lieutenant Thomas Wright] wounded badly, and twenty-nine men killed and wounded of the light company; tho' unavoidably a good deal scattered, they individually stood firm to the cavalry and bayoneted some of them; I had five men cut with sabres, but none killed. Col. [George] Vigoureux was wounded early in the day, and Colonel Hill soon after; our wounded in general are doing well. The fire the cavalry received from the regiment when formed, and their charge, astonished the whole army. Captain [Hon. Mark] Napier was not touched; his company suffered severely.'

6. Cannon, Richard, *Historical Records of the Ninety-Second Regiment*: 24–25. Gardyne, *Life of a Regiment* 1:105, quotes a letter dated 15 March by Captain John Cameron of Fassfern, which lists the same number of officers dead and wounded and cites eight sergeants and 119 men killed and wounded. Mackesy: 92 for some unknown reason gives a wholly unwarranted eighteen officers and 150 men killed and wounded!

The wounded officers were: Lieutenant Colonel Charles Erskine (subs. Dead), Captains the Hon. John Ramsay, and Archibald McDonnell, Lieutenants Norman McLeod, Charles Doule (dead). Donald McDonald, Tomlin Campbell (dead), Alexander Clarke (dead), Ronald McDonald, and Alexander Cameron, and Ensign Peter Wilkie – the latter was the 14-year-old son of Quartermaster Peter Wilkie. Quickly recovering from his wound, he served with the regiment throughout the Peninsular War, was wounded again at Waterloo and became a regimental major in 1819.

7. The 'hussars' in this case were actually in fact the 22e *Chasseurs a Cheval*, who had taken advantage of their remoteness from Paris to give themselves airs and add hussar-style apple green pelisses to their regulation bright green dolmans and breeches.

213

8. Moore, *The Diary of Sir John Moore* Edward Arnold (London, 1904) 2:8–10.

9. Walsh: 89 and App 2*10–12. The returns attached to Abercromby's dispatch of 16 March need to be treated with caution since they are rather unhelpfully broken down by brigades, of which the 1st and 2nd brigades apparently suffered the heaviest losses with 205 and 501 casualties respectively. However, more than half of the former belonged to the Gordons, who were detached from the brigade at the time. As for the 2nd Brigade on the other hand, its quoted loss must actually include the 244 killed and wounded of the 90th Regiment, who were evidently treated by the brigade major as being attached to it during the operation.

10. Walsh: 90. The curricle guns referred to were light cannon (in this case the two 4-pounders attached to each demi-brigade) mounted directly on to the bed of a small two-wheeled cart or curricle, whose shafts doubled as a trail. These were once very popular but rapidly fell out of favour as heavier cannon were phased in.

11. Moore: 2:10.
   Abercromby was evidently unaware at this point that he had actually been fighting General Lanusse, while the latter obviously saw no reason to enlighten him.

12. Wilson: 41–43. Walsh's account (p.93) in fact appears to be largely lifted directly from Reynier (p.259), who also provides a brief paragraph on the fight, usefully confirming the identities of the French units involved, while very pointedly making absolutely no mention of his hated rival, General d'Estaing:
   '... 50 hussars of the 7th regiment, detached with a company of the carabineers [grenadiers] of the 21st to reconnoitre their position on the canal. The light horse charged the hussars who, rushing at the same time against them, broke through their squadron; then, suddenly wheeling, on their excellent Arabian coursers, took the English on the rear; who, unable to check their horses, were thus driven, on the carabineers, whose fire completed their destruction.'

13. The official return (Walsh App 3:16*) lists the following casualties (including horses) in the skirmish:
   12th Light Dragoons. – 5 horses killed; 1 officer, 1 sergeant wounded; 2 officers, 7 rank and file, 7 horses missing.
   26th Light Dragoons. – 1 quarter-master, 7 rank and file, 18 horses killed; 2 officers, 1 sergeant, 6 rank and file, 12 horses wounded; 1 officer, 1 quarter-master, 5 rank and file, 7 horses missing.
   Total. – 1 quarter-master, 7 rank and file, 23 horses killed;

2 officers, 1 sergeant, 6 rank and file, 12 horses wounded;

3 officers, 1 quarter-master, 12 rank and file, 7 horses missing.

Officers killed. – 26th Light Dragoons: Quarter-master John Simpson.

Officers wounded. – 12th Light Dragoons: Colonel Merwyn Archdall.*

26th Light Dragoons. – Lieutenant and Adjutant John Harte.

Officers missing (taken prisoner).

12th Light Dragoons: Honourable Captain Pierce Buller, Cornet Earl Lindsay Daniel.

26th Light Dragoons. – Captain Charles Turner (Brigade Major), Quarter-master Abraham Moulton.

*Despite losing an arm, Colonel Archdall subsequently returned to command the regiment

14. Thus far the British had encountered French infantry dressed in red, or something like it, and cavalry dressed in green. The fact that d'Estaing's infantry were dressed in light blue and his cavalry in red ought to have rung some alarm bells.

Chapter 6: Kasr Kaisera

1. Although British authors traditionally refer to the battle of Alexandria, and those regiments involved proudly bear the name on their colours as a battle honour, French and other continental historians know the battle as *Canope*, naming it after the presumed site of the ancient seaport of Canopus, which seems to have been largely destroyed by natural disasters in antiquity, leaving most of it beneath the shallow waters of Aboukir Bay. Nevertheless, given the fact that a number of quite different engagements took place around Alexandria during the campaign, distinguishing this particular one as *Canope* appears sensible.

2. Reynier, Jean Louis Ebenezer *State of Egypt after the Battle of Heliopolis, Preceded by General Observations* … G. and J. Robinson (London, 1802): 262. 'General Lanusse, indirectly applied to for a plan by General Menou, sent him, by a third person, one drawn up in concert with General Reynier, which was reduced into the order of the day, and delivered to the generals at ten in the evening.' – and a rather hurriedly botched plan it was, too.

3. Speaking of the later position at El Hamed, Wilson helpfully pointed out that 'it must be understood, that these canals are not like those of Europe, as they have no water in them, except at high

Nile, the level of the country forming their bed, and the banks being raised above it'. The channel of the Alexandria Canal, according to Walsh, was 7ft (2m) wide and lined with bricks, although somewhat choked with drifting sand. Unfortunately, he neglects to note how high it stood above the surrounding countryside, but it must have been about 2m, or even more in places.

4. The rest of the 26th Light Dragoons were still back at Aboukir Castle. Dismounted light cavalry normally paraded with their short 28in (71cm)-barrelled, small-bore carbines, but although these were perfectly adequate for arming sentries and quarter-guards, they were quite unsuitable for infantry work and it is more than likely that the dismounted cavalry in Egypt were actually provided with full-sized Sea Service muskets borrowed from the Royal Navy.

5. Some of the classically inclined chroniclers of the campaign such as Wilson, even rather hopefully identified the ruins as those of Ptolemy's palace, but there is no doubt of its being the remains of a fortress.

6. Wilkinson, Sir John Gardiner *Modern Egypt and Thebes: Being a Description of Egypt* … J. Murray (London, 1843), 1:172–3. Originally published in 1835, Wilkinson's book was the fruit of twelve years' survey work in Egypt carried out between 1821 and 1833, and at that time the remains of the fort will have been little changed since the battle. The reference to its being surrounded by a sea water-filled ditch is interesting, for no mention is made of such a feature in accounts of the battle, and no trace of such a ditch can be seen in Walsh's plan, but it does emphasise how close it lay to the sea. By the time John Murray published an updated edition of what had become the *Handbook for Travellers in Lower and Upper Egypt* in 1880 the site had been almost totally obliterated by the building of the Khedive's palace.

7. The very substantial walls are also depicted in near contemporary paintings by Edward Orme and Philip Loutherbourg, both emphasising the defendable condition of the ruins and the way in which they dominated this part of the battlefield.

8. Walsh: 104. These figures did not include the 500-strong Turkish contingent, which was posted safely out of harm's way down at the depot by the northern end of Lake Maadje.

9. *1/21e Légére* were still in Upper Egypt at this time and so missed the battle, while the *Grenadiers Grecs* was a locally recruited regiment supposedly comprising volunteers of Greek origin who resident in Egypt although the term Greek was probably a rather elastic one. An error by Walsh (or his printer) confuses matters by giving

d'Estaing the command of 'the 21st brigade, and two companies of grenadiers, those of the 25th and the Greeks'. In fact, Menou's orders actually say that d'Estaing's column *'composee de la 21me brigade; de deux compagnies de grenadiers de la 25me brigade, et des grenadiers Grecs'*. Elsewhere in his correspondence leading up to the battle Menou very clearly confirms that the latter formed a battalion, not a mere company.

10. Although not referred to in Menou's orders, Hutchinson's official report on the battle (Walsh App 4: *17) credits d'Estaing with having one demi-brigade, some light troops and a detachment of cavalry. The 'light troops' were presumably the grenadiers, who were frequently employed in this role, while the latter will have been the same detachment of *7e(bis) Hussards* who had been under his command on the Alexandria Canal three days earlier.

11. Reynier: 264.

12. Mackesy (254 n.14) errs in stating that Menou's orders did not place Reynier in command of the French right wing. On the contrary, after directing that the attack was to be begun on the left and by the centre, the orders explicitly state that; 'At the same time the right of the army, commanded by General Regnier, will refuse itself a little, till the left is closely engaged with enemy.' Walsh App 8:41*.

13. A copy of the orders was afterwards found on General Roise's body and is published in full with a translation in Walsh App 8: *37–42*.

14. The time of 3.30 am was apparently an hour ahead of that laid down in Menou's plan, but as everyone on both sides is agreed that the action began an hour before sunrise, we may safely conclude that the British and French watches and chronometers were set to different times.

15. Captain David Stewart identified them as belonging to Stuart's Minorca Regiment, but he may have confused the regiment with the brigade. As was customary, they were recorded as 'missing' in the initial casualty returns.

16. *'Un corps leger se portera fur la gauche de l'ennemi, poure faire une fausse attaque, qui commencera a la meme heure que la veritable.'* 'A light corps will advance on the enemy's left, to make a false attack, which will commence at the same hour as the true.' Walsh App 8: 38*, *41.

17. Wilson 1:48.

18. Moore, *Diary* 2:12–13.

19. It is unclear how many cannon were actually in the redoubt. Walsh says there were intended to be two of them but according to David Stewart of the 42nd, he second one had not yet been mounted.

20. In order for Rampon's 32e to become entangled with Sylly's brigade they would first have need to pass to the other side of d'Estaing's column, which was advancing down the road on their right.

21. The traditional French uniform of long-tailed coats and cocked hats had by now been replaced in Egypt by a much simpler one, better suited to the local conditions; it featured a short Austrian-style single-breasted jacket, in a confusing variety of colours, and a peaked soft leather cap (not unlike a modern baseball cap in appearance) topped by a woollen caterpillar crest. In the poor pre-dawn light the shape of these peaked caps will have been easily distinguished from the taller cylindrical caps worn by most British infantrymen.

22. Walsh: 97–8. In actual fact, according to Dr Larrey (*Memoirs of Military Surgery and Campaigns of the French Army*, Baltimore 1814 1:378), General Lanusse's right knee was shattered by a small ball from what must have been a discharge of grapeshot. Larrey recommended immediate amputation, but despite being in agony the general refused until it was too late, dramatically declaring he did not wish to outlive such a defeat.

23. Reynier: 266.

24. David Stewart *Sketches of the Highlanders of Scotland*. 1:465. The 'white frocks' seen by Stewart's soldier will have been the white canvas greatcoats worn by all French infantry in Egypt. Many of the short Austrian-style jackets they had adopted were red or near-red in colour and therefore the white greatcoats were often worn over them in action to avoid confusion when fighting against British troops. The 'large hats' rather than caps may possibly be accounted for by the *21e Légére* coming from far-off Upper Egypt.

25. Stewart 1:465–467. Stewart is at some pains in his narrative to emphasise that; 'it is proper to explain, that it was only the rear rank of the left wing that faced about and charged to their rear; the front rank kept their ground to oppose the enemy in their immediate front'. This very helpful statement also answers the perennial question as to whether, despite their professed enthusiastic adherence to the teachings of David Dundas, the British infantry in Egypt were formed in the two ranks that had served them so well in America and would do so again in the Peninsula and at Waterloo, rather than standing in the outdated three ranks so very firmly prescribed by Dundas.

26. There was an unusual sequel to this incident when General Reynier later returned home and wrote his rather mendacious account of

the campaign, stating that d'Estaing (against whom by then he had a grudge) 'retired from the field, after being slightly wounded' (p.266). In fact, according to Larrey (1:152), d'Estaing was badly wounded 'by a ball of large size' that passed through his right arm, paralysing it and resulting in 'anguish general debility and difficult respiration'. He subsequently developed tetanus and while Larrey managed to save him, his hand and forearm remained paralysed. Not surprisingly, d'Estaing took exception to the slur, and challenged Reynier to a duel, only to be shot dead.

27. Mackesy, following Wilson, renders his name as 'Crowdje', but Crowgey is the form in which it appears both in the *Army List* and in his own manuscript return of service (NA WO25/3998).
28. Hill's statement of service 1816. Royal Welch Fusiliers Museum.
29. Reynier: 266–7. Wilson on the other hand (1:58–59) was quite scathing about this; 'General Reynier states, that the battalion to which these colours belonged was composed chiefly of Copts; but how Copts came to carry a standard, on which *le Passage de la Serivia, le Passage da Tagliamento, le Passage de l' Isonzo, la Prise de Graz, le Pont de Lodi*, are inscribed, General Reynier can only explain.' In fact, the *21e Légére* while indubitably French, was indeed one of those units boosted by local recruiting.
30. Walsh's map does, however, show two small units trailing off the right flank of *3/21e* as they climb the slope. These are not identified and may simply be part of *3/21e*, but it is also possible that they may be Eppler's grenadiers.
31. Reynier's statement that 'The second battalion effected their retreat' might be considered decisive, if he had not already confused them with *32e Ligne*. It is unclear what subsequently happened to the errant battalion, but it seems improbable that it would have managed to disengage itself from the assault on the redoubt and then move around in the dark in time to join d'Estaing and Hausser in their ill-fated attack on the fort. More likely that *2/21e* 'escaped' the debacle by not being involved in the attack in the first place.

Chapter 7: The Dawn's Early Light

1. Stewart 1:467.
2. And curiously enough no more is heard thereafter of Rampon himself during the battle.
3. Hope's movements at this time are rather uncertain, but Moore saw him near Abercromby before the cavalry attacked. The nature of

his injuries – he lost his right index finger and was bruised by a spent musket ball striking him in the groin – does suggest he was facing infantry and that he was no longer with Abercromby when the latter was hurt.

4. Honeyman was the second son of Sir William Honeyman of Armadale, West Lothian, and had earlier served in the Reay Fencibles and then on Moore's staff in Ireland. He was now present in Egypt as a volunteer on the staff but he was afterwards rewarded with the brevet rank of lieutenant colonel and the appointment of major in the 93rd Highlanders. He subsequently served in South Africa before dying of fever on Jamaica in 1809.

5. Reynier: 268.

6. Reynier: 270. In all the circumstances, just how accurately Reynier reported Roise's supposed words might be a little open to doubt.

7. Wilson 2:193 (Black Watch regimental report).

8. Stewart 1:468.

9. Stewart 1:469.

10. Larrey (1:380) records that he was actually shot in the abdomen close to the groin by a large ball (perhaps part of a canister or grapeshot round). Nevertheless, he survived and went on to serve with distinction in Spain and in Germany. A very intrepid officer, he was wounded many times and eventually died of his many injuries in 1813.

11. Stewart 1:469–70.

12. Wilson 2:191–199 provides transcripts of the inquiries into the matter by both the 42nd and Stuart's Regiment: The dragoon who had seized the colour from Sergeant Sinclair was himself shot down, leaving it to be picked up from the ground by one of Stuart's men, Private Anton Lutz. Claiming to have recaptured the flag in a heroic feat of arms, Lutz very prudently obtained a receipt for it from the DAG. This earned him an immediate reward of 24 dollars (being illiterate he was not judged fit for promotion), an elaborately embroidered badge to wear on his arm and what later amounted to a get out of jail free card. The incident later occasioned some bad feeling between the regiments since 'ownership' of the flag was disputed by the 42nd and eventually Sergeant Sinclair was rather pointedly commissioned in the regiment in 1804 before being promoted into the 81st three years later and retiring on to the half pay as a captain when his battalion was reduced in 1816. The implication, of course, is that he may in fact have been more actively involved in the original capture of the colour than Stewart suggests.

Interestingly the centre point of Loutherbourg's splendid painting of the battle depicts Sinclair and Lutz disputing ownership of the colour before a wounded Abercromby.

13. Although earlier speaking of Abercromby being set upon by dragoons, Moore (2:18–19) very explicitly refers to them here as being hussars. As Roise had none in his brigade these men probably belonged to the detachment of 7e(bis) Hussars that was originally attached to d'Estaing's column when it was designated as the advance guard. The soldier of the Black Watch who rescued Abercromby is identified in regimental histories as a corporal named Barker, and he was assisted by two others.

14. Including, it would seem, General Roise himself (although Larrey says he was struck by a cannonball) for his body was discovered there after the battle. Larrey also recorded that Roise's chief of staff, Adjutant General Blaniac, was 'wounded in the breast by a ball. His ribs were fractured but there was no organick lesion'.

15. Wilson 2:193–4 (Black Watch regimental report). Mackesy (141) in discussing how little we actually know of Abercromby's role in directing the battle, speculates: 'Was it by his orders that Stuart began to march his foreign brigade towards the left on the first alarm, and then counter-marched towards the valley to intervene at the crisis of the battle?' As he rightly concludes, we simply do not know, but on the evidence it seems unlikely. Stuart, just as the other brigadiers and regimental officers, was acting on his own initiative, and certainly took the credit for the result.

16. Reynier simply says that Sylly's leg and thigh were shot away, but Larrey, who actually treated him, comments that his left leg was completely carried away at the knee, but because he was evacuated swiftly and the amputation was completed while he was still in shock and only semi-conscious, he quickly recovered, despite being aged over 60. (Larrey: 1:379).

17. Oddly enough, although nearly two-thirds of the casualties occurred in the Minorca Regiment, Walsh depicts *32e Ligne* attacking Dillon's Regiment in the centre of the brigade, but perhaps when the offensive was halted they deployed to their left in an attempt to link up with Sylly's *18e Ligne*.

18. Wilson 1:54.

19. This statement might appear to be contradicted by Captain David Stewart's assertion (1:459) that the final shot was fired from the redoubt by Major Alexander Duncan (who was *Captain* Duncan at the time), but there is no reason not to suppose that the guns were

indeed laid by subalterns during the action and that Duncan only came up with the resupply that enabled them to recommence firing at the close of the action.

20. Reynier: 270.

21. Larrey, however, says that Baudot was fatally wounded at about the same time as Lanusse, which suggests he may have been felled by a random cannon shot long before Reynier's advance actually began. The calf of his leg was shot away, but like Lanusse he refused to submit to amputation and so died of gangrene within days (Larrey 1: 379).

22. For some reason, Walsh's meticulously plotted map does not appear to have been much studied in any detail by historians, yet it is absolutely invaluable in clarifying this and a number of otherwise obscure but important issues.

23. Captain John Cameron of Fassfern, cited in Gardyne, *Life of a Regiment*, 1:108.

24. The military crest (as distinct from the topographical crest) of a hill or ridge is defined as the point from which a defender can most effectively observe and bring down direct fire on an attacker toiling upwards, while conversely it is also the limit of upward visibility for an attacker.

25. Walsh: 98.

26. Walsh: 102–3. The most notable of these long-range casualties was Lieutenant Colonel David Ogilvie of the 44th Regiment, who was fatally wounded.

27. Moore *Diary* 2:16–17.

28. Walsh: 103–4. One gun was, of course, taken at the head of the *21e Légére*, while the other (identified as a captured Austrian piece) was found abandoned in front of the redoubt after its horses and crew had all been cut down by a single discharge of grapeshot when they inadvertently strayed too close in the darkness.

29. Larrey: 1:378. He adds that 'a great portion of these wounds were severe, and required important operations'.

30. Colonel Dutens was a well-connected young officer of Huguenot descent. Wilkinson *op. cit*, records that in the 1820s there was still a memorial inscription to him on an upright stone within the ruins of the Roman fort. Other memorials to casualties that were carved on the walls of the fort were also noted although not recorded, which suggests that after the battle the interior of the fort may have become a formal burying ground for the British dead.

Chapter 8: Up the Nile

1. His father, John Hely, took the additional name of Hutchinson on his marriage in 1751 to Christiana Nickson, who was herself the financially well-endowed heiress of her uncle, Richard Hutchinson. Despite the rendering of his name in secondary sources, the general did not employ a hyphen. Instead he appeared in the *Army List* under the name Hutchinson and invariably signed himself J.H. Hutchinson.

2. As it happens, at the last minute the 77th Highland Regiment was earmarked to go to India and accordingly transferred from the Irish to the British Establishment. However, this intention was frustrated when the men flatly refused to embark at Portsmouth on the not unreasonable grounds that since they had only enlisted for the duration of the war, the ending of hostilities with the Americans on 20 January entitled them to their discharge. Hutchinson's paper transfer, taking effect from 13 March, came after this incident and in the full knowledge that the regiment was about to be disbanded.

3. General officers were entitled to have aides-de-camp on a sliding scale according to their rank. Major generals were entitled to have one at public expense (in this case Abercromby's own son John) and lieutenant generals had two, but any number of additional or 'Extra' ADCs could be also taken on at the general's own expense.

4. At any rate Cornwallis, who took over as CinC Ireland, thought so and later remarked on learning that Hutchinson was to go to the Mediterranean, that 'he is a sensible man, but he is no general – at least he was not one in 1798'. Cornwallis, *Correspondence of Charles, first Marquis Cornwallis* (London, 1859) 3:360.

5. *The Military Panorama or Officers Companion* (London, 1814) 3:514.

6. Mackesy: 104; quoting NAM *Abercromby MS*. Abercromby to Brownrigg 16 March 1801.

7. Walsh: 107. The digging of *trous de loup* was obviously a lesson very promptly learned after the problems encountered by the French cavalry in traversing what had been the 28th's lines.

8. TNA WO 1/292.

9. Wilson 1:81.

10. Wilson 1:83. There is a possible mystery here. The garrison, according to Reynier, comprised only 3/85e *Ligne* and three companies of *61e Ligne*, and even allowing for a flock of rear-area personnel they cannot have amounted to anything like the 800 troops seen by Spencer and his men. Wilson (op. cit.) specifically links 'certain

intelligence that the French had detached [reinforcements] to Rosetta' to the decision to add the Queen's Regiment to Spencer's force on 6 April, yet according to Reynier (p. 283), General Valentin was only sent off with the 700-strong 69e *Ligne* and 180 men of the *7e Hussards* two weeks later on the night of 20 April, long after Rosetta was captured. However, Reynier's statement appears in the course of a characteristically violent diatribe anent Menou's alleged incompetence and may not be true as to the date. Curiously enough, there is a circumstantial clue in a later passing remark that the British infantry in Egypt proved themselves greatly superior to the French in everything except in the matter of marching, which would support the possibility that Valentin's relief force actually left much earlier than Reynier claimed and had won the race to reach Rosetta and evacuate its garrison before Spencer arrived.

11. Wilson 1:92–93.
12. Walsh: 116.
13. Wilson 1:86–88.
14. Walsh: 114, 118.

In a footnote he observed that: 'This canal is now probably ruined for ever, in consequence of the cut made by us to let the waters of lake Aboukir into the bed of the Mareotis; as the violence of the current has increased the opening to such a width that the apathy of the Turks cannot be expected to attempt repairing the damage.' In fact, it was repaired afterwards.

15. Walsh: 120.
16. See Walsh: *47 App No. 11 Correct Statement of the Division of the Army under the Command of Major General Hutchinson, 6 May 1801.
17. Walsh: 113. 'Three men of Hompesch's dragoons, while vedettes, deserted to the enemy on three successive mornings. This was a bad example, especially when it is considered that we had a brigade entirely composed of foreigners, great part of them deserters, whom it was well known the enemy would do all in their power to entice over to them. Accordingly, general Hutchinson, wishing to stop the evil at its commencement, ordered the corps to be immediately dismounted, and sent to do duty in the rear at Aboukir. The service required this measure, though apparently severe on the officers and privates of the regiment, who had hitherto, and on all occasions, behaved with gallantry.' Wilson, while also recording the incident, coyly relates only that that his hussars were withdrawn from the outposts, without admitting that they were dismounted and sent all the way back to Aboukir.

18. Wilson 1:127.
19. Wilson 1:126. 'At El Aft the first accurate statement of the French force opposed immediately was obtained, and in such a manner that the story ought to be recorded. As the soldiers rambled amongst the huts to find anything useful which might have escaped the conflagration, one of the 40th flank company saw a piece of paper, marked with figures, lying amongst the ashes; he could not read, but with a consideration which cannot be too much commended, went instantly to his officer. Captain D'Ancer [William Danser] who, perceiving the paper to be a return, delivered the same to the general; it proved to be a detailed statement of the French army, as certified by the commissariat and commanding officer, making their force amount to 3331 men, including artillery, sappers, and miners, but exclusive of the cavalry, which was near 600 men.'
20. Wilson 1:133.

Chapter 9: The Heart of Darkness

1. According to Wilson, the original intention was to leave only fifty men to guard the sick, but the 'surplus' had been abandoned there helplessly drunk after breaking into the magazines.
2. Wilson 1:141–142. There is some confusion as to the regiments involved. Wilson begins the story by recounting how Colonel Browne of the 12th turned up at headquarters with a report that an officer of his regiment on a watering party had fallen in with and captured a French detachment. Wilson then goes on to specifically identify the officer in question as a Lieutenant Drake of the 12th Light Dragoons and the French party as belonging to the *22e Dragoons* 'the best and heaviest regiment in the army of Egypt'. However, according to the *Army List*, William Drake actually belonged to the 26th Light Dragoons, while as to the French; the *22e Dragoons* did not serve in Egypt at all. Mackesy suggests that this was a mistake for the *22e Chasseurs a Cheval*, but Wilson had, of course, met the latter before, at Mandara and Alexandria, and moreover 'the heaviest regiment in the army of Egypt' is an unlikely description for a dashing light cavalry unit, dressed and equipped as hussars. More likely then that the regiment in question was actually the *20e Dragoons*.
3. To be precise, just 167 men of the 86th Regiment under Lieutenant Colonel James Phillips Lloyd and fifty artillerymen belonging to the East India Company service.
4. Moore 2:12–24.

5. Thomas Gage Montresor is not to be confused with his elder brother, Lieutenant Colonel Henry Tucker Montresor, the commanding officer of the 18th Regiment. He actually became major of the 89th Regiment with effect from 28 March 1801, but this was probably not known until sometime afterwards.
6. Wilson 1:160–161. Major Montresor does not appear to have taken part in the conference, although he certainly brought the news of the battle to Hutchinson.
7. Wilson 1:183–4.
8. The Albanians remained in Egypt after the campaign, filling the void created by the eclipse of the Mamlūks and, although Tahir Pasha was killed in the subsequent manoeuvring, Mehmet Ali ended up as *khedive* or viceroy of Egypt and founded a dynasty that lasted until 1952.
9. Holloway to Elgin, Benerhassett (Benha) 20 May 1801 (Wilson 2:241–45 and Walsh App 13: 51*–54] Elgin to Hawksbury, Constantinople, 21 June 1801. 'The modest and unassuming manner in which this deserving officer [Holloway] has mentioned himself and the British under his orders, imposes upon me the obligation of stating to your Lordship, what I learnt by their private communication to me from Jaffa and Gizah; that as soon as the determination was formed for the Vizier to advance into Egypt, Lieutenant Colonel Holloway proposed that distribution of the Turkish army, and that order of march, which have effectually insured this unlooked-for success over the French.' Holloway's role in fact subsequently earned him a knighthood. Lacey and Leake were also Royal Artillery officers, but while the latter had indeed served as a gunner at the outset of his career in the West Indies, he was thereafter employed in secret service work in Greece and the Levant before commanding the Albanian infantry at El Khanka. Afterwards he was again employed in secret service work in the Balkans and in 1815 in Switzerland. Leaving the army at the end of the war, he became noted as a traveller and antiquarian before dying in Brighton at the ripe old age of 83! (ODNB)
10. Wilson 1:174. In his usual sardonic style, he dismissed Reynier's bombastic claim that the French captured two cannon and commented that: 'With the same accuracy which distinguished his other observations, he augments the Vizier's army with five hundred English artillery, thus clothing twenty-nine men with five hundred buckram jackets.'
11. Wilson op. cit.

12. Wilson 1:165–9.
13. Wilson 1:190–192. The *Mamlūks'* fears of retribution were entirely justified in due course and Wilson notes that the envoy was one of those murdered by the Turks at Alexandria after the campaign was over.
14. Wilson 1:200. A *feu de joi* – literally fire of joy – was a traditional form of victory celebration in which the troops were lined up and every gun, firelock musket and trooper's pistol fired off one after the other in a ripple up and down the line. In this case it apparently celebrated a wholly imaginary 'capture of Ireland'.
15. Wilson 1:262. The 'plague' had struck while they were at Jeddah, and while Wilson did not expand on his remarks, it is possible that they may by now have been clad in Arabic style with long shirts, drawers and perhaps even turbans.
16. Walsh: 175. Abercromby was in turn succeeded as DAG by Captain John Taylor of the 25th Regiment, one of Hutchinson's ADCs.
17. Wilson 1:178–9. To be precise, eventually there were 10,856 cavalry, infantry and artillery of all ranks embarked at Rosetta, along with another 2,816 other personnel (including a detachment of 177 *Dromedaries* who had not been in Cairo and might, technically, have been excluded from the terms of the surrender) and eighty-two civilian employees.
18. Wilson 1:242–48.

Chapter 10: Another Part of the Field: The Fall of Alexandria

1. Walsh: 226–229.
2. See Walsh: *43 App 9 State of the Troops under the immediate command of Major General Coote, 25 April 1801.
3. In fairness, most of those who were forwarded to Hutchinson will, of course, have been recruits and recovered convalescents belong to the Nile regiments. 1/27th was employed for a time as a garrison for Rosetta, but on 16 June they were relieved by the 13th Regiment and then proceeded up the Nile to reunite with 2/27th Regiment.
4. Walsh claims that the water was introduced into the canal by cutting it at a different point in order to draw off water from Lake Mareotis.
5. Walsh: 169. It is implied that the 'mistake' alluded to was in not trying to run straight in to Alexandria.
6. Reynier: 301. '… the only well-concerted military expedition in the whole campaign was executed on the night of the 23d and 24th of Floreal (12–13 May). 300 infantry, 50 horse, with one piece of cannon,

and miners, were assembled, but ignorant of their destination, when they were ordered to invest the house of general Reynier, to convey him on board a vessel ready to sail for Europe, on board of which were at the same time sent general Damas, Daure principal commissary, Boyer adjutant commandant, and several other officers.' The officer in charge of the troops sent to arrest Reynier was General d'Estaing, against whom Reynier took a petty revenge by accusing him of being shy in the battle of 21 March – and then shooting him dead when he resented it.

7. Promotion to the substantive rank of lieutenant general had to wait until 25 September 1803.
8. Fencible units, first raised in Scotland to cover for that kingdom's lack of a militia, were originally intended only for home defence, but the letters of service issued for some later units, such as the Ancient Irish, allowed them to be employed anywhere in Europe.
9. Walsh: 197–8.
10. Moore, *Diary* 2:40–42.
11. The nickname was used by almost everyone present, although no one reckoned the hill was actually green. Indeed Stewart 1:483 refers to it as 'a piece of ground covered with a white sparkling sand, which the soldiers jocularly called the 'Green Hill'. Although the popular hymn would not be published (at least in its present form) until 1848, it is very tempting indeed, given its situation outside the walls of Alexandria, to look at an allusion to what would then be the opening line of the hymn: 'There is a green hill far away, without a city wall ...'
12. Moore, *Diary* 2:40–42. As to his own losses, Moore recorded: 'We had five men killed, one officer and thirteen men wounded.'
13. Colonel Jöst Durler was the commanding officer of the Regiment *De Roll* and had formerly been an officer of the *Garde Suisse*. He had commanded the detachment stationed at the Tuileries on 10 August 1792, but managed to escape the massacre that followed after Louis XVI ordered him and his men to lay down their arms. He died at Alexandria 18 September 1802 – over a year after the campaign ended – presumably of natural causes while still on occupation duties.
14. Supposedly this structure had once been a mosque and its single tall watchtower, a minaret, but given its situation at the mouth of the harbour, it is more likely to have originally been built as a lighthouse, before being adapted first as a mosque and then later as a fort.

15. According to Walsh, they were firing on the French guns at pistol range, which is not particularly helpful given that in combat it was still common to jam the muzzle of a pistol into an opponent's body before pulling the trigger. He may perhaps have been alluding to the ten or twenty paces customarily allowed to duellists, but whatever the actual distance, no one was in any doubt as to the effectiveness of the sharpshooting by men armed with smooth-bored common firelocks.

16. Walsh: 208–9 and App.23. The garrison had comprised a total of 195 men. About thirty were reckoned as having been killed or wounded, but none of the besiegers were returned as casualties.

17. Not to be confused with his older brother, Major Charles Norris Cookson RA, who did not serve in Egypt. Both, oddly enough, had been gazetted major on the same date, 1 January 1800.

18. According to Walsh's map, they were all detached units, from left to right *1/32e Ligne, 3/61e Ligne, 1/23e Ligne* and *3/18e Ligne*.

19. Walsh App 23: *87; also: *Return of the names of the officers in the army who receive pensions for the loss of limbs, or for wounds*; WO 30 April 1818.

20. Wilson 2:25.

21. Walsh App 20. It will be noted that this 'new arrangement' did not include the 13th Regiment out at Rosetta.

22. This particular alteration was a direct result of Ludlow's being appointed to the colonelcy of the 96th Regiment on 8 May. By long-established tradition, the Guards insisted on always being commanded by one of their own, so the Earl of Cavan (a Coldstream officer) took over the brigade, while George Ludlow was given the new 1st Brigade by way of compensation.

23. The rank of brigadier was a local one, to be held in Egypt only, and with effect from 25 June. The promotion, however, was actually moot, for the brigade was actually led in the last weeks of the campaign by Colonel Brent Spencer, presumably because the newly arrived Blake was sick.

24. That the reserve was organised into two discrete brigades is confirmed by the appointment of two brigade majors; Captain George Groves of the 28th Regiment and Captain George Bowles of the 8th Regiment. The exact composition of the two brigades is not entirely clear, but it is likely that Oakes' brigade had the 2nd, 28th, 42nd and 58th Regiments, while Spencer would have had his own 40th Regiment flank companies, the 23rd Fusiliers and all the foreign light infantry units – although the position would

shortly be complicated by the assignment of a wing of Lowenstein's riflemen to Coote's operation west of Alexandria, and by Spencer's temporarily taking command of the 6th Brigade.

25. To the great confusion of historians, this unit is simply listed in Walsh's version of the *New Arrangement* as a 'Rifle Corps', leading to the bizarre suggestion that this was an otherwise unrecorded remnant of the Experimental Rifle Corps – a forerunner of the famous 95th Rifles. Mackesy suggests instead they may have been a greatly reinforced Hompesch Hussars, on the grounds that the unit was officially listed as Mounted Rifles – but at the same time confuses the *Löwenstein Chasseurs* and the entirely different *Chasseurs Britanniques*! A simple process of elimination confirms that the unit in question was indeed *Löwenstein's*; a rifle-armed German mercenary unit in British pay, and indeed Moore puts the identification beyond doubt in his own transcript of the *New Arrangement* by explicitly referring to them as *Löwenstein's Jaegers*.

Chapter 11: Abercromby's Legacy

1. *A Foreign Office Affair* (1894): The protagonist, a French agent, abducts the messenger in order to delay the news of the fall of Alexandria until the preliminaries have actually been signed.

Appendix 1: Opposing Forces March 1801

1. The practice, although widespread in the eighteenth century, virtually disappeared in the British Army after the creation of dedicated Light Infantry regiments in the first decade of the nineteenth century. In fact, Colonel Spencer's mixed flank battalion, drawn from both battalions of the 40th Regiment, was one of the last instances. The French army clung to the practice for much longer. While flank battalions were undoubtedly an elite, they had the age-old faults of not only drawing the best men from their parent units, but tended to get them killed off at a much higher rate.
2. *Sketches of the Highlanders of Scotland* (Edinburgh, 1822) 1:448.
3. The younger son of the Earl of Ludlow, born in 1758, he was a typical hard-fighting Guardee whose first commission came in 1778 as an ensign in 1st Footguards, with whom he served in North America until the surrender at Yorktown in 1781. A captain and lieutenant colonel in 1790, he went to Flanders in 1793 in command of one of the newly formed light companies, but was wounded at Roubaix in

the following year, losing his left arm. A colonel by brevet, in 1795 he served on the home staff until promotion to major general on 18 June 1798 gave him command of 2 Guards Brigade, serving in Ireland and then at Ferrol before being assigned to the Mediterranean and the expedition to Egypt. On 8 May 1801, Ludlow was appointed colonel of the 96th Foot and the officers of his brigade thereupon insisted that he be replaced, since by tradition they could only be commanded by a Guardsman. Accordingly, Ludlow took over the 1st Brigade instead, while the Guards Brigade passed to Lord Cavan, whose own weak brigade was disbanded.

4. A nephew of the rather more famous Sir Eyre Coote, who did so much to secure Britain's position in India, he entered the Army as an ensign in the 37th Regiment and within four years was a captain. Service throughout the American War ended with the surrender at Yorktown in 1781, but two years later he was major of the 47th Regiment and then lieutenant colonel of the 70th in 1788. A colonel by brevet in 1795, he became a major general on 1 January 1797. In the meantime, he had served with some credit in the West Indies, first commanding a light infantry battalion under Sir Charles Grey and again under Abercromby. He then commanded the land forces in the Ostend debacle in 1798, but although badly wounded and forced to surrender he was subsequently exchanged and so served at the Helder in the following year before being assigned to the Ferrol expedition and then to the Mediterranean. Sadly, Coote's career ended very badly. After Egypt he served again in the West Indies and as second in command at Walcheren in 1809, where it became increasingly clear that he was becoming mentally unfit for command, supposedly as a result of repeated bouts of sunstroke or heatstroke in the West Indies. He was not employed again and eventually in 1816 he was dismissed from the service after an extraordinary incident in which he was discovered in the act of sexually assaulting schoolboys at Christ's hospital in London.

As an unrelated aside, his ADC in 1801 was the Captain Thomas Walsh, who would write and compile the absolutely invaluable *Journal of the Late Campaign in Egypt*.

5. The son of a Bishop of Dublin, Cradock was first commissioned a cornet in the 4th Dragoons in 1777 at the age of 15; was an ensign in the Coldstream Guards two years later; a lieutenant and captain on 12 December 1781; then briefly a major in the 12th Dragoons in 1785, before transferring to the 13th Foot on 16 June 1786. Promoted to lieutenant colonel on 16 June 1789, he went with the

regiment to Jamaica, before serving more widely in the Caribbean, commanding a grenadier battalion under Sir Charles Grey. He was then quartermaster general in Ireland in 1797 before becoming a major general on 1 January 1798 and serving in India and the early days of the Peninsular War. *WO25/3998; Royal Military Calendar*. (NB: his entry in the *Oxford Dictionary of National Biography* is rather eccentrically found under Caradoc, a spelling of his name he only assumed in 1820!) All four of his battalion commanders went on to later hold active commands as general officers, and in the case of Rowland Hill eventually died as Commander in Chief of the Army.

6. Born in 1762 Cavan was a Guardsman; commissioned an ensign in the Coldstream on 2 April 1779, he was a lieutenant and captain two years later and a captain and lieutenant colonel on 30 November 1790. After service in Flanders in 1793, where he was wounded at Valenciennes, he became a colonel by brevet on 21 August 1795 and then major general on 18 June 1798 while serving in Ireland. However, he still remained a member of the Coldstream and was successively appointed second major of the regiment on 9 May 1800 and first major on 19 November 1800. As a Guardsman he was suitably qualified to take over command of the Guards Brigade from Ludlow when the later was given the colonelcy of a mere regiment of the line.

7. John Doyle was born in 1756, the fourth son of Charles Doyle of Bramblestown, Co. Kilkenny. He was an ensign in the 48th Regiment in 1771 and a lieutenant two years later before transferring to the 40th in 1775 and serving throughout the American War. There he helped raise a provincial corps named the Volunteers of Ireland and at the end of the war retired on to half pay as a major. There he remained until 1793, when he raised the 87th Regiment, successively being appointed lieutenant colonel commandant and then colonel of the regiment (by brevet) on 3 May 1796. In the process he was badly wounded while serving in Holland under Lord Moira. Having been brevetted colonel, he was also named to command the land forces in a proposed raid on the Dutch fleet in the Texel, but after it was cancelled due to bad weather he accepted a political appointment as Secretary at War in Ireland before being appointed to the local rank of brigadier general at Gibraltar with effect from 27 June 1798.

8. His father, Colonel John Stuart of the Southern Indian Department, originally came from Inverness, but he himself was born in the colony of Georgia in 1758. Educated at Westminster School, he obtained an ensign's commission in the 3rd Footguards on 7 August 1778

and served in America until the end of the revolution, becoming a lieutenant and captain on 6 November 1782 and a captain and lieutenant colonel in 1793. That same year saw him go to Flanders and then on 3 May 1796 he received a brevet promotion to colonel and in November an appointment as brigadier general to go first to Portugal under Sir Charles Stuart (who was not related) and afterwards on to Minorca. He was to serve very creditably in Egypt and returned to the Mediterranean in the next war, spending the rest of his career there, where his most notable feat was winning the battle of Maida. Despite his activity, his handsome victory and his proven competence, for some reason he seems to have attracted a fair amount of personal hostility.

9. As a lieutenant general, he would command a substantial part of the Dutch army at Waterloo.

10. Born in 1761, John Moore was the son of a fashionable Glasgow doctor who counted the Duke of Hamilton among his clients. Originally commissioned an ensign in the 51st Regiment on 2 March 1776, he was appointed captain-lieutenant in the Duke of Hamilton's newly raised 82nd Regiment on 8 January 1778 and first made a name for himself in a raid on Penobscot, Maine, in the following year. At the war's end the regiment was disbanded and he was placed on half pay but quickly became a major in the 60th Regiment on 23 November 1785, before exchanging back to his old corps, the 51st Regiment, on 1 October 1788, and rising to become its lieutenant colonel on 30 November 1790. He then commanded the regiment on Corsica before falling out with the governor and being sent home. This contretemps did no harm whatsoever to his career and he next served under Abercromby in the West Indies as a brigadier general. Elevated to become a major general on 18 June 1798, he served against the rebel forces in the south of Ireland and then in the following year he was wounded in the head during the Helder campaign. Soon recovered, he next went with Abercromby to Minorca and there helped form the army that would go to Egypt.

11. Hildebrand Oakes was himself the son of a soldier, born in 1754 and first commissioned into the 33rd Regiment 23 December 1767. He was a captain in the regiment by 8 August 1776, and there he stayed despite serving through the American War until a brevet promotion to major in 1790 was followed by becoming major of the 66th Regiment in September of the following year. Another brevet promotion to lieutenant colonel on 1 March 1794 was followed this time by becoming lieutenant colonel of the 26th Regiment on

1 September 1795. In the meantime, he was successively appointed QMG in the Mediterranean on 13 June 1794, then QMG Portugal on 30 November 1796. From there he went to Minorca, having become a colonel by brevet 1 January 1798 and a brigadier general under Sir Charles Stuart with effect from 29 August 1798. After Egypt he was lieutenant governor of Portsmouth for a time, QMG Mediterranean in 1806, CinC Malta 1808 and then Civil Commissioner on the island until 1813 and afterwards Lieutenant General of the Ordnance until his death in 1822.

12. In his list David Stewart names the commanding officer on the day of the Aboukir landing as Major James Mackenzie, but the 7 March state records that three field officers were present and an anecdote refers to a conversation between Abercromby and Lieutenant Colonel Hall.

13. As noted above, despite their outward difference in role and their distinctive uniforms, it was quite common for elite 'flank battalions' to be formed of mixed grenadiers and light infantry and Colonel Spencer had first made his name while commanding just such a flank battalion on St Domingue in early 1794.

14. Officially this particular unit was part of Ferdinand von Hompesch's Light Dragoons (or mounted Rifles) and in theory ought not to be confused with the different Hompesch Hussars, raised by his brother, Franz Karl von Hompesch. That regiment was disbanded in late 1797 due to heavy losses on St Domingue, but the remnants appear to have been drafted into Ferdinand's regiment, because Major Wilson, who led the detachment in Egypt, invariably refers to his men as Hussars!

15. Formed in 1799, the Staff Corps was responsible for logistical engineering, such as the construction and maintenance of roads and bridges, rather than military engineering proper. Accordingly, its officers wore the red uniform of the QMG department rather than the blue then worn by the Royal Engineers. Abercromby had called for 500 Maltese volunteers to form a corps of pioneers to go to Egypt, but they are not evidenced in any of the returns, so those who did volunteer were presumably carried on the strength of the Staff Corps.

16. Lawson's antecedents are unknown, but he entered Woolwich in 1758 and was first commissioned a lieutenant fireworker on 25 December 1759. He first served at Belle Isle in 1761, then at Gibraltar until 1776, when he went to North America. Afterwards he was CRA on Jamaica from 1700 to 1700. On 5 November 1795 he reached the regimental rank of major, was a lieutenant colonel 30 August

1794, then a colonel by brevet on 1 January 1900, qualifying him to hold the local rank of brigadier under Abercromby with effect from 26 June 1800.

17. British and French brigades differed in that traditionally the former were ad hoc formations formed from different single battalion regiments. French regiments, on the other hand, were normally multi-battalion units and the terms regiment and brigade were therefore synonymous. In practice, the actual terminology was sometimes used quite loosely. In Menou's orders for the battle of Alexandria, for example, individual units are carelessly referred to very promiscuously as demi-brigades, brigades and as the ( ) *Ligne*.

18. Reynier, Jean Louis Ebenezer *State of Egypt after the Battle of Heliopolis, Preceded by General Observations ... G. and J. Robinson (London, 1802).*

19. Born in Switzerland in 1771, Jean-Louis-Ebénézer Reynier (or Regnier) originally volunteered to join the Artillery as a gunner in September 1792, but less than a month after that he was serving as a *capitaine* in the Army of the North and in early 1794 he received a promotion to *chef de brigade*. Most of the next three years was spent in a variety of staff posts in Germany before becoming a *général de division* in 1796 and being selected to go to Egypt in 1798. After General Kléber's assassination, he found himself increasingly at odds with General Menou, especially in the Alexandria/Canope campaign. Eventually he was arrested and deported, and subsequently wrote an extremely useful if tendentious history of the campaign. In bad odour for a time with Napoleon after killing a rival, General d'Estaing, in a duel, he later served in Italy, where he was defeated by John Stuart at the battle of Maida, and in the Peninsula and Russia. Captured at Leipzig in 1813, he was eventually exchanged but died of exhaustion in the following year.

20. At this point, due to an embarrassing administrative error, there were actually two regiments in the French army bearing the title *7e Hussards*. In 1803 it was all straightened out by recasting the 7e (bis) regiment as the *28e Dragoons*.

Appendix 2: The British Army in Egypt

1. Tie-on sun-visors were issued to the Black Watch and 79th Highlanders, but refused by the 92nd Highlanders.
2. The 54th were not one of the regiments originally designated to receive volunteers from the Militia and it will be noted that there was apparently no restriction on their service.

3. Both watercolours are held by the National Army museum and in one of them a few figures appear who do not belong to the 61st, indicating that this style of dress was common to all of Baird's regiments – and probably to the Mediterranean regiments with the main expeditionary force.
4. Wilson 1:262.
5. Delavoye, Alexander *Records of the 90th Regiment (Perthshire Light Infantry); with Roll of Officers 1795–1880* (London, 1880) :53.
6. Henry Dundas to Marquis of Huntly 3 December 1796, see Bulloch, J.M., *Territorial Soldiering in the North East of Scotland* (Aberdeen, 1914): 220–221,
7. Stewart 1:481. The Irish Fencibles were enlisted for European service only, and were ordered from Ireland to Minorca, where they were quartered in 1801. When more troops were required in Egypt, this regiment was treated in the same manner as at different times the Highland regiments had been, and without regard to their terms of service, was ordered to embark for Africa. The men complained, and stated the nature of their engagement, but to no purpose; and being less refractory than the Highlanders had showed themselves in similar circumstances, they embarked, though reluctantly. However, when they found themselves fairly landed in Egypt, and were ordered to march forward from the beach to join the army before Alexandria, making a virtue of necessity, and with characteristic good humour, they pulled off their hats, and, with three cheers, cried out, 'We will volunteer now.'
8. The regiment was actually formed by Colonel John Ramsay, a British agent who was then the Inspector General of Foreign Troops. The clothing probably came from the same depot in Germany that furnished Watteville's Regiment, in which case the jackets will have been single-breasted with black facings, the pantaloons sky blue and the caps Austrian in style – see Watteville below.
9. Gould, Robert. *Mercenaries of the Napoleonic Wars* (Brighton, 1995): 71–74.
10. Thomas Graham to Lord Cathcart 18 November 1798 (Dalavoye, A.H. *Life of Thomas Graham, Lord Lynedoch*, London, 1880) '… and for the Swiss I should have been quite hurt at destroying them, many of them my friends of the Aust-Italian army in the very clothes they wore when I saw them taken, afterwards basely sold for two hard dollars a-piece to the Spaniards by these rascally French'.
11. Confusingly, ten years later they were renumbered the 90th Foot before being disbanded at Limerick in 1816 and then re-raised in

1824. At the time they were officially recognised as successors to the original and eventually relied upon this to successfully claim possession of the colour taken from *3/21e* in Egypt.

12. Although broadly similar, the jackets differed from the British style in having turned-back skirts in the facing colour. The caps were again very similar to British ones but differed in not having a large brass plate on the front. There was, however, a black turban around the base.

13. The use of the French grey jacket at this time is confirmed by the regimental history, see Smet, John Francis, *Historical Record of the Eighth King's Royal Irish Hussars* (London, 1874) and an example of the regimental helmet is still extant.

14. Cannon, Richard *Historical record of the Eleventh, or the Prince Albert's Own Regiment of Hussars* (London, 1843): 33–37. Money had only been promoted on 3 May 1800. The rank of captain-lieutenant was held by the lieutenant commanding the colonel of the regiment's own troop or company. As that worthy was invariably absent, day-to-day command was actually exercised by his lieutenant, and acknowledged by his dual title. The rank was abolished in 1803 and henceforth all companies and troops were commanded by captains – with those who had previously held the dual rank taking precedence from their original appointment.

15. This only applied to ADCs employed at public expense. Extra ADCs, whose appointment was only temporary, wore their own regimentals. Although the regulations are silent on this point, their status was probably marked by shifting their single epaulette to the left shoulder.

Appendix 3: The East India Company in Egypt

1. British India was at still at this time privately managed by the East India Company, but from 1784 the Company's governance of India was overseen by a government appointed Board of Control. The Company's possessions were grouped under three Presidencies; Bombay, Madras and Bengal, each with its own military establishment and governor. (Ceylon, having recently been seized from the Dutch, belonged to the Crown.) Of those, the Governor of Bengal was regarded as the senior one and as such styled Governor General.

2. Volunteers were necessary due to the presence of so many Brahmins or high-caste Hindus, who had a religious aversion to travelling by sea, serving in the ranks of the Bengal regiments.

3. Weller, Jac, *Wellington in India* (London, 1972): 106–113.
4. Not all of the Indian troops came down to Rosetta. Colonel William Ramsay of the 80th Regiment had been left as commandant at Giza, with detachments totalling 150 men from the 10th, 61st, 80th and 88th Regiments, and five companies of the 7th Bombay Native infantry.
5. While they arrived too late to take part in the campaign properly, the regimental history relates that they were employed in rounding up shoals of French deserters making their way south to join with the *Mamlūks*.

Appendix 4: The French Army in Egypt

1. The listing is primarily based on Elting, John and Knötel, Herbert, *Napoleonic Uniforms* Vol.1 (New York, 1993) Haythornthwaite, Philip *Uniforms of the French Revolutionary Wars 1789–1802*: 115–117, 142 and Grant, Charles *Napoleon's Campaign in Egypt* 1:97.
2. An oblique clue may lie in Wilson's description, singling out the *20e Dragoons* as 'the best and heaviest regiment in the army of Egypt', which may imply they were unusual in still retaining helmets.
3. Reynier: 107–8.

Index

NB: French ranks are distinguished by italics.

Mandara, 55-63, 132
Marabout [fort], 139-40
Mareotis, Lake, 68-69, 107-8, 136
Marmaris Bay [Anatolia], 28-32
McKerras, Major William
[RE], 40
McKinnon, Captain John
[Minorca Regt], 66
McNair, Captain John [90th], 58
Meade, Ensign Frederick
[40th], 47
Mehmet Ali Pasha [Albanian],
118-9
Menou, General Abdallah de,
37-41, 66, 68-71, 84-5, 88-91, 94,
102-3, 134, 143-4
Middlemore, Captain George
[86th], 166
Minorca, 8-9, 22
Monet, Captain-lieut. Archibald
[11LD], 173
Montresor, Lieut. Col. Henry
Tucker, 150
Montresor, Lieut. Colonel John, 178
Montresor, Major Thomas [ADC],
117, 120, 124
Moore, Major General John,
22-24, 35[Aboukir], 44-5, 50-1,
52-3, 56-63, 74-94, 135, 137-9,
142, 146, 152
Moore, Major James [26LD], 141
Morand, General Charles, 127
Murray, Lieut. Col. George
[DQMG], 18, 19, 33-5
Napier, Major Alexander [92nd], 92
Napoleon Bonaparte, 1-8, 13-14, 26
Nelson, Rear Admiral Horatio,
4-5, 7, 10, 11, 14
Nicopolis, Heights of / Lines, 53,
55, 60, 61, 102, 104, 106-9, 142
Nile, Battle of [Aboukir Bay], 7

Oakes, Brigadier Hildebrand, 46,
52, 75, 77, 94, 124, 135, 146, 152
Ogilvie, Lieut. Colonel David
[44th], 152
Oswald, Lieut. Colonel John
[35th], 14
Paget, Colonel Edward [28th],
75-6, 138-9, 152
Panatini, Captain [Corsican
Rangers], 47, 50
Perponcher, Baron Henrick
Georg, 152
Perponcher, Captain
[Lowenstein], 140
Pigot, Major General Henry, 14
Popham, Rear Admiral
Sir Home, 176
Portugal, 24, 27
Pulteney. Lieut. General Sir
James, 22-6, 100
Pyramids, Battle of the, [Imbaba],
5-7
Quarrell, Lieut. Colonel Richard
[10th], 161
Ramanieh, 5, 107, 110-112, 114,
116, 135
Rampon, General Antoine-
Guillaume, 40, 72, 80, 83, 88, 91,
155-6
Ramsay, Lieut. Colonel William
[80th], 166
Reynier, General Jean Louis, 6,
40-41, 72, 84-5, 90-1, 93, 102-3,
134, 156
Roise, General Cesar-Antoine, 73,
84-86
Roman Ruins [Kasr Kiasera], 65,
68, 70-1, 72, 75-90
Rosetta, 104-5, 127, 133, 135-7
Rowe, Lieut. Colonel Benjamin
[50th], 151, 164

244